Prophetically
INCORRECT

Prophetically
INCORRECT

A Christian Introduction to Media Criticism

Robert H. Woods and Paul D. Patton

FOREWORD BY
Quentin J. Schultze

PREFACE BY
Clifford G. Christians

BrazosPress
a division of Baker Publishing Group
Grand Rapids, Michigan

© 2010 by Robert H. Woods and Paul D. Patton

Published by Brazos Press
a division of Baker Publishing Group
P.O. Box 6287, Grand Rapids, MI 49516-6287
www.brazospress.com

Printed in the United States of America

Library of Congress Cataloging-in-Publication Data
Woods, Robert H., 1970–
    Prophetically incorrect : a Christian introduction to media criticism / Robert H. Woods and Paul D. Patton ; foreword by Quentin J. Schultze ; preface by Clifford G. Christians.
        p.   cm.
    Includes bibliographical references and index.
    ISBN 978-1-58743-276-7 (pbk.)
    1. Mass media—Religious aspects—Christianity. 2. Christianity and culture. I. Patton, Paul D., 1952– II. Title.
    BV652.95.W66 2010
    261.5'2—dc22   2010004402

Unless otherwise indicated, Scripture quotations are from the HOLY BIBLE, NEW INTERNATIONAL VERSION®. NIV®. Copyright © 1973, 1978, 1984 by International Bible Society. Used by permission of Zondervan. All rights reserved.

Scripture so indicated is taken from *The Message* by Eugene H. Peterson, copyright © 1993, 1994, 1995, 2000, 2001, 2002. Used by permission of NavPress Publishing Group. All rights reserved.

Scripture quotations labeled NEB are from *The New English Bible.* Copyright © 1961, 1970, 1989 by The Delegates of Oxford University Press and The Syndics of the Cambridge University Press. Reprinted by permission.

Scripture quotations labeled KJV are taken from the King James Version of the Bible.

10   11   12   13   14   15   16   7   6   5   4   3   2   1

green
press
INITIATIVE

Contents

Acknowledgments

Our debts on this project are numerous. Thanks to Spring Arbor University (SAU) for granting a sabbatical request that allowed us to finish on time. Our research assistant, SAU student Sarah Byrne, spent months running back and forth between our offices and the library with arms full of materials, and always with a smile. Several SAU students, staff, and faculty reviewed various chapters and in many cases the entire manuscript to help make the book more readable and compelling: Marsha Daigle-Williamson, Rachel Decker, Cheryl Hampton, Julie Devine, Kaitlin Shelby, Abigail Wood, Sarah Byrne, and Jason Thiede.

Other non-SAU colleagues and friends provided similar feedback as well: Quentin J. Schultze (Calvin College), Clifford G. Christians (University of Illinois, Urbana-Champaign), Kathy Bruner (Taylor University), Kevin Maness (Eastern University), Craig Mattson (Trinity Christian College), Stephanie DeLano Davis (Northwestern Michigan College), Steve Patton (Missouri Valley College), Samuel Ebersole (Colorado State University, Pueblo), Ronnie Ferguson, Beth Patton, Emily Patton, and Rebekah Woods.

SAU's library staff (Roy Meador, David Burns, Karen Parsons, Susan Panak, Kami Moyer, and Robbie Bolton) provided ongoing and timely research support that allowed us to stay on schedule.

Marsha Daigle-Williamson's masterful copyediting work and substantial feedback throughout the process made us write more clearly and reinforced the unity among the chapters. John Muether, library director at Reformed Theological Seminary, made sure that our index was helpful to our readers. William D. Romanowski, Calvin College, provided us with several key examples, quotes, and sources that appear in chapter 4.

Clifford G. Christians met with us over a three-year period to share ideas and provide sage advice. His generosity of spirit and scholarly support are seen all over the final product, including but not limited to the preface. Portions of chapter 2 and chapter 7 include material from Clifford that we updated and expanded to fit the scope of our current project.[1] Quentin J. Schultze was involved at the proposal stage and helped to organize three years of material in about two days. He encouraged us to have fun and always keep our audience in mind, and graciously agreed to write the foreword. Both Clifford and Quentin were writing and thinking about prophetic communication in popular media long before we arrived on the scene. We are eternally grateful for the contributions and friendship of these "soul brothers."

Our wives, Rebekah Woods and Bethany Patton, challenged us to be patient with the project and one another. They gave up many weekends to let us work. They are constant sources of joy.

Our friends at Brazos Press enthusiastically supported this project from beginning to end. Special thanks to Rodney Clapp for championing the project and providing assurances along the way that we were headed in the right direction. We also thank Lisa Ann Cockrel who patiently and expertly shepherded us through the final stages of the editorial process.

We absolve all our friends and colleagues of any responsibility for the weaknesses that remain.

Foreword

The Audacity of Prophetic Truth

QUENTIN J. SCHULTZE

Arthur H. DeKruyter Chair in Faith and Communication, Calvin College

The Danish philosopher Søren Kierkegaard (1813–55) had a knack for irritating the state church. He claimed an unusual gift: namely, perceiving the lengths of the noses of Christendom's Pinocchio-like prelates. When their noses grew, Kierkegaard reported it publicly in books and articles. In Kierkegaard's view, church leaders were self-righteously playing God rather than humbly following God. As he once put it, "Christendom plays the game of taking God by the nose: God is love, meaning that he loves me—Amen!"[1] By "Christendom," Kierkegaard meant the established, bureaucratic, self-serving institution that had become increasingly irrelevant to the real spiritual vitality of everyday citizens. Christendom was a godless church, more like a country club than a place for submitting to the one true God. "Christendom," wrote Kierkegaard, "is a society of people who call themselves Christians because they occupy themselves obtaining information about those who a long time ago submitted themselves to Christ's examination—spiritlessly forgetting that they themselves are up for examination."[2]

Beginning with the story of Adam and Eve in the opening chapters of the book of Genesis, the biblical drama shows that human beings have always been liars. We like to fib. To exaggerate. To misrepresent. To pretend that we know more than we really do. For instance, self-serving deception is a common malady in the modern advertising business. Deceit runs throughout contemporary political discourse of the Right and Left. Like politicos, we appreciate opportunities to enhance our own ethos so that others will look at us more kindly or respectfully—even if all we get is fifteen minutes of media fame. In short, we humans dwell east of Eden, in ever-evolving but rarely progressing cultures that are based on one or another pack of lies about God, ourselves, others, and the creation. As Augustine discovered, our collective, self-serving, socially shaped lies foul up our personal desires. We desire the wrong things—or the right things in the wrong ways. We love things the way we should love only God, and we pretend to love God while treating God as another thing to control. We become tragic characters in our own puny, picayune dramas. Which came first—real life or reality TV? What difference does it make to us? After a while, we can hardly distinguish between our adventures and our misadventures. We imitate the oddities that we have created in the media. Imagine Adam and Eve watching their fall unfolding on TV and enjoying the drama. This would have been the first reality TV series (as long as God was not there to narrate).

Into this mess steps a prophet, himself or herself fallen but simultaneously carrying a God-given ounce of dangerous, culture-upsetting, society-challenging wisdom. This prophet's wisdom runs deeper than data or information. The wisdom could be only one word: Stop! Outlandish! Unjust! Folly! The Decalogue itself is essentially ten word-phrases that might please a modern German linguist. Here's a slippery translation of one command: "No-idols-or-you're-dead-meat." I can imagine Arnold Schwarzenegger mouthing this line in a movie. The problem is that the word *idol* would not work. It is not commercial enough for prime time. Especially in a literal translation: "No-nothings-or-you're-dead-meat." An idol is, literally speaking, a nothing. The insightful prophet perceives the connection between no-nothings and the know-nothings who worship them. Didn't Jesus say something like "I'll be Bach"? A reporter could answer that question properly without parroting Arnold Schwarzenegger's famous line in the movie *The Terminator*, "I'll be back."

The Hebrew and Christian traditions offer a prophetic means for human beings to find their way amid the miasma of mediated mendacity. This way requires humans to do something outrageous, even foolish by many of today's standards: to be faithful (or to be true to the One who is the truth). This kind of faithfulness is based on assumptions at odds with Christendom. First, we truthseekers assume that there is a living, personal God of the universe. There is a God who knows, who sees through the lies that we hold dear. Second, we assume that God has and will continue to speak to us through wise, God-fearing mediators. Third, we give witness to particular people and other means by which God speaks the truth in our midst; instead of merely listening to God as individuals, we listen as communities of prophetic discourse in which we can hold each other accountable. We affirm prophetic critics' gifts to identify and speak the truth, but we also question them as to whether they are speaking truthfully. We might not like everything they say. We will not always appreciate words of wisdom that hit too close to home, challenging our misplaced desires and reminding us that we cannot control our own fate. The prophetic way is inherently communal, testing the words of truth through ongoing proclamation, discussion, and sacrificial living.

Obviously I have ducked several of the most difficult questions related to the specific times, places, and means that God uses to speak prophetically (or, to put it less tribally, the ways that God appropriates human beings' language for God's own purposes). When Augustine claims that "all truth is God's truth," he reminds us that there is always gold as well as dross in any culture; truthtelling cannot be limited to any one social group. Does God "speak" through an individual person's conscience? Do some people hear the literal voice of God? Neither my foreword nor this book claims to solve these problems. Indeed, such difficulties are probably necessary for faith. To borrow another quote from Kierkegaard, "Christianity has been abolished somewhat as follows: life is made easier."[3]

My own view is that God can appropriate anything for the purpose of speaking to humans. Here I am borrowing from Nicholas Wolterstorff's fine book *Divine Discourse*, which uses speech act theory to support the thesis that God speaks.[4] As Wolterstorff argues, God does not just reveal truth or inspire people to speak the truth. God asserts things, commands things, promises things, and so forth. God accomplishes such speech acts, first, through prophets who proclaim the source of their speech: "Thus says the Lord." Prophets are deputized to speak in the name of God—just as an ambassador might (or should!) speak in the name of the head of state that he or she serves.

Moreover, God speaks not just through such deputized prophets but, second, by appropriating others' truthful messages. These truthtellers need not be prophets in the sense of being directly called by God to declare the Lord's word. For example, God appropriates King David's speech in the psalms. David never says, "Thus says the Lord," as if he were a prophet who heard the words directly from God. Nor was he merely inspired by God to write psalms. Nor was he simply revealing more about God by writing the psalms. God appropriated David's language in order to speak the truth. The Hebrew and Christian Scriptures certainly include both prophets and apostles deputized by God to speak in the name of God, but the same Scriptures include other human discourse, like the psalms and epistles, which God appropriated in order to say what God wanted to say.

Now Robert H. Woods and Paul D. Patton are playing the role of deputized prophets by appropriating others' words—words spoken by God, rabbis, scholars, and cultural critics, among others—for the sake of truthtelling about the purpose and nature of prophetic media criticism. Their purpose is to speak truthfully about the state of contemporary media criticism by offering a renewed vision of the critic as prophet. Their own guides include the insightful Rabbi Abraham Joshua Heschel (1907–72), who descended from European rabbis and whose family was decimated by the Nazis. He escaped Poland before the Nazis could send him to the death camps, but the emotional scars remained: "If I should go to Poland or Germany, every stone, every tree would remind me of contempt, hatred, murder, of children killed, of mothers burned alive, of human beings asphyxiated."[5] In effect, Heschel and the other sources of wisdom in this book are Kierkegaardian gadflies in the midst of today's Christendom. While monitoring their own noses, they are busily yanking the planks out of each other's eyes and using the wood to build a bridge between the prophets of old and the media critics of today. Moreover, they are building a bridge over which we too can journey back and forth, appropriating words that help them and us to understand our plight in societies dominated by consumerism. Heschel's daughter recalls of her father,

> Words, he often wrote, are themselves sacred, God's own tool for creating the universe, and our tools for bringing holiness—or evil—into the world. He used to remind us that the Holocaust did not begin with the building of crematoria, and Hitler did not come to power with tanks and guns; it all began with uttering evil words, with defamation, with language and propaganda. Words create worlds, he used to tell me when I was a child, and they must be used very carefully. Some words, once having been uttered, gain eternity and can never be withdrawn. The Book of Proverbs reminds us, he wrote, that death and life are in the power of the tongue.[6]

One problem (or is it an opportunity?) that Professors Woods and Patton necessarily face is avoiding the existing shibboleths that religious and nonreligious groups simplistically equate with God's truth. The language of "prophecy," "the prophetic," and "prophetic voice" have been co-opted by disparate groups acting like psychological, theological, and ideological thought police. This is particularly true for media criticism, which is highly predictable given the theo-moral background of the critics. For instance, mainline Protestant and Roman Catholic media criticism has been co-opted by what we might call "secular elite culture." Sometimes it is hard to distinguish between the words of the *Times* (almost any *Times*) or National Public Radio, on the one hand, and the words of the mainline critics on the other. Meanwhile, much evangelical media criticism has been co-opted by "inspirational" popular culture. There is a fine line between evangelical media criticism and evangelical celebrity culture; the celebs are the de-facto, trusted critics. Why? Partly because their predictable, tribe-affirming criticism sells well. Who can argue with the marketplace, the great adjudicator of Christian truth? If you want to operate a successful "ministry," you have to find a leader whose words confirm what the tribe wants to believe is true. Christendom, both on the Right and the Left, increasingly resembles gaggles of gawkers with their own penchants for self-styled, self-induced "Christian correctness." Like all fallen human beings, Christians tend to seek media content that confirms what they already believe or wish to believe. This is far more than what psychologists call *selective perception*; it is a form of self-delusion.

This book's splendid title, *Prophetically Incorrect*, captures the authors' shibboleth-questioning perspective. The playful title captures a kind of extra-tribal or cross-tribal vision that refuses to bow down to the commonplaces *de jour*. TV celeb Bill Maher claims to be "politically incorrect" but is far more politically predictable. When his program was on Comedy Central, it was less predictable (and less profitable) than it became on ABC. He serves on the board of a humble organization called The Reason Project (religiously dedicated to spreading scientific knowledge and secular values in society). Maher once referred to religion as a "neurological disorder"—similar to the phrase "psychological disorder" that conservative radio talk show host Michael Savage, on the other end of the thought police divide, uses to describe liberalism. Fans of Maher or Savage love to see evil people's oxen get gored. Again, we all do, as long as we are not among the evil people. A second problem the authors face is the self-deceptive nature of propaganda in mass-mediated societies. Most citizens, whether they are religious or not, naively assume that propaganda is simply the easily identifiable lies and deceptions promulgated by a few really bad people (like a Hitler). This simplistic, good-bad notion of propaganda is actually part of the propaganda by which we all live. Augustine in the fourth century battled against Manichaeism, which held a dualistic worldview in which the flesh was evil and the spirit was good—period. Today the villains are said to be members of one or another social group: fundamentalists, liberals, feminazis, neocons, and so forth. The specific labels come and go as new dualisms emerge from media discourse. This self-deceiving criticism lacks prophetic discernment. Like toddlers, we stuff square or triangle blocks into their respective holes on the top of a plastic can—round is good and goes here, whereas square is bad and goes here. We self-servingly employ favorite moralistic categories to simplify the complex, confusing, and often incongruous aspects of culture.

Along the way, we completely miss some deeply biblical categories. For instance, some critics' concerns about immoral media content focuses on obscenity and profanity but ignores racism and sexism. Others focus on materialism but ignore gratuitous sex, violence, and profanity. In short, we critics tend to carve up the world into classifications that reflect our desire for self-righteousness more than they do our faithful quest to become selflessly wise. We propagandize ourselves. The media join in, telling us what we already believe or what we want to believe—regardless of whether or not such belief is ultimately true. The media do not cause us to believe one thing or another; that idea is itself too simplistic, more like scapegoating than critical analysis. Media and culture are synergistically dependent on one another; both the media and our lives are complicated mixes of good and bad motives and misordered desires, many of them institutionalized in bestseller lists, fan and critic awards, audience ratings, and YouTube rankings.

Prophetic wisdom invariably prods people to ask themselves what it is that they truly want—and why. Often it uses satire and parody, frequently in the form of questions. God begins the fun with a whopper directed at the newly fallen couple in the garden of Eden: "Where are you?" The question was ontological and ethical rather than merely geographical. When I was growing up in Chicago we used to ask one another, "What's shakin'? What's going on? What's happening?" Most of the time our friendly greetings were not meant to be interrogations. But when we knew that something significant was happening, we were quick to follow up with more questions. "Was Jim suspended from school for drinking in PE again?" We did not want him to get booted out. But we did desire to drink in PE without getting caught. Surely we needed a higher vision based on a deeper understanding of the nature and purpose of life. We did not respect school officials, some of whom might not have completely deserved such respect. But who merited our respect? How should we have fulfilled our mimetic desires? In a spoof interview in the Christian humor magazine *The Wittenburg Door*, Superman complains,

> I used to be this untouchable, all-powerful being. I always did the right thing. I never struggled with the decision. Now people want someone more down to earth, easier to relate to. So I have this relationship with Lois I can't figure out. And I make little moral misjudgments, like sleeping with Lois, leaving my elderly mother alone for five years while I go search for Krypton, things like that. I'm just an ordinary guy with the powers of a god. That's what people want from Jesus nowadays, too. Not an all-powerful, all-knowing, all righteous God. They want an affable, easy-going guy who just happens to have superpowers and uses them for good.[7]

We could have used those superpowers to get off the hook in high school. Imagine the opportunities!

There is something delightful about self-deprecating prophetic wisdom when it reveals our foibles with gentle love and open curiosity about our plight in this good but fallen world. As the authors of this volume indicate, prophets sometimes have to call down the roof, overturn the tables, and "call 'em as they see 'em." Still, the more subtle, inquisitive style of prophetic critique has its place. For one thing, we are curious creatures—even curious about what troubles us and why we continue on our wayward paths individually and collectively. Perhaps partly because of what Augustine called original sin, we are born with what J. Richard Middleton calls a "desire to learn, a passion to explore, to stretch the boundaries of the known, to go new places, to discover new insights, to ask probing questions that maybe we hadn't asked before." According to Middleton, this curiosity is a "natural part of life. It's a developmental task God has put before us, and it's a blessing God has gifted us with—to be playful as kittens in our curiosity."[8] We need to learn measured styles of prophetic criticism that bring others into the conversation rather than drive them away from the discourse. This partly means not taking ourselves so seriously that we fail to take others seriously enough.

Perhaps the underlying basis for all prophetic criticism must be humble gratitude. Gratitude to God, first, and to other faithful critics, second, melts away our self-righteousness. The fact is that we cannot save ourselves even by knowing the prophetic truth; salvation is beyond our rhetorical, ethical, and hermeneutical abilities. The kingdom of God and all of its prophetic insights are gifts worthy of accepting before we get overly exercised about anything that appears to be wrong with media and culture. "Everything changes," writes Evan Drake Howard, "when we realize that the only rewards that matter can't be earned. This is how prophets and righteous persons and children live—not out of shoulds but out of thanks."[9] Much Jewish humor—from Seinfeld to Stiller—simultaneously pokes fun at human beings' nuttiness while gently reminding audiences that things could be worse. We ought to be thankful for the fact that our situation is not even more desperate, that we can still smile and laugh rather than merely hate. Speaking at the Oslo Conference on "The Anatomy of Hate" in 1990, the former Czech Republic President Václav Havel said, "The man who hates does not smile, he merely smirks; he is incapable of making a joke, only of bitter ridicule; he can't be genuinely ironic because he can't be ironic about himself. Only those who can laugh at themselves can laugh authentically."[10] Kenneth R. Chase insightfully says that Christian discourse "emerges out of a double humility: the humility that comes from acknowledging the inexhaustibility of God's abundant grace, and the humility that arrives from a posture of silence before the Almighty."[11]

In Brian Friel's play *Translations*, Irish bureaucrats are remapping the country and changing the long-standing place names that carried the histories of the local people and their common experiences of the land and its related cultures. The bureaucrats' outlandish aim is to create for the entire country a simple, understandable, six-inch map largely devoid of any of the cultural memory of specific places. In the name of progress, they are destroying what one character calls "a rich language . . . full of the mythologies of fantasy and hope and self-deception—a syntax opulent with tomorrows."[12] Just as playwright Friel serves as a kind of prophet, revealing culture-robbing folly and warning about its implications, the contemporary media critic can help us to identify what we lose and gain in the mediatization of practically every aspect of modern life. Without such audacious critics, we can become "imprisoned in a linguistic contour which no longer matches the landscape of . . . fact."[13] The perennial task of the prophet is understanding the contours of the present in the light of God's wisdom. The critic thereby mediates our understanding of the media world by proclaiming and warning, satirizing and tracking the ongoing remapping of God's world. The Christian critic always does so self-reflexively as part of a community of Christian discourse, aware that he or she might indeed be part of the problem. As Kierkegaard wrote, "There is something frightful in the fact that the most dangerous thing of all, playing at Christianity, is never included in the list of heresies and schisms."[14] May this book help all of us to attend to the sizes of our own noses as we monitor the noses in the media.

Preface

The Moral Order

CLIFFORD G. CHRISTIANS

Charles H. Sandage Distinguished Professor and Research Professor
of Communications, University of Illinois, Urbana-Champaign

While you read this book, Friedrich Nietzsche is the elephant in the room. Professors Woods and Patton work in the most difficult terrain possible for communication studies—that established by Nietzsche in nineteenth-century Europe. In the history of ideas in the West, a moral order was assumed. In ethics, rationalism was the dominant paradigm. Through reason humans were distinctive as a species, and through rationality moral canons were considered legitimate. In this view, there are different theories of the good life, but no conceptions of any kind are possible unless a moral order can be discovered and systematized.[1]

German thinker Friedrich Nietzsche (1844–1900) developed a scorched-earth attack on this ethical rationalism and the moral order it presumed. His total assault was directed not only against the rational character of ethical principles but against the idea of moral values per se. He announced a philosophy beyond good and evil that "places morality itself not only in the world of appearances but even among deceptions, as semblance, delusion, and error."[2] The history of thought had postulated a moral order, but Nietzsche argued that moral values had become worthless. In his *Will to Power* there is no longer an answer to the human "why," and this nihilism means the "end of the moral interpretation of the world."[3] Because he was questioning God's existence, and with it the validity of moral commands, Nietzsche turned to aesthetic values that need no supernatural sanction and do not require moral obligations of any sort. As Walter Kaufmann observes: "One can speak of beauty without implying that anything ought to be beautiful or that anybody ought to create the beautiful. Beauty can be construed as a factual quality which either is or is not present."[4]

Nietzsche was one of the most influential European impresarios of the nineteenth century. His ideas have been of interest to philosophers, sociologists, literary theorists, and artists ever since. He was a philologist and an amateur composer of music, and students of communication are often fascinated with his work. Professors Woods and Patton wrestle within his domain too. Rather than dismissing ethics or thinking of popular culture only in aesthetic terms, they insist on keeping the two together and in harmony. Instead of agreeing that a moral order is no longer credible, their prophets demand justice, truth, and mercy—nonsense unless a moral order exists. They agree with Nietzsche's claim that without God morality is absurd, but they believe in a living God as guarantor of prophetic truth. Nietzsche sought a world beyond good and evil; for this book, good and evil are the axis around which the prophetic imagination revolves.

Prophetically Incorrect takes on Nietzsche's world and commands our attention for doing so. But to become a classic of enduring value, it must do more than stimulate our intellectual interest. Is it actually sound and fury signifying little over the long term, or a *tour de force* that reclaims for us a domain Nietzsche and his circle brought to its knees? In other words, in an age of relativism, why should anyone take prophetic certitude seriously? A credible assessment requires an elaboration of Nietzsche's legacy in terms of the wall-to-wall argument in this book. Popular culture is one crucial laboratory for addressing the predicament Nietzsche presents. He was a professor of classical languages, and the conundrums typically come to a head in language theory and communication practice.

For Nietzsche, developments in science and the increasing secularization of Europe killed the Christian God who had served as the basis for morality and meaning in the West throughout its history. He recognizes that without a theistic perspective, there is no coherent ground for truth or a universal framework. Life is then tragic, because we are all alone in the universe without a higher being to help us in our suffering. For Nietzsche, humanity has no greater challenge than finding a robust philosophy of life to replace the antiquated Christian one.

On the Genealogy of Morals contends that Christian morality was formed from revenge and hatred. It is a madness that lives by condemning others as wicked. In addition, Nietzsche argues, Christian morality is unhealthy since it stifles our natural inclinations by calling them evil. Western culture has suffered for two thousand years under a moral system born of sickness. Over against the traditional belief that ethics was essential for social order, Nietzsche contends that biblical values cripple the imagination and restrict human growth.[5]

Therefore, he threw himself into artistic experience for replacing religious belief. Art was sacred for him. It preserves the best in human values and inspires us to new horizons. Art gives non-religious existence the qualities of eternity. In Nietzsche's view, art provides release from the tensions of everyday life. Art, for him, is the human being's highest task and a "truly metaphysical activity."[6]

In denying God's existence and with it the viability of moral commands, he turns to aesthetic values that need no supernatural sanction. We can speak of beauty, he says, without commands or beliefs. In *The Birth of Tragedy*, Nietzsche puts it this way: "Only as aesthetic phenomena are life and the world justified eternally."[7]

Nietzsche's oppositional voice in the nineteenth century has burgeoned into a wholesale attack, so much so that in our own time, ethical imperatives have been generally invalidated. Defending an abstract good is no longer seen as beneficence, but rather as imperialism over the moral judgments of diverse communities. The concept of norms itself has eroded. Metaphysical certainty has been replaced by philosophical relativism. Moral principles are presumed to have no objective application independent of the societies within which they are constituted. Just as there are a profusion of conflicting values, there are multiple conceptions of the good life based on those values.[8]

In our day, morality has appeared to reach the end of the line. The social fashion is to be emancipated from moral standards and to disavow moral responsibility. We are witnessing the demise of the ethical, living in what Nietzsche called the era beyond good and evil.[9] In summarizing the postmodern argument against ethics, Zygmunt Bauman uses Nietzsche's perspective that ethics has been replaced by aesthetics.[10]

Cultural relativity is unquestioned and celebrated—that is, the right and valid are only known in local space and through native languages. A context that is intelligible, an argument that is valid, a television entertainment program that is artistically genuine, and judgments of right and wrong are accepted as such by a culture's internal criteria. Therefore these concepts, propositions, and judgments are considered to have no validity elsewhere. Moral values are situated in the social context rather than anchored by philosophical abstractions that cut across cultures. Contextual values replace ethical absolutes. If phenomena situated in space and time contain everything of consequence, the search outside the immediate and particular is meaningless. Popular culture gets caught up in the technological imperative, producing the visually interesting, creating new programs at times of artistic wholeness, but driven by the conditions of aesthetics rather than ethics. In defining today's society as aesthetic space, popular arts of the eye and ear re-create a spectacle in which amusement values are supreme.

Consider the status of values in academia. Social constructionism is the dominant pattern in today's social science.[11] Relativism requires a constructivist methodology in the liberal arts and sciences. Scholars make, construct, and fabricate both problems and their solutions. They create new knowledge. For the interpretive turn in social science, the idea of humans as constructors and deconstructors is presumed.

Professors Woods and Patton offer a distinct alternative. They integrate ethics and aesthetics through a theocratic framework that contradicts the relativism of the Nietzschean tradition. But notice carefully: they are not simply declaring that God is alive when Nietzsche concludes that God is dead. The biblical God of the Old Testament prophets is the Creator God, and the creation is a created order. And with the created order is the possibility of a moral order. The heart of the issue is whether a moral order exists, with Nietzsche's relativism denying its possibility and the book's realism defending its credibility.

The prophetic truth of this book is broader than the words of the Old Testament prophets and explicit biblical teaching. Stewards of an *alternative consciousness*,[12] the prophets are called—media critics who understand the human ethos, educators, entertainers, managers, and film producers. Prophets are those who speak the truth with integrity, call for accountability, and champion justice. Prophetic messages are anchored in the moral domain, and small-p prophets are grounded in it.

God made a world that is stable and permanent. With biblical faith, one knows the created order in its wholeness, but all human beings as God's creatures find it ineluctable. Insisting on a divine Creator would be meaningless if creation were no more than undifferentiated energy. Creation is not merely raw material but is ordered by its Creator's design. There is a world that exists as God's creation and in no other way.[13]

Therefore, instead of operating within a constructed world of values in which humans create their own systems of meaning, our creative ability works within the limits of an established natural order. We possess an irresistible creative imagination and the unusual capacity to interpret experience, to evaluate action, and to transmit such to public discussion. Symbols open up reality by making the invisible perceptible. Within the broad constraints of our natural existence, human beings grasp their own outline and implant intelligent systems for themselves. In the theistic worldview, God creates and extends that ability to his creatures so they can work with their immediate world imaginatively. But this is creativity within a structured whole. In Paul Tillich's terms, all knowledge and experience cannot be groundless or totally open to every configuration. Something irrevocable must be claimed for everything else to make sense—in this case, God as the ground of being.[14]

People shape their own view of reality, and we are under obligation to take each other's meanings and beliefs seriously. But this fact does not presume that reality as a whole is inherently nonstructured until it is shaped by human language. A world that exists as a given totality forms the presupposition of historical existence. Reality is not pure energy, but it is ordered vertically and internally among its parts. The creation forms an ordered whole as determined by its Maker. A complex and intelligible network of relations binds natural reality into a cosmic oneness outside of both the Creator and human beings. Vegetables are available to people as food, and rocks are ordered to trees as the foundation for the soil in which they grow. Some kinds are hierarchical, subspecies within species, and species within genus, but relations among humans are horizontal. There is no slave race to serve a master race, and the human species will not metamorphose into something else. This coherent whole is history's source. We are born into an intelligible universe that enables our lived experience to be intelligible. While God alone is omniscient and humans only know in part, the doctrine of creation affirms that truth is knowable and life ultimately makes sense.[15]

In other words, the realism of a created order in *Prophetically Incorrect* is a different paradigm than the radical relativism of the *Genealogy of Morals*. There is a moral domain that makes prophecy coherent in one and the demise of moral norms in the other. The philosophical issue in coming to judgment is the logic and status of values. For Paul Ricœur, human valuing can only be in two modes: we either discover values or we create them. On the one hand, creating values appears as a human activity; we construct society and its institutions with them. On the other hand, values appear to have an essential status, and while working in the world we find them.[16]

Upon denying the existence of a moral domain, Nietzsche began constructing a world of values of his own. In *The Birth of Tragedy*, he advocated artistic energy to bring joy into our painful existence. He composed music to give himself harmony. "Nietzsche insisted that art, particularly music, should be approached with the same earnestness with which St. Paul, Augustine, and Luther had approached religion."[17]

For the worldview of this book, where values are discovered, the moral domain is known through special and general revelation. Nature itself communicates its character, and biblical revelation provides the ultimate meaning of all things. Truth from the Old Testament prophets is known by special revelation. But small-p prophets speak creational truth that by God's common grace is known to everyone created in his image.[18]

Ricœur is correct in calling this divergence an antinomy. He insists that this dilemma in the philosophy of culture is incommensurable—an antinomy in the sense that both sides independently can be justified as self-evident. Those who believe that values are discovered do so authentically, and the opposite view does not discredit it—an antinomy. Both sides are credible, and the systematic coherence of the one does not by itself destroy the validity of the other.[19]

Thus my endorsement of the Woods and Patton perspective. They do not seek to dismantle the values-as-constructed view. They do not engage in an apologetics that argues for the existence of an eternal being against its detractors. Their intention is not to demonize other approaches to media criticism but to build the prophetic mode in both its theory and practice. The values-as-discovered option needs strong demonstrations of this sort—consistent from presuppositions to concepts to application.

Its validation internally is the issue. Does it recommend itself as conceptually and empirically valid? When it meets that test, it does not mean that it has thereby discredited the social constructionist option. *Prophetically Incorrect* has gravitas. It is deep and wide, and it opens insights on media institutions and programs that are richer than Nietzsche's work on art and more comprehensive than other approaches, such as the economic or sociological. It sees issues as whole units, and in so doing interprets popular culture around the central problem of consumption. It gets at matters of substance rather than the marginal and superficial. This book exhibits the quality the redeemed mind can produce, and it enables those who believe in a moral order to walk tall. In realist terms, Woods and Patton discover truths about the world that exist within it. This philosophy of values is as solid as a rock intellectually in its own terms and not discredited by relativism. But again, values-as-constructed retains its own identity.

While defining and applying the prophetic to popular media engagement with a thoroughness not seen heretofore, biblical realism avoids the huge problems in secular relativism. The latter continues to exist with coherence, but the luminosity of *Prophetically Incorrect* is transparent. Relativism with its empty center faces an insurmountable paradox. Relativists can only declare that all ideas are relative to their culture by rising above their own. And in rising above it, they have given up their absolutes. The naturalistic fallacy seems inescapable too: what we establish as *is* cannot be simultaneously considered an *ought*. The communities we describe ethnographically are not necessarily good. What we observe scientifically cannot be called normative without confusing two different categories. And Nietzsche's understanding of the human is problematic. For Woods and Patton, the human species is unique as God's image-bearers. Nietzsche's *Übermensch* ("superman" or "superhuman") is an elevated being of power without the constraints of a divine Master. Rather than be preoccupied by objections of this sort, *Prophetically Incorrect* gives us a detailed account of a worldview free of these weaknesses and dilemmas.

Knowledge is finally faith-conditioned. Differences in theory and methodology are basically matters of belief. Nietzsche takes his approach because he believes it to be true, as do Woods and Patton for theirs. Our theoretical world is grounded in first beliefs. All human knowledge must accept something as given. Theories of morality arise from and explicate our fundamental beliefs about the world. A faith commitment is the very condition through which human cognition is intelligible. Therefore, different paradigms articulate what one believes, while the faith commitments of others are not necessarily emasculated. When dealing with other faith systems, Woods and Patton correctly choose to give witness to their own beliefs rather than search out and destroy those of their opponents.[20]

The foundations of our knowledge are deeply interiorized. As we integrate particulars, we do not understand them externally but make value judgments regarding them nonetheless. When scientists discover new knowledge and accept these discoveries as true, they become committed to them and thereby embody them in their beliefs. Anything explicit presupposes a fund of inexplicit knowing. Thinking begins with core beliefs, though human knowing is not restricted by them. Our theoretical models are propositions about human existence. They represent a set of basic beliefs about human destiny.

In this sense, scholarship is encompassed by its presuppositions. Nietzsche's humanism is faith-based in the same formal sense as Woods and Patton's theism. Scholarly work, as in this book, is confessional in character. Integrity requires that we choose issues and develop interpretive perspectives that are consistent with our beliefs about truth, the nature of humans, and axiology. Understanding our worldview in thick terms illuminates our own pathway and the journeys of others.

In this inspiring book, the theistic perspective enriches our understanding of the way the media work. It enters academia as a serious option for teaching and learning. In the imagery of Jesus's parable, confessional scholarship lets the wheat and tares grow up together until the *eschaton* (Matt. 13:24–30). And in the debates on this side of heaven over presuppositions, over realism and relativism, over the aesthetics and ethics of popular culture, this book will turn heads and contribute a compelling voice.

Introduction

Prophetically Incorrect

First things first. This is not a book about politics. It is not a book that teaches you how to develop a gift of prophecy. Nor will you learn how to identify signs of biblical promises regarding the end times. Our lack of discussion about such things does not mean we think they are unimportant. They simply reside outside our scope of expertise.

Instead, as students and teachers of communication and media, we are interested in how individuals might interact with popular media prophetically, or with a prophetic voice. More specifically, how can we, in the tradition of the Old Testament prophets, engage popular media? And how can we identify such prophetic media engagement when we see or hear it from others, whether inside or outside the church?

A New Take on What Would Jesus Do? (WWJD)

We are drawn to the bold, faithful truthtelling of the Old Testament prophets. They said things we wish we could have and hope we would have said in the same situations. We are also drawn to their rage—not rage as in bitterness, or being out of control, or feeling dwarfed by the accomplishments of others, but rage as in: "Can you believe it!?!" "Enough is enough!" "Someone has to say something!"

We recognize that the word *prophet* causes discomfort for some. The list of false prophets grows daily, and cultlike nightmares led by counterfeits live in our collective memories. Plus, the word is used today to describe a dizzying array of individuals, from entertainers to politicians. It seems that just about any cherished figure in a particular tradition is dubbed *prophet*. We are right to be wary.

But the place of the prophet as one who speaks truth, calls for accountability, and champions justice is too important to give up in light of the global and local crises we face, even with the threat of counterfeits. So, we distinguish capital-P Prophets from small-p prophets. Capital-P Prophets include Isaiah, Jeremiah, Ezekiel, Amos, and others like them in the biblical record who heard a direct, supernatural word from God and later spoke on his behalf.[1] Small-p prophets are individuals tied intimately with, and accountable to, specific communities, who passionately and courageously interpret their life and times from the perspective of faith—and in that sense "read," or interpret, "the signs of the times." Regardless of their skill, however, they do not necessarily presume a direct, supernatural word from God.[2]

In the small-p sense, all Christians are called to be everyday prophets: to interpret events from a biblical perspective, to tell it like it is and how it should be. The Old Testament prophets often are thought to be tellers of the future, in a category with Nostradamus, Jeane Dixon, or more recently John Edward. But the biblical prophets were not primarily foretellers. Rather, they were *forth*tellers, or truthtellers: messengers who brought a message that was sorely needed for a particular time.

In this light, the prophetic vocation today is not a calling to be modern-day Jeremiahs, and it is not reserved for those with special gifts. Rather, it is an overarching directive as part of the "prophethood of all believers"[3] to demonstrate resistance thinking—that is, thinking that resists the dominant forces of our culture while simultaneously helping others imagine alternative, hope-filled ways of thinking and being.[4] In this setting, "What Would *Jesus* Do?" (WWJD) becomes "What Would *Jeremiah* Do?"

Since we see Jesus in the prophets and the prophets in Jesus, we are comfortable turning this popular phrase (WWJD) to ask how the prophets' communication practices and traditions might inform our interaction with popular media. In the Old Testament, prophecy served the same functions that the apostle Paul lists in the New Testament: edification, or building up (and tearing down, e.g., Jer. 1:10, in which God's word overthrows and restores nations); exhortation, which can include criticism and rebuke; and consolation, or comfort and hope (nearly all Old Testament prophets, no matter how focused they were on judgment, included a message of consolation and hope).[5] It is easy to imagine the prophets only as thunder-bearers, but they were also critics motivated by compassion and deep concern for their fellow community members.

Moreover, our emphasis on Jeremiah and other Old Testament prophets does not mean we see them as simple alternatives or superior role models to Jesus, or that we think that Jesus is simply part of a larger list of prophets. Jesus Christ was the last great prophet, the "ultimate prophet who conferred gravely and in transcendent glory"[6] with two of his prophetic predecessors on the Mount of Transfiguration. The necessary emphasis for Christians on the salvific work and words of the Savior, Jesus of Nazareth, the chief prophet, does not lessen, let alone negate, the urgency and relevance of the Hebrew prophets.[7] Even though Jesus and the apostles do some social criticism, the Old Testament prophets give more sustained attention to issues of social justice than the figures in the New Testament.[8]

The Day Jeremiah Visited a Theme Park

We are not the first to examine closely the relevance of the Old Testament prophets' communication traditions and practices to today's world. For instance, scholars trace the source of much of the rhetoric of radical reform in North America—from slavery to civil rights—to the prophetic books and therefore study closely their form and style of speech.[9] Others use the prophets to develop models for politics[10] and preaching.[11] Still others consider the presence of prophetic voices in certain forms of artistic expression, including poetry, music, and theater.[12] Our current project benefits greatly from their thinking.

There are few attempts, however, to develop models that address popular media's "prophetic witness." Such a model would use the prophetic as an organizing concept to analyze media content as well as media institutions and technologies.[13] So, applying a prophetic model to popular media, we might ask the following questions: How would the prophets critique popular media programming and its advertisements? What questions would they ask media owners and operators? What would they blog about or include on their Facebook walls? What music, video games, or comic books would they buy? Which movies or concerts would they attend? Would they visit a cyberchurch? And what about nontraditional media like multidimensional Christian theme parks?

Rabbi Abraham Joshua Heschel says a real biblical prophet is "bowed and stunned at man's fierce greed."[14] Fighting greed? Would a Christian theme park give Jeremiah a parking-lot soapbox to criticize greedy people and institutions? What would he say about the SUVs and designer jeans as people streamed from the lot to the main doors? Or about the cheap religious trinkets available in the Holy Land gift shop?

Heschel adds that a prophet's words "are often slashing, designed to shock rather than to edify."[15] Like Ezekiel's description of Jerusalem's harlotry,[16] the contemporary prophet's work would not be family-friendly. Imagine Jeremiah standing on top of a lemonade stand, angrily shouting at the picture-taking, spiritually lukewarm tourists who just skipped church to celebrate a Sunday together at the "sacred" theme park. The little kids are crying, pleading to go home. Some adults are shouting back at him, telling him to clean up his language.

Prophetic? Yes! Easy to swallow? No!

If Rabbi Heschel is even partly right, few of us are in the mood for anything deeply prophetic. The prophets are watchmen. They do not hesitate to draw attention toward our leaders' hypocritical actions and attitudes. They attack idolatry, pride, and complacency. They speak out particularly against those who would "eat my people's flesh" (Mic. 3:3), who would make "widows their prey" (Isa. 10:2).[17] They warn of doom, but hold out hope of redemption. Their message is not likely to be very entertaining, especially when we see the finger pointing at us. Nor would it be, on its face, overtly evangelistic. And it probably would not be very good for the theme park business. We may not be ready for it, but faithful media stewardship demands the presence of such "prophetically (in)correct" voices.

Faithful Media Stewardship

The cautious reader may conclude that our prophetic approach to popular media adds up to little more than a warmed-over social gospel, or that we are underemphasizing evangelism or compromising on bedrock values like the sanctity of life. Not so. We simply cannot escape the words of the Old Testament prophets and Jesus about love, justice, peace, and righteousness.[18] Both called for individual *and* cultural transformation. Faithful media stewardship thus recognizes wisdom in the affirmation of both voices at work in the church today. In addition, faithful media stewardship recognizes the following:

1. *There is a close relationship between critiquing, creating, and consuming popular media.*[19] Throughout this book we move reflexively among these three modes since how we critique media influences—and is influenced by—what we create and what we consume. *Critiquing* media is guided by the overarching responsibility of living redemptively, moment by moment, acknowledg-

ing the responsibility of love and good deeds.[20] *Creating* media is sustained by one's critical faculty: an act of the will to choose this word, or that color, or that contour, or that next musical note. *Consuming* media—choosing which program to watch or which song on iTunes to download—is also a by-product of one's critical faculty. Thus, whether we are critiquing, creating, or consuming popular media, we have opportunities to develop our prophetic sensibilities.[21]

2. *Criticism of popular media is not license to critique, create, or consume any kind of mass media in the name of challenging the status quo.* The Old Testament prophets, as will be explained in chapter 2, operated within interpretive communities that held them accountable for their criticism. Prophetic criticism takes seriously the biblical principle that although everything is permissible, not everything may be beneficial.[22] This principle, along with certain aesthetic traditions and personal sensitivities toward media content, can be used to establish practical guidelines when it comes to making everyday media decisions.[23]

3. *Both popular media content and media technologies matter.* Media content is an easy target for Christians, and for good reason. Concerns about the coarsening of cultural life through excessive displays of sex and violence are legitimate. But the technologies that deliver the content are also made by human beings, and as such reflect human values, desires, and aspirations. Each communication technology has its own unique DNA, or characteristic predispositions that shape human communication.[24] So, while your cell phone does not make you do anything, it does influence the way you interact with others and the world around you. Playing video games is fun, but it may desensitize us to violence. Television delivers important news and rich entertainment, but it encourages us to think that seeing is believing. Each technology, then, comes with benefits and burdens apart from the content it delivers. We highlight these benefits and burdens throughout, and offer a special case study on one technology (television) in chapter 7.

For now, note that developing technological literacy begins by asking at least three key questions: (1) "What values are inherent in this medium (my TV, PC, and cell phone)?" (2) "What impact does this medium have on my relationship with others and with God?"[25] And since each technology is part of several social institutions that guide our use of the technology, we also ask, (3) "What impact do various social institutions such as the family, business, or government have on why and how we use certain technologies?"

4. *Prophetic voices come in different shapes and sizes and from unexpected places.* We do not offer a cookie-cutter approach in answering, "Who is the popular media prophet?" In chapter 2 we identify characteristics that distinguish the prophetic critic of popular media from other kinds of critics. None of the characteristics, however, presume membership in a particular Christian denomination. We offer names and suggest certain prophetic voices throughout that might not fit comfortably in church pews. But Old and New Testament examples illustrate that God used unexpected individuals prophetically at times to describe how bad things were and how good they might be. All popular media artists—and nonartists—have a spiritual orientation that frames their approach to everything. To the extent that popular artists' moral offerings to their audiences align with a biblical perspective, we consider the prophetic possibilities of such offerings.

Therefore, in this book, we refer to non-Christian media as *mainstream media* rather than *secular media* to avoid making knee-jerk or superficial judgments about media that do not seem to be very religious, at least on the surface. We use *Christian media* to refer to the grouping of all media that claim to be Christian by one or another Christian subcommunity, or tribe[26]—including Roman Catholic, mainline Protestant, and evangelical tribal media.

5. *Good criticism is grounded in tradition and history, not trends.* A lot of media criticism is driven by popular opinion or the latest fad. Many critics believe they are saying something new or expounding new morality. Competing voices clamor for attention,

seeking converts to their unique brand of media criticism.[27] It is difficult sometimes to distinguish legitimate critique from political commentary or self-promotion.

In contrast, the prophets avoided faddish, fragmented critique by grounding their message in a particular tradition. Their critique was not radically new; it depended on previous messages. They called the people to be faithful to the particular tradition in which they were placed. For the most part, the prophets disclaimed originality; yes, they had heard from God in a fresh way, but the message was fueled by their confidence that they were speaking for Moses and the patriarchs. This in no way means their work lacked creativity; rather, it was important to situate their criticism within history, since the past gave meaning to the present.

6. *No special training is required.* At this point you might say, "I'm not a pastor. I cannot sing or write poetry. I do not blog. I do not have my own television show or weekly column. Nor do I understand the inner workings of the television industry or the fine art of filmmaking. Besides, the DNA of technology sounds way too complicated. I plan to leave this stuff to the experts!"

Nevertheless, we are all popular media critics regardless of our training. It is unavoidable. The shows we watch and video games we play (or let our children watch and play) are moral statements about the media. When we consider a song's deeper meaning or chat with a friend about a movie, we are doing media criticism. Prophetic media criticism is open to anyone willing to make a commitment to steward his or her affections toward popular media—whether a book, photograph, article, painting, or news story—and ask important questions, such as "Why do I hate or love this? What does it provoke or confirm for me? Defy or confront? How is it consistent with biblical values?" Whether we share our answers to these questions as self-reflections or in conversations with others, each offers opportunity for reflection about, and subsequent movement toward, the great biblical prophetic values of peace, freedom, love, truth, and justice.

Heschel and Brueggemann

At the start our readers must know of our indebtedness to the voices of two Old Testament scholars, one Jewish and one Christian, whose writings on the prophets have influenced our work: Abraham Joshua Heschel and Walter Brueggemann. Their work will be referenced numerous times throughout this book, with fuller details in many cases included in the endnotes.

Abraham Joshua Heschel, who died in 1972, was a philosopher of religion and of Judaism, with a "broad knowledge of the whole of Judaism, and with a worldwide impact on Jewish and Christian thought."[28] He was professor of Jewish ethics and mysticism at the Jewish Theological Seminary of America, New York, and, coincidentally, a colleague of Martin Buber. Heschel's two-volume series on the prophets is considered a significant classic in the field of Old Testament studies, and his life and work are regarded as formidable instruments in the reengagement of prophetic work and its possibilities in a contemporary setting. Heschel "reintroduced in our time the prophetic tradition" and "exemplified it."[29]

The four characteristics that make up our profile of the prophetic critic of popular media in chapters 3–6 are taken from Heschel's monumental two-volume work, *The Prophets*. This is not to say that Heschel lists them numerically, or that there are only four, or that he applied the four we use to popular media. We chose these four characteristics because they represent Heschel's overall emphasis, and because they are not tied to the unique historic mission of the classical Hebrew prophets of the eighth through the fifth century BC. We use these four characteristics as a launching pad to extend our thinking about what it means to engage popular media prophetically as faithful media stewards today.

Walter Brueggemann is a North American Old Testament scholar and professor at Columbia Theological Seminary, Decatur, Georgia, and ordained minister in the United Church of Christ. As with Heschel, Brueggeman's work on the prophetic does not include a direct emphasis on, or application to, popular media, yet it is extremely helpful for considering ways to develop a prophetic sensibility in a contemporary setting. From Brueggemann's now-classic book *The Prophetic Imagination* we apply several key concepts, including but not limited to dominant consciousness, alternative consciousness, achievable satiation, religion of optimism, and prophetic imagination. These phrases are defined early on and used throughout the book to build our arguments.

Reading Heschel is an immediate workout in cultivating a prophetic voice; reading Brueggemann is a similar experience. We hope for anyone not familiar with either scholar that our application of their works will encourage a closer reading.

The Big Picture and Other Helpful Reminders

Part of our interest in cultivating a small-p prophetic sensibility came as we realized that most popular media involvement, in our own lives and in the lives of our students, occurred out of boredom. We realized that our participation lacked intentionality and a clear sense as to how our media involvement related to the lordship of Jesus and the call to do all things in his name.[30] Therefore, we have become increasingly interested in exploring how our dance with popular media avoids turning us into passive participants, robbed of the energizing strength to actively lead and reflect on our dance as unto the Lord.

With that said, our book seeks to introduce readers to the possibilities of cultivating a wise prophetic sensibility as they engage popular media and its technologies. We hope that advanced readers already immersed in such thinking and activity will encounter fresh insights and discover new sources for study in our endnotes. Like the Hebrew prophets whose "whole being was involved in their message,"[31] the prophetic sensibility can be a way of seeing, hoping, and experiencing all of life.

Also, the prophetic sensibility must be understood as working in tandem with a priestly sensibility. We do not seek to elevate one sensibility over the other in the pages that follow. The priestly sensibility, as described in chapter 1, can reinforce what is good and wise in our families, churches, and all of a society's institutions, including mass media. This is a natural and necessary part of faithful media stewardship. At the same time, the prophetic sensibility confronts lovingly what is not wise and good, including our relationship with media, and courageously offers constructive correctives. The prophetic sensibility lives with a disquieting irritation that disallows the possibility of becoming too enmeshed with any existing order.[32] Both voices are needed in the church today.

Additionally, both priestly and prophetic voices may be attributed to the same individual. In other words, the same voice that speaks prophetically on one occasion may speak with a priestly voice on another occasion, for better or worse. For instance, in chapter 1, we offer an example of priestly communication by Father Michael Pfleger, a Catholic priest who was speaking at Trinity United Church of Christ in Chicago. We are well aware that on other occasions, Father Pfleger's criticism of the dominant cultural order resonates with strong prophetic overtones. In chapter 2, we suggest that Bono, lead singer of rock band U2, has a prophetic voice. This does not mean that everything Bono says (or that all of U2's music) is prophetic. The point is that the prophetic (or priestly) voice is not an all-or-nothing proposition. Each act of communication must therefore be judged on its own merits, and not on past expressions or the general reputation of the individual communicator.

Finally, it should be clear by now that this book is more than an exercise in abstract thinking. Such an exploration would be in vain (and inconsistent with the prophetic tradition) if it did not produce some practical suggestions for coping with our current media environment. We thus make periodic recommendations: sometimes by asking what we think are the right questions, other times by offering examples and exercises to help cultivate prophetic sensibilities. Of course, all of these should be considered carefully in the cultural and theological context of a reader's own church community.

Organization of the Book

In chapter 1, we explore the priestly role of popular media in North America. We define the character, or *ethos*, of modern North American culture as consumerism and consider how it shapes our lives, how popular media reinforce it, and how it opens the door for prophetic possibilities. In chapter 2 we look more closely at the prophetic critic, asking what motivations and core commitments specifically define his or her *talk* about popular media. We conclude chapter 2 with a profile of the modern prophetic critic of popular media as one who (1) becomes inconsolably burdened by greed and arrogance, (2) is consumed by humanity's fallen plight and the alienating effects of greed and arrogance on individuals and institutions, (3) rejects a spirit of acceptance among individuals and institutions toward the dominant cultural order, and (4) emotionally burns with critical images that shock the complacent out of their numbness toward the effects of the dominant cultural order. In chapters 3–6 we further describe each characteristic in the profile and demonstrate its application in the popular media context. Then, in chapter 7, we offer a special case study of one technology (television) to demonstrate in greater detail how the critique of media technologies themselves might open new and exciting avenues of thought for prophetic critics, creators, and consumers. In our concluding chapter, we identify several occupational hazards related to prophetic criticism and offer advice on how to avoid such hazards.

We suppose that the goal of every author is to write something that serves readers for a long time. We hope and pray that this book does just that. To the small-p prophets among us and to those yet to come, welcome to the conversation.

1

Communicating Faithfully in a Culture of Ideological Division

In 2006, *Crash* won the Academy Award for best picture and original screenplay. Set in present-day Los Angeles, *Crash* explores what happens when characters from different racial and socioeconomic backgrounds "crash" into one another. Its overall tone is unsettling. Its R-rated content would keep it off many Christians' "must see" list. And this film about racism does not provide clear solutions to life's problems.

Yet many Christians consider *Crash* to be as religious as *The Passion of the Christ* or *Facing the Giants*. Why? Because it is *prophetic*: that is, it draws attention to social sins often overlooked by mainstream and Christian media and, like the Old Testament prophets, "draws viewers into an experience of death—startling them into an awareness of their own mortality, and bringing to consciousness the possibility of the death of our society."[1] *Christianity Today* considered *Crash* one of the ten most redeeming films of 2005.[2]

If *Christianity Today* is right, then *Crash* challenges those who narrowly define Christian media as "family-friendly" media produced or consumed primarily by Christians. Furthermore, if

1

Christianity Today is right, then Christian journalists, playwrights, filmmakers, and talk show hosts preoccupied with evangelism and edification on one hand, and news or public relations on the other, may be overlooking an important function of Christian communication in society. The redemptive possibilities of *Crash* challenge Christians to bring clarity to the definition and role of prophetic communication in popular media.

In this chapter we argue that mass media in consumer-driven, market-oriented economies play a priestly rather than prophetic role in an attempt to attract audiences for advertisers by mainly reinforcing rather than challenging a culture's *dominant consciousness*.[3] (We argue that North America's dominant consciousness is characterized by the ethos of consumerism.) Given this priestly function, popular media function like churches, insofar as they connect people with stories that reflect what they believe.

Second, we argue that Christian media also play a priestly role and follow fairly predictable patterns of consumption and criticism. In the process, Christian media on the Left and Right practice what we call *tribal correctness*, confirming what their audiences already believe and amplifying their group's existing prejudices. Many Christian media are more preoccupied with maintaining audiences than addressing wider societal issues.

Before concluding, we suggest that to challenge truthfully a culture's dominant consciousness, Christian media professionals and lay communicators must reclaim an understanding of the prophetic role of church in society and the redemptively subversive potential of media and technology. Like *Crash*, prophetic communication challenges Christians to be prophetically (in)correct—to transcend ideological divides and grasp a comprehensive focus of Jesus's call for justice, mercy, and faithfulness.[4]

Media as Priestly Propaganda

Mass media are storytellers that produce and present myths for public consumption. The word "myth" comes from *mythoi*, which refers to stories that people in a particular community use to understand themselves.[5] A myth packages beliefs and values that are vital and long-lasting to the culture, such as the rags-to-riches (North American Dream) myth, portrayed in *Erin Brockovich*, *Rudy*, *Waterboy*; the romantic messiah myth, depicted in *Pretty Woman*, *An Officer and a Gentleman*, *The 40-Year-Old Virgin*; or the individual freedom myth, shown in *The Fugitive*, *Cider House Rules*, and *The Shawshank Redemption*, to name a few.[6]

Myth does not necessarily have anything to do with the truth or falsity of the value or belief. The events described in the myth may never have happened. Instead, a myth creates shared experiences by capturing a particular community's beliefs and feelings about life. "Instead of sitting around the fire recalling tales of our own cultural tribes," suggests media scholar Quentin J. Schultze, "we gather around the television, read newspapers and magazines, attend movies, and listen to the radio."[7]

As a major source of popular mythologies, media function like ecclesiological structures, or religious institutions. Media are like a "secular bible," Schultze writes, the "sacred stories" of which provide a shared map of reality and instruct individuals about a culture's rules for living.[8] In fact, "the average congregant spends more time watching television in one day than he spends in all spiritual pursuits combined for an entire week."[9] Shows like *Entertainment Tonight* become televised worship services that summarize the latest commandments and epistles of celebrity "priests." As comedian Jim Carey said in the movie *The Cable Guy*, we are "learning the facts of life from *The Facts of Life*," a 1980s sitcom.

Media perform a priestly function in that they confirm and exploit what the community wants to believe about itself. The word "priest" is related to the Latin *pontifex*, which describes the priest's role as mediator or "bridge builder." Media perform rituals and build bridges that connect us to our culture's broader beliefs. For instance, investigative info-tainment shows like *Dateline NBC* and *60 Minutes* confirm our belief in the need to unmask villains and protect individuals from evil corporations. *Rocky* confirms that rugged individualism and self-determination are the ways to overcome hardships in life. *It's a Wonderful Life* and *Forrest Gump* confirm that God helps those who help themselves. Like real priests, priestly media let us take part in rituals about happiness, success, romance, and other such mythologies. They are part of our "culture's liturgy," presenting "ritualistic stories that assure us of the promise of the myth repeated over and over again."[10] This is why one media scholar calls television viewing, in particular, a ritual at the video altar.[11]

Finally, as French sociologist and lay Christian theologian Jacques Ellul explains, priestly media are propaganda: they tell people what they want to believe more than they try to challenge or change their beliefs. Ellul further distinguishes between the gospel truths of the Christian faith and the everyday popular mythologies we accept as truth. Commercial media are not interested in speaking truth as much as they are concerned with economic gain. Popular media tell stories in an effort to maintain old and gain new audiences. In the process, they reinforce the existing cultural system's beliefs about its own power and goodness.[12]

Media and the North American Dominant Consciousness

Our culture's dominant consciousness is composed of the core values and beliefs that dominate the way we live, the way we understand and make sense of the world and our place in it, our understanding of who has power and who is powerless, and our understanding of how things work and how they should work. The dominant consciousness represents a culture's *Zeitgeist*—its "spirit of the age."[13] If *worldview* is a culture's perceptual map, then *Zeitgeist* is the expressed reason for the ride.

The North American dominant consciousness—and one that likely applies to most Western capitalistic cultures—is *consumerism*, characterized by a cycle of acquisition-consumption-disposal. This framing story, or metanarrative, says we are godlike creatures "free to live without moral or ecological limits and that we exist merely to consume products and experience maximum pleasure."[14] It further proclaims a messianic promise in technological advancement.

That ours is a culture based on consumption is a commonplace maxim that startles no one. But in generations and centuries past, self-identity and social integration were based primarily on production, or what someone produced, and on the workplace. Today the things we consume are the dominant prerequisite of individual self-identity and organized society. We use our purchases as ways to identify with certain individuals, communities, and lifestyles, purchasing items to help establish affiliation—"I shop, therefore I belong." We are not what we make anymore, we are what we buy—"I shop, therefore I am." Such is our national character.[15]

Christian author Brian McLaren describes the consumerist narrative as a "suicide story," one that is both powerfully destructive and covert. Beneath the surface it drives the dominant systems of our culture and is responsible for many of our world crises today.[16] It is deeply embedded in symbols, institutions, and cultural practices, and it orients our thinking in such a way that we accept the current way of doing things as natural. The ethos of consumerism parallels Solomon's *royal consciousness* in the Old Testament and even exceeds its commitment to *achievable satiation*—or confidence in the culture's ability to satisfy hungers, whatever their size and propriety.[17]

While overt propaganda is explicit about its message, covert propaganda conceals its intentions, subtly pushing populations toward certain views and affirming certain visions of goodness, responsibility, and beauty. Advertisers do not shout, "Buy this product and you will receive individual freedom, power, and happiness." Instead, they pair products with appealing images and music that target emotions and short-circuit critical thinking. Rocky Balboa does not say, "Yo, Adrian. The meaning of my life and actions is to shake free of a limiting past in a struggling ascent to an open and gracious future."[18] Instead, this rags-to-riches myth is reinforced through characters' actions and carefully edited images. In short, covert propaganda is not a conspiracy; rather, people simply choose images that seem natural and commonsensical within the culture.

Cultural analyst Christopher Lasch explained that the ethos of consumerism—which he calls the "modern propaganda of commodities" and the "good life"—has sanctioned "impulse gratification and made it unnecessary for the id to apologize for its wishes or disguise [its] grandiose proportions."[19] Within North America's dominant consciousness, getting what we want when we want it is the main problem to be solved, and "God has no other business than to maintain our standard of living."[20] Efficiency is the highest good, and getting things done is elevated above most other values. Meanwhile, consumerism assimilates all protests against the dominance of its "total cultural worldview," co-opting and thereby weakening them—making it difficult for opposing ideas to be disseminated.[21] A recent credit card commercial assimilated critics' concerns about achievable satiation when it said, "We are a nation of consumers, and there's nothing wrong with that. . . . After all, there's a lot of cool stuff out there."[22]

Priestly mass media informally, and chiefly, sanction our culture's ethos of consumerism. Each year North American advertisers roll out billions of ads that reinforce the same basic message: "We are what we buy; and only when we have bought enough will we accomplish the American dream and be content."[23] From commercial ads to what we see in popular programming, "It is tough to shake the notion that what counts is our comfort."[24]

Especially in a commercially driven system, priestly media must appeal to the broader community's dominant consciousness since they require faithful participation to build audiences and attract advertisers. (See figure 1 below.) The "Popular Culture Formula" explains that the "popularity of a given cultural element (object, person or event) is directly proportional to the degree to which that element is reflective of general audience beliefs and values."[25] In the television industry, *least objectionable programming* (LOP) is the term used to describe popular programming by network gatekeepers who "pander to mediocrity by airing bland, disposable programming that will not disturb or challenge a typical viewer."[26] Media that ignore the formula and challenge the culture's mythic beliefs and values risk losing popularity.

> **FIGURE 1**
>
> **North American Dominant Consciousness**
> (Our culture's *Zeitgeist*)
> ⇕
> **Ethos of Consumerism**
> ("Framing Story")
> ⇕
> **Mass Media**
> ("Priestly" Function)

In this setting, it is not surprising that commercial media mythologies repackaged in an ethos of consumerist frenzy are often incompatible with gospel truths. For instance, individual independence and success often come at the expense of the biblical value of the redemptive development of the family, church, and community. Many advertisements suggest that external beauty determines one's worth, whereas Scripture emphasizes internal beauty and the heart. The mass-media worldview tells North Americans that they are "basically good, that happiness is the chief end in life, and that happiness consists in obtaining material goods,"[27] whereas Scripture emphasizes that legitimate happiness is unselfishly oriented.

In our experience, American Christians in the United States suffer from a kind of dualism as it relates to the ethos of consumerism. We are good at using the rhetoric of "integration, worldview, and kingdom service," according to John Van Dyk, but often foster instead "an accepting attitude toward the typical North American priorities: a luxury home, gadgets and paraphernalia we don't need, an almost religious dedication to the world of sports, and the glorification of celebrity and financial success, no matter what the pressure in our personal or family life."[28]

In the church, consumption communities turn cheap trinkets into Jesus merchandise. They peddle everything from "Christian" weight loss programs to coffee mugs to breath fresheners. Christian publishers create demand for special Bible translations, including leadership Bibles, gender-specific Bibles, adult and teenage Bibles. Many tribal bestsellers are by Christian celebrities known for their megachurches or broadcast ministries, music careers, or politics. Although consumption communities can help strengthen tribal members' faith, they also run the risk of commercial exploitation of spiritual desires.[29]

The Popular Culture Formula gives an introductory picture of the difficulty in promoting an *alternative consciousness*[30] (or alternative framing story) and resisting the near-omnipresence of the dominant consciousness. So, how do Christians engage media in a culture in which popular media progressively strengthens an individual's identification with the dominant consciousness?

Christian Media Use and Criticism

Christians gather together in subcultures, or *tribes*. Christians carve up Jesus's diverse, worldwide church into movements and minichurches. Each tribe thinks that it has special, and often superior, insights about relating faith to culture. One tribe says *Crash* is prophetic, while another considers it profane. Who is right? It depends on which tribe someone belongs to.

Christians' engagement with media technologies and media content is based on their understanding of the role of church in society and what it means to be in the world but not of it.[31] Broadly speaking, apart from tribes that outrightly reject media and those that accept it with few limitations, most North American Christian tribes fall into two consistent categories: *Proclaimers* and *Transformers*.

Proclaimers. Proclaimers promote evangelism and edification as chief functions of Christian media. The church is viewed primarily as a herald that received an official message and passed it on; therefore, media should be used for a kind of "first proclamation."[32] Proclaimers are among the first to adopt new media technologies in service of Christ's Great Commission to spread the gospel faith.[33] To remain separate and apart in an ungodly media environment, Proclaimers recommend avoiding morally questionable content—mainly sex, violence, and profanity; boycotting media with the most offensive content; and choosing family-friendly programming.[34] They create Christian versions of nearly every form of popular media as a way to teach, encourage, and strengthen resolve.[35]

Proclaimers' media criticism tends to be moralistic.[36] It is usually not grounded in a full review of the particular event or media content, its context, or its apparent meaning for a given audience. Criticism appears rules-based at times and often says more about the critic's personal biases or his or her tribe's fears than about the Christian metanarrative.[37] Proclaimers' criticism seems insensitive to the ways believers can receive valuable religious truths from popular media.[38]

Transformers. Transformers do not deny that evangelism or edification are important, but avoid placing the church in opposition to society and instead see the church in dialogue with the world.[39] God not only gave Christians the Great Commission but a mandate to form and inform culture, which calls them to redeem not just individuals but cultural institutions, including the media. Since all truth is God's truth, Christians should search for faith-affirming interpretations among all types of popular media content.[40]

Transformers' media criticism tends to be analytical, i.e., exegetical or hermeneutical.[41] By exegetical we mean that they perform close readings of myths found in popular media. They first define the event or media content, then explain its context, and then identify a dominant reading or interpretation. Finally, they look for "points of tension, synergy, allegory, and irony between the TV series' [or other stories'] meaning and Christian faith." This cultural critique is "lower criticism with a higher purpose, or using a religious metanarrative to exegete the patterns and meaning of mass media's mythological formulas."[42]

Strengths and Weaknesses. Both Proclaimers and Transformers do media criticism with one foot in mainstream popular culture and the other one in their tribe's beliefs. Both try to subvert popular notions of truth while asserting their own contrary notions of reality consistent with biblical truth. Both support critical functions of Christian communication and the church in the world, including evangelism, edification, and cultural critique.

Yet Proclaimers' overemphasis on evangelism and edification often means there is little room for popular art that might be devoted to battling "falsehoods" and "lies of corrupt regimes."[43] In assuming that most mainstream media are evil at worst, unedifying at best, Proclaimers underestimate the value of this world's culture and government, although there is common grace by which even unbelievers are able to discover truth, create objects of beauty, launch worthwhile social projects, and perform humanitarian efforts with integrity and skill.[44]

Transformers sometimes walk a fine line between understanding the world without surrendering to its mold. Some deceive themselves when they think they can rise above harmful media content in the name of critical analysis. And sometimes their calls for cultural transformation overshadow calls for personal holiness.

Both Proclaimers and Transformers tend to place too little emphasis on the various social institutions surrounding popular media that reinforce the dominant consciousness. Popular media are always a combination of content, technology, and social institutions. Television technologies—such as cameras, lights, and computer-editing software—are part of several social institutions. These institutions have certain values that guide media producers' use of such technology and determine what content is delivered and how it is delivered.

In the United States, for instance, commercial television networks, production companies, and advertising agencies "have decided that the technology of television should be used primarily to attract audiences and to sell those audiences to advertisers," writes Schultze. Based on the Nielsen ratings, advertisers pay for the commercial time to reach the audiences they want. Nearly everything on commercial television done with cameras, lights, and editors "reflects the goal of building audiences for advertisers." Compare this to public television, which tends to educate and inform audiences with somewhat less attention paid to audience size.[45]

Of course, other social institutions are also involved in television. Family values influence the content of shows that networks air and when they air them. In the United States, television has its own government organizations that monitor "appropriate" programming. (The Federal Communications Commission plays this role.) Nongovernmental groups provide rating systems that give viewers an idea of the suitability of certain television programming for children.[46]

Not only do both Proclaimers and Transformers place little emphasis on the various social institutions surrounding popular media, but both also pay little attention to the media technology itself. Many suggest that technology is neutral, meaning it is morally neutral, or amoral.[47] They believe that technology, like rocks and trees, is soulless; only humans have souls and are capable of sin.[48] Accordingly, what makes a particular technology good or bad is the actual use to which it is directed. (As we explain later in chapter 5, this position often leads to media idolatry.)

Although much has been written to demonstrate that technology is not neutral,[49] we can best serve our readers by offering a simple but helpful explanation of two foundational ideas.

First, a belief in technological neutrality confuses inanimate objects in nature with objects created by human beings. Popular media technologies are human creations and as such are cultural artifacts, or products, that nurture the values and biases of their human inventors. For instance, personal computers were created by people like Bill Gates, who valued organizing vast amounts of information, sending messages (at high speeds), and connecting individuals and businesses worldwide.[50] Thus, regardless of the actual messages sent, computers nurture efficiency, information sharing, speed, and globalization. These values are the additional *message* of the computer system that accompanies any content, regardless of whose hands the system is in.[51]

Moreover, computers indeed consist of soulless microchips and motherboards, but the values they nurture still affect human life and consciousness in positive and negative ways. For instance, computers let us organize and send vast amounts of information, but also encourage *informationism*—an almost religious "faith in the collection and dissemination of information as a route to social progress and personal happiness."[52] Computers create jobs and allow us to work efficiently, but heavy users typically communicate differently from the rest of us.[53] And despite our reported "global village" sense of belonging, our collective sense seems to be that community is diminishing rather than increasing. As Benjamin Barber put it, "The planet is falling precipitately [abruptly] apart and coming reluctantly together at the very same moment," a phenomenon described as "McWorld."[54]

Second, although technology does not speak directly, it has its own language apart from the content it delivers. By language we mean that each communication technology has its own unique way of capturing and presenting reality to audiences that involves a structural bias in its communication. In this sense, the potential of any technology is limited not just by social institutions or by its human operators, but by the very language of the technology itself.

For instance, we cannot watch radio—its bandwidth is too narrow to carry pictures. We can only listen to it. Theater requires a different kind of acting than film or television does. In most instances, the theater audience is far away from the actors' faces. Audience members must be told in a loud voice what is going on, and plot movements must be marked vividly rather than gently shaded by subtle facial expressions.[55] And filmmakers must decide whether their work will be released in its original format or reformatted to fit the different aspect ratio of the television set. If reformatted, it loses some of its original image quality; if not reformatted, images may be too small for people at home to see adequately.

We agree that a communicator's message may be aimed at improving or demeaning the human condition whether it is carried by voice, print, or electronic technology. We also acknowledge that technology is not determinative: our computers or cell phones do not make us do anything. People still act or fail to act based on their interpretation of certain messages. Despite these acknowledgments, however, we maintain that technology is not neutral. It clearly affects how messages are constructed and delivered, and it shapes the individuals who are immersed in its use.

It is helpful, then, to view faithful media criticism as a type of social criticism that addresses (1) the *content* of media itself, and how such content affects individuals, groups, and organizations in society; (2) the communication *technology* (or channels) that distribute songs, novels, newspapers, movies, and other cultural products or artifacts to large numbers of people in society; and (3) the practices and process of various social *institutions* that surround and regulate the channels of communication and determine how and when content is delivered. (See figure 2 below.)

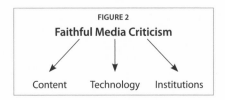

FIGURE 2
Faithful Media Criticism

Content   Technology   Institutions

Generally, the most incisive tribal critics are Transformers. Most Transformers recognize that each technology influences society and individuals in particular ways no matter how it is used. They are more likely than other tribal critics to recognize popular media as deeply embedded social institutions that both form and inform culture. They also tend to avoid knee-jerk reactions to mainstream media content and frame popular media myths in terms of tribal "control beliefs"[56] rather than couching criticism in separate or simple moralistic language that cuts short conversations. When tribal critics slip into moralistic labeling or media bullying, they often end up "preaching to the choir."

Preaching to the Choir

In a sermon at Trinity United Church of Christ in Chicago, Father Michael Pfleger pretended to be a sobbing Hillary Clinton in the aftermath of her loss for the 2008 democratic presidential bid to Senator Barack Obama: "She just always thought that, 'This is mine. I'm Bill's wife. I'm white.' Then out of nowhere came, 'Hey, I'm Barack Obama,' to which Hillary replied, 'Oh, damn, where did you come from? I'm white. I'm entitled. There's a black man stealing my show.'"[57]

What was Father Pfleger thinking? "Like many preachers before him," suggests syndicated religion columnist Terry Mattingly, he "fell for the temptation to 'preach to the choir,' their listeners who already agreed with them."[58]

In their approach to media, Christians often create their own religious broadcast ghettos. Christian books are consumed by those who are "born again" and Christian radio "rocks the flock."[59] Tribal television attracts overwhelmingly older, already committed evangelicals.[60] Nearly all tribal magazines and newspapers speak to specific audiences intensely interested in their content.[61] The audience of most Christian media is composed of Christians who desire to reinforce and supplement their beliefs and experiences. Christian media can be priestly too.

Christian media are under the same pressure as mainstream media to build and maintain audiences—perhaps even greater pressure, since much of their support comes from the audience and not the advertisers.[62] Consequently, Christian media often self-propagandize, telling already-loyal viewers what they want to hear. They promote political agendas and take sides on hot-button issues such as abortion, health care, and gay rights, while avoiding other important topics such as racism, poverty, and the environment.[63] The late Jerry Falwell said that "there's no need for the church of Jesus Christ to be wasting its time gullibly falling for all of this global warming hocus-pocus." Instead, he claimed, we should focus on "reaching this world with the Gospel of Jesus Christ."[64]

Like mainstream media, Christian media must transform their brands into "destinations," serving their targeted audience "better and in more ways than anyone else."[65] *The Christian Century* magazine, for instance, often confirms for readers that Jesus is a Democrat who cares about social justice and that the Far Right is imposing its values on everyone else, while *World* magazine often confirms for its conservative base that they can please Jesus by voting Republican and help the poor by promoting personal responsibility rather than governmental programs.[66] Each practices its own form of *tribal correctness* for avid audiences who devour specialized content and targeted ads.[67]

But in preaching to the choir, Christian media further promote ideological divisions already present among Christian tribes. Ideological divisions, in part, revolve around "competing ways of understanding and presenting the Christian gospel in America."[68] One side emphasizes individual salvation while the other side emphasizes social reform. Battle lines are drawn. Tribes concerned with large-scale social injustices are stereotyped as "liberals" who dilute the church's dominant purpose of winning souls, while tribes looking for converts are stereotyped as "fundamentalists" who emphasize patriotism and personal piety at the expense of cultural transformation. Not surprisingly, popular religious media are regularly dismissed by the mainstream press as Right or Left wing.

More important, perhaps, preaching to the choir means that few tribes effectively transcend the ideological divide. Innovative tribal artists who challenge tribal correctness get marginalized or pushed underground for fear of losing supporters. Christians who criticize or challenge their own tribal media become victims of harsh and often unfair condemnation. As a result, there is little sustained community discourse about media. On the whole, the actions and attitudes of tribal media mean that "Christian communities give up an attempt to act as a unified body, choosing instead to function according to the idea of 'local options,' thus losing ties to other Christians past and present."[69]

To transcend the ideological divide and speak in response to the forces of the dominant consciousness, Christian media must ultimately be less concerned with evoking applause from their audiences than provoking thoughtful, sometimes uncomfortable, reflection. Whether Christian media are preaching to liberals or conservatives, "it's hard to tell people truths that they don't want to hear. But if your people are smiling and applauding all of the time, that's when warning flags need to go up." If not, we may end up "defanging the gospel,"[70] and the "mantle of the prophets" might descend upon "secular shoulders."[71]

Prophetic Possibilities

The "Television Heisenberg Principle" says media can do more than just reflect reality or reinforce beliefs; they can also question widely accepted North American values such as individualism, consumerism, and the legitimacy of violence as a routine part of everyday life.[72] The Television Heisenberg Principle points to the tribal critic's responsibility to analyze the mass media's view of society.

Prophetic tribal critics neither *reject* mainstream media mythologies nor aim merely to *deconstruct* them; rather, they aim to imaginatively "*reconstruct* tribal liturgies of shared understanding and to reassert tribal expressions of hope" that cut across ideological divides and speak to wider audiences.[73] Using his or her own "prophetic imagination," the tribal critic casts an alternative framing story (or alternative consciousness) that confronts the dominant consciousness. The prophetic voice aggressively challenges our culture's dominant narrative at the subideological level while groups on the Right and Left push for their own agendas.

The prophetic critic imagines a different and presumably better world, and considers whether the media are moving us toward or away from his or her tribal concept of the good life. In some cases the prophetic critic illuminates the existing roadblocks and articulates the means that the tribe should use to achieve that better world. Patrick O'Heffernan, for instance, not only deconstructs the media coverage of the Los Angeles riots but asks his readers to "reconstruct" or consider what kind of world they wish to inhabit. The tribal critic can thus help the community to imagine an alternative vision of social reality that is in tune with its tribal beliefs and sentiments. In other cases, as in *Crash*, the prophetic critic, like the prophet Jeremiah, brings "viewers to a point of despair and thereby frees them to imagine a new alternative" without giving them that alternative just yet.[74]

One of the most prophetic Christian voices addressing the role of media technology and propaganda in modern life was that of Jacques Ellul.[75] According to Ellul, a culture with only priestly media is a dangerous place filled with arrogance and ignorance: "Day after day the wind blows away the pages of our calendars, our newspapers, and our political regimes, and we glide along the stream of time without any spiritual framework, without a memory, without a judgment, carried about by 'all winds of doctrine.'"[76] Without critical discernment, "a tribe implodes with its mythological self-delusion or explodes with its own conflicts."[77]

Here and there we see tribal media seeking to transcend what we described earlier as local options. The World Association for Christian Communications' (WACC) statement on prophetic communication says, "Prophetic communication stimulates critical awareness of the reality constructed by the media and helps people to distinguish truth from falsehood, to discern the subjectivity of the journalist and to disassociate that which is ephemeral and trivial from that which is lasting and valuable."[78] WACC backs up its statement with workshops, public statements, and publications that increase awareness of the negative effects of media monopolies and media's impact on women and the poor. Many tribes have organizations similar to WACC that take up issues of social justice. Other independent groups of lay Christian media workers demonstrate a "passion for prophetic truth" with their own brand of investigative journalism that targets Christian media activities.[79] Also, Christian magazines like *Geez*, *Relevant*, and *First*

Things regularly challenge priestly periodicals with a prophetic sensibility.

To inspire North American Christians and Christian media to engage prophetically requires "a profound transformation in our worship life, and the kinds of sins we confess."[80] Christian media must address a wide range of important cultural issues including materialism, consumerism, self-deification, gluttony, ethnic stereotypes in films, sexism in soap operas, and violence in sports, and not focus solely on individual, isolated instances of morally objectionable content.

Prophetic engagement also requires that tribal critics *speak truth to power*, which refers to the action of the biblical prophets and their courage in challenging those who became preoccupied with maintaining their power at the expense of truth—as well as justice, fairness, and compassion.[81] The prophetic critic "follows the rhetorical way of Jesus, turning popular wisdom on its head and standing up for the victims of society."[82] Jesus exposed and confronted the dominant consciousness in his own day and offered a radically different narrative. His radical faith and prophetic voice included attacks against institutional power and injunctions against his disciples' pursuit of self-interested power. These attacks in no way diminished his message of personal salvation.

A prophetic communication model can help Christians to defect faithfully from the culture's dominant narrative while providing a message of hope in a hopeless time. It can encourage believers to rise above the supposed supremacy of any particular tribal agenda and address issues that arise out of core religious values and a common biblical heritage. It brings together mainline Protestants and Catholics as well as African American, Latino, Asian, and Native American faith communities that desire both spiritual revival *and* social change. The idea of a *prophetic blessing* for the community at large is an important concept in the prophetic tradition and offers direction in a culture characterized by ideological division. In a culture of polarization, in which "powerful and powerless groups often both feel as though the other is winning," a commitment to traditions that "bless whole communities may be an important exercise of faithful Christian authority and power."[83]

In brief, the dominant consciousness is certainly strong, but it can be changed. While popular media articulate dominant mythologies, they are not simply vehicles of the dominant; the issues are much more complicated. It is useful to think of popular media as sites of struggle, where ideologies are articulated but also worked on and potentially transformed. In other words, mainstream media typically advance the dominant consciousness, but frequently provide material that offers opportunity for prophetic resistance by faithful media stewards.

Crash and Burn

Back in the theater, *Crash* has just ended. We do not feel entertained. We will not give away tickets to our non-Christian friends as an evangelistic outreach. Yet *Crash*'s passionate "invitation to grief" embodies the "first moment of prophetic ministry."[84] It burdens us and makes us burn, begging for an alternative consciousness or way of seeing. This "energizing alternative"[85] is the sequel that we hope to realize. Are we ready for it? Or "could it be that we, in the affluent West, bathing in the comfort and appeal of our secular, advertising-soaked, sports-crazed culture, are too easily blinded to our calling to be prophetic?"[86]

One thing is for certain: unless we cultivate an alternative consciousness, newly emerging ideological conflicts will threaten to tear the remaining fabric of societal neighborliness. More than ever we need prophetic voices. But what characteristics define such a voice, and how do we begin to cultivate it? We take up these questions in our next chapter.

2

Cultivating a Prophetic Voice

Amos. Jeremiah. Isaiah. Bono? Including rock band U2's lead singer alongside cherished Old Testament prophets seems a bit odd and perhaps even irreverent. But after spending time with the band, Eugene Peterson (bestselling author and translator of *The Message*) declared that "when Bono sings, I can hear the voice of the prophet in pop culture."[1]

Prophet is used frequently today to describe individuals outside the biblical record. Even in Christian communities, where prophetic roots run deep, there is little consensus about what a prophet is. Some tribes consider prophecy to be a supernatural gift available only to Christians, while others say that the gift is no longer available today—to anyone. Also, while African American churches make frequent reference to the prophetic preacher, this phrase is typically not used in other traditions. What sense can we make of this?

In this chapter, we argue that the prophetic critic of popular media should be a social critic who most closely resembles the Old Testament prophets. As stewards of an alternative consciousness, such critics—whether inside or outside the church—challenge North America's dominant consciousness (described in chapter

1 as the ethos of consumerism). Contemporary prophetic critics provide perspectives that challenge popular media mythologies, self-complacency, and institutional self-righteousness.

Second, we describe prophetic media criticism as *prophetic talk* that requires individuals to cultivate certain foundational commitments that distinguish their communication from other tribal critics. Prophetic critics are connected to a tradition of criticism rather than acting like freewheeling, socially disconnected elitists. They develop a certain habit of thinking, writing, and speaking about popular media that provides other individuals, including themselves, with opportunities for reflection and repentance. Their communication is frequently provocative and arises out of a deep sense of concern for members of their community.

Finally, we describe briefly how prophetic talk in popular media might create moral literacy that is rooted in biblical values. Prophetic talk in popular media explains, in part, why U2's Bono and others like him are sometimes considered modern-day prophets.

Ancient Prophetic Roots

The revolution forged by Moses in Egypt, a revolution both religious and political, existed as a viable reality until approximately 1000 BC. Moses had challenged Egypt's dominant consciousness by presenting a "free" God: free to "come and go," free to lift up the downtrodden.[2] Moses's alternative framing story confronted Pharaoh's grip on the people and was later embodied in the covenant (Mosaic Covenant) made between God and the nation of Israel at Mount Sinai.[3]

But by the time of King Solomon's reign in 962 BC, there was a radical shift in the foundations of Israel's life and faith. Although begun by King David, the shift, finished and stabilized under Solomon, abandoned Moses's radical, alternative vision. The effects of this shift can be traced to the united kingdom of Israel's "incredible well-being and affluence,"[4] which dulled the vision of a redeeming, exceedingly just future. Like the dominant consciousness of

Pharaoh's Egypt, Solomon's dominant framing story endured because of an encased, domiciled God, inherently incapable of saying anything abrasive about Israel's "golden age."[5]

The prophets in the centuries following Israel's golden age sought to steward the imagination of Moses's alternative consciousness. Most of the prophets lived during the eighth to sixth centuries BC, times of extreme peril. The leaders of Israel and Judah refused to acknowledge that their kingdoms were disintegrating from within as a result of greed, injustice, and the worship of false gods. In response, the prophets' vision was one of reconciliation to the "free" God, thereby combating the institutional and personal corruption in the everyday life of the country. They called for collective responsibility and reminded the people of the covenant they had made with God.[6] The prophets would, however, watch and wail as Israel decayed. Although the prophets were considered laughingstocks by the general public and often subjected to harsh treatment, they refused to be silenced.[7]

For Whom Do You Speak? Around Israel's and Judah's leaders stood a core of professional prophets: bureaucratic soothsayers who claimed to speak in God's name yet told the leaders what they wanted to hear. These were false prophets who did not speak for someone larger than themselves, and kings who sought confirmation of their own wisdom courted them. Jeremiah warned about them: "Do not let the prophets and diviners among you deceive you; do not listen to the dreams that you encourage them to have" (Jer. 29:8).[8] Jeremiah begged the people to ask, "For whom does the prophet speak?"

Isaiah, Jeremiah, and Amos, among others, were of a different prophetic stripe. They were outside the royal court, lacking professional credentials and credibility among the people. They did not inherit the office, nor receive it by human (or self-) appointment, but were chosen, prepared, and called of God—as his "mouthpiece"—and the call was often discovered through "soul-searching."[9] Even though they spoke for God, they did not refer to themselves as prophets. Instead of reassuring Israel's leaders, they resisted the powers that sought to rip out their tongues. They took a direct view of the social and political realities and the dismal consequences that awaited. The priests, soothsayers, and politicians detested them for it.[10]

So how might Jeremiah and others describe themselves if not as prophets? Try *dissident thinkers*. Not as in the disillusioned scholar who retreats from the masses, but more like a nonconforming group member or faithful dissenter. As stewards of an alternative consciousness, the prophets played a socially destabilizing role in taking an independent, critical, or alternative line over against the state's dominant ideology.[11]

"Acting" Prophetically. While some individuals like Isaiah, Jeremiah, and Amos were called and appointed by God as prophets, other individuals at times acted prophetically without holding the prophetic office: for instance, Abraham, Moses, Miriam, and Balaam.[12] Moreover, that the prophet was to be raised up from the people of Israel alone did not stop God from sending a dream to an occasional Philistine, Egyptian, Midianite, Chaldean, or Roman.[13] Even Balaam, who was a soothsayer and as such was invited by the king of Moab to curse Israel, was temporarily and prophetically used by God.[14] These foreigners were in momentary contact with the kingdom of God and provided God's perspective on events. In addition, in the New Testament, Paul gives the title of prophet to a heathen writer who so correctly describes the immoral character of the Cretans that he proved himself to that extent a mouthpiece of the truth.[15] Speaking or acting prophetically, then, was not limited to a full-time career or to individuals who were part of a particular religious tribe.

Forthtelling versus Foretelling. The prophet was sometimes called a *seer* who made known the secret counsel of God, including future judgments.[16] Although *seeing* was an important part of the prophet's work, more important still were the prophet's tasks in dealing with every aspect of social life and instructing people in God's ways.[17] Samuel, for instance, went out among the people as an authoritative teacher of the nation sent by God, and this public proclamation was the distinctive idea in his prophecy.[18] The teaching function, as seen in Moses several centuries earlier, became prominent again. Beginning with Samuel and his followers, the prophet was a constant teaching presence in the national life, "a preacher of righteousness, interpreter of past and present history on its moral slide, and an admonisher of the consequences which God attached to conduct."[19] Describing future events remained a function of the prophet, to be sure, but a comparatively small part of his work. The prophet was primarily a teacher, a *forth*teller more than a *fore*teller.[20]

A Company of Critics. Prophets often formed companies or associations. These were communities of prophetic discourse in which individuals learned together how to cultivate a prophetic voice. Samuel was the head of a company of prophets who gathered to nurture their own spiritual life in common worship, "to praise God together as the Spirit gave them utterance, to engage in united prayer in behalf of the nation, and to go forth in companies for the revival and instruction of the people."[21] Sometimes prophetic companies arose in direct response to idolatrous worship to confront the problems and provide a community of dissent. Some may have even formed as a direct response to military threats. Many individual prophetic figures in the Old Testament were associated in some way with such communities of support, accountability, and wisdom.[22] Prophetic companies connected prophets with one another interpersonally and socially, but to a larger religious tradition as well.

In short, the Old Testament prophets give rise to a model of prophetic criticism. The prophets were social critics. Some consider them to be the very "inventors of the practice of social criticism, though not of their own critical messages."[23] Sometimes they spoke from within the tribe and other times from outside the tribe, but in each case they were used by God to confront injustices among individuals and within religious and governmental institutions. From them we learn "something about the conditions that make criticism possible and give it force, and something too about the standing of [prophetic critics] among the people [they criticize]."[24] From them we gain insights into how we might talk about modern social institutions, including the mass media.

Prophetic Talk

Prophetic media criticism is a special kind of talk about popular media, what we refer to as *prophetic talk*, with its own tone and style.[25] There are several core commitments of prophetic talk that in one form or another appear in multiple writings on the topic presented below. We refer to these commitments as prophetic *threads*, because each strand weaves in and out of descriptions on the topic—whether in politics, preaching, or poetry—that might otherwise seem unrelated. The threads, or strands, that we identify below deal with both the content (what we talk about) and process (how we talk about it) of prophetic criticism.

It Is Truth-to-Power Talk. The biblical prophets were committed to truthtelling. They called the people to reject false gods and to remember who they were as the children of God. But they did not focus their attention solely on individual conduct or belief. They also set themselves in opposition to the social order itself. Hosea's angry line, "They have set up kings, but not by me" (Hos. 8:4 KJV) indicates that something is "wrong with monarchy itself, not merely with this or that king."[26] The prophets were committed to *speaking truth to power*, or being critical of the systems, processes, and rituals used by the powers-that-be to maintain their current position and standing among the people.

For some, *speaking truth to power* is becoming a worn-out phrase in mainline North American Protestantism. There is ready reference to it in the black church, but it is frequently ignored or looked upon with suspicion by many evangelical tribes.[27] The phrase "speaking truth to power" can be as blinding as revealing, explains L. Gregory Jones, dean of Duke Divinity School: "It can induce self-deception as often as courage. . . . [W]e assume we are the ones with the truth and someone else has the power."[28]

But when we take the biblical tradition seriously, speaking truth to power has both relevance and timeliness. The prophets encourage us to be suspicious of concentrations of wealth and power, whether in our neighborhood, city government, or local church. They encourage us to be sensitive to the poor, the marginalized, and the oppressed, and to be wary of any sensibility that diminishes our neighborly concern. Amos's main charge is not that the rich live well, but that they live well at the expense of the poor. Their wealth deadens their capacity for sensitivity to others' needs. In essence, according to Amos, they forget the laws of the covenant, of collective responsibility, and the principle of charity.[29]

It Is Imaginative Talk. The prophet imaginatively describes *what is,* and in so doing, helps us to see the ugly side of the dominant consciousness, where our affluence shields us from others' pain, where the powerful abuse the powerless, and where there are no mysteries, only problems to be solved. These descriptions, as one might expect, are not always G-rated.

But in describing what is, the prophet does not morally scold or reprimand; instead, she brings to expression the "dread of endings, the collapse of our self-madeness, the barriers and pecking orders that secure us at each other's expense, and the fearful practice of eating off the table of a hungry brother or sister," writes Brueggemann. The prophet invites others to "engage their experiences of suffering to death."[30] Until and unless we can own up to the inevitable consequences of the dominant consciousness, a different, and better, possibility is difficult to imagine.

For such reasons, it is easy to think of prophets as gloomy doomsayers. But the prophet asks us to move beyond *what is* to *what if.* U2's Bono talked about the need to develop an "empathic imagination" so people could understand each other: "To tell our stories, to play them out, to paint pictures, moving and still but above all to glimpse another way of being," is what he aims for, "because as much as we need to describe the world we do live in, we *need to dream up the kind of world we want to live in.* In the case of a rock-and-roll band that is to dream out loud, at high volume, to turn it up to eleven. Because we have fallen asleep in the comfort of our freedom."[31]

It is the prophet's job to keep alive the "ministry of imagination," to keep on conjuring and proposing biblically compatible future alternatives "to the single one the king wants to urge as the only thinkable one."[32] The prophet recognizes that we are so enmeshed in the dominant consciousness, so numbed by its effects, that imagining differently is unimaginable without some help. Meanwhile, the prophet does not worry about how everything can be implemented, for such questions do not matter until the vision can be imagined. The way of the prophet, then, is that of poetry and lyric, which is why *prophetic imagination* can be used interchangeably with *poetic imagination*.[33] This does not mean, of course, that one must write poetry or play music to express one's prophetic voice. It simply means that imagination precedes implementation. And where imagination is free to envision alternatives, there is hope.

It Is Hopeful Talk. The prophet is not a manipulative hope-peddler. He does not offer visions of utopia, or some idealized, "best" society or system free from history or the realities of everyday living.[34] The hope he offers is a fuel for life's various journeys, a common grace available for anyone needing help "sticking with it." We liken hope to a giant bird with expansive claws that lifts us up by our shoulders and flies us to a higher perch to see our promised land. In valleys of despair, one often loses sight of the journey's end. For Israel wandering in the wilderness, the Promised Land was Canaan; for the unemployed mother of four on welfare, the Promised Land may be a decent paying job with benefits. Whatever the exact circumstances, in the midst of overwhelming despair the prophetic critic reminds his community of a Promised Land filled with greater justice and reconciliation.

The prophetic critic, explains Michael Walzer, must believe at some level that his tribal members' conduct "can conform more closely to a moral standard than it now does, or that their self-understanding can be greater than it now is, or that their institutions can be more justly organized than they now are. For all his foretelling of doom, a prophet like Amos must hold open the possibility of repentance and reform: else there would be no reason to prophesy."[35] Prophetic hopefulness is always associated with images of justice, mercy, and relational faithfulness—unlike an optimistic confidence that profit margins, technological savvy, and management miracles will pave the road to utopian bliss.

It Is Connected Talk. Prophetic criticism requires critical distance. But how much? In the conventional view, the critic is an unattached spectator, a dispassionate outsider. In contrast, the prophet is a *connected* critic: someone who is connected to the people she criticizes through a shared tradition and group identity. So, "critical distance is best measured in inches, not miles."[36]

Although radically detached critics have their place in critical history, they are overshadowed by the *local judge*: someone who is intensely immersed in the life and identity of the community and who judges the people's relationships with one another and the internal character of their society. This kind of prophetic critic speaks not because she is a traitor or enemy of the state, but because she is passionately intertwined with the people and cares deeply about their well-being. As Amos demonstrates, the prophet's concern was locally focused: for this people, their own family that came up out of Egypt (see Amos 2:10).[37] The prophet earns her authority, then, by quarreling with her own people.[38] The sense of what is at stake pushes the prophetic critic close enough to her community of compatriots that they feel her breath.

What motivates the prophet's audience to repentance is more than the impending doom of judgment; it is also a sense of their own history, or shared tradition. By drawing on authoritative texts, shared memories, values, practices, and agreements familiar to those in the community, prophetic voices arouse remembrance and repentance. Behind the prophet's demand for justice, peace, and charity is a sense of unity, which makes it easier for the prophet to avoid supporting the superiority of one tribal agenda over another. When the prophets address their audience, for instance, they always use inclusive proper names—Israel, Joseph, Jacob; their focus is always on the fate of the covenanted community. Although prophets serve a particular tribal tradition, they also serve the larger society as a whole.

Some try to deny the value of the prophetic example by arguing that Israel had an unusually coherent moral tradition, whereas today, as members in a pluralistic society, we have only competing narratives and endless disagreement. But as Princeton University professor Michael Walzer explains, "The coherence of Israelite religion is more a consequence than a precondition of the work of the prophets." Their prophecies begin the creation of "normative Judaism." It is important to stress the preexisting moral and legal codes, the sense of a common past, and the depth of popular religiosity that characterized ancient Israel. These characterizations similarly describe the way that we talk about the United States today as a "Christian nation." But all this was still "theologically inchoate, highly contentious, radically pluralistic in form," much like the ideological divisions and denominationalism that characterize North American Christianity. In the face of such pluralism, the prophets tried to "work up a picture of the tradition that brought together the fragments, one that made sense to and connected with the experience of their own contemporaries."[39]

It Is Provocative Talk. Christianity Today recently identified "Prophetic (or at least Provocative)" rhetoric as one of the five key streams flowing into the emerging church movement. The movement is "consciously and deliberately provocative. Emerging Christians believe the church needs to change, and they are beginning to live as if that change had already occurred."[40]

In his passion for truth or outrage at injustice or sympathy for the oppressed, the prophet's voice is seldom described as *nice*. *Edgy, bold, confrontational,* or *jarring* fit better—something along the lines of Nobel Prize–winning author Alexander Solzhenitsyn's remarks to Harvard University graduates in 1978, in which he unapologetically denounced the West for its "lack of courage and personality, its legalism, moral decadence, intellectual and social shallowness, enslavement to fashion," and more. Solzhenitsyn traced such sicknesses to the West's embrace of the Enlightenment's materialistic humanism, which he defined as "the proclaimed and practiced autonomy of man from any higher force above him."[41] Needless to say, he was not invited back.[42]

Although the prophet speaks out of a genuine desire for the community's well-being, his criticism is sometimes blunt and even painful. Ezekiel tells the people that they are thick-skulled or hard-headed, and if they really listened to God they would listen to him![43] Amos tells Israel that they would rather buy designer shoes and expensive sofas than take care of the poor and needy.[44] Prophetic voices are also at times accused of overstatement, exaggeration, generalization, and absolutist rhetoric.[45] In this regard, none in the emerging church is more effective than Brian McLaren: "Often I don't think Jesus would be caught dead as a Christian, were he physically here today. . . . Generally, I don't think Christians would like Jesus if he showed up today as he did 2,000 years ago. In fact, I think we'd call him a heretic and plot to kill him, too."[46]

It Is Courageous Talk. Truth-to-power talk that is connected to a community and a tradition, and which is often provocative, requires courage. Sometimes the courage required is physical; persistence in the face of imprisonment, violence, and even death, as demonstrated by the Old Testament prophets. Matthew 10:34–36 describes the radical commitment that criticism requires, and Jesus's death suggests the risks of that commitment.

At all times, moral courage is required. The prophet must condemn her fellow citizens for their complicity in the face of tyranny and oppression and withstand accusations of being a traitor. The task of being alert to hypocrisy also requires courage, explains cultural critic and Princeton University professor Cornel West, because "one must remain open to having others point out hypocrisy of your own." The prophetic voice in our time thus cannot be one who claims "unmediated access to God." Rather, the prophetic critic recognizes herself as a fallen vessel who may be, consciously or unconsciously, an unwitting accomplice of the very thing she criticizes. As West concludes, radical self-examination, or self-criticism, is a form of "intellectual humility."[47] Courage in prophetic talk is born in the realization that something sacred is at stake in every moment of human interaction.[48]

It Is Compassionate Talk. After hearing our description of prophetic talk, one of our friends said, "The Bible says to be kind to one another—this prophetic stuff sounds unkind. Unloving. Mean-spirited. Even cruel." At first glance, maybe. But the prophet talks to us like Hamlet to his mother: "I must be cruel only to be kind."[49] He does not criticize to feel superior or to demonstrate his intelligence, but to relieve the suffering and injustices placed upon society's victims, whether victims of tyranny or religious or sexual bigotry. Since his talk does not always sound kind and may lead others to label him a traitor, he would rather remain silent; hence, he is the reluctant critic, the prophet who would refuse God's call if he could.[50]

Without a deep sense of compassion for humanity's plight as a motivating force, criticism may become inaccurate and untimely.[51] Prophets must have some knowledge or sense of human suffering— first, so their rage or prophetic thunder "is properly focused, and second, so that it is properly expressed."[52] Anger without compassion is chaos. Prophetic empathy means never losing sight of the frustrations and anxieties of others, since the need to lend a voice to suffering is a condition of all truth.[53] Compassion is a "profoundly moral moment."[54]

In brief, the prophetic vocation today is to keep the ministry of imagination alive as part of a company of critics. So instead of asking, "Do you have the gift of prophecy?" we ask, "What community are you intimately connected with? Do you courageously and compassionately demonstrate your concern for your community by speaking truth to power? Do you provocatively describe where your own community is falling short of prophetic biblical values and imagine ways to narrow the gap? Are you training your ears to listen to the prophetic voices in the popular media that surround you?"

Nurturing a prophetic voice toward popular media requires the courage to stand alone and the humility to subject oneself to the wisdom of a company of critics. Such tempering humility provides a cushion against the presumption of a single pair of eyes and ears. Humility in the prophetic voice prevents the elevation of independence at the expense of the redemptive development of the community.

Prophetic Talk and Popular Media

Prophetic media criticism uses prophetic talk to articulate a moral order rooted in the great prophetic biblical values of justice, mercy, and humble service.[55] Put another way, through prophetic talk, tribal media critics can offer a "prophetic witness" that engenders moral literacy by calling popular media content, institutions, and technologies to their appropriate role in opening windows on the moral landscape.[56] (See figure 3 below.) Such a witness would demonstrate the ways popular media confirm the wisdom and necessity of North America's dominant consciousness. To the extent that prophetic critics stimulate the moral imagination about both *what is* and *what if*, they fulfill a transformative purpose.

Christians have much to offer here, but one would never discern it from their typically moralistic content, which closes rather

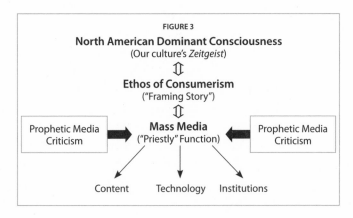

FIGURE 3
North American Dominant Consciousness
(Our culture's *Zeitgeist*)
⇕
Ethos of Consumerism
("Framing Story")
⇕

| Prophetic Media Criticism | → | **Mass Media** ("Priestly" Function) | ← | Prophetic Media Criticism |

Content   Technology   Institutions

than opens windows. Christian media are consumed mainly by Christians and appear uncreative before the very culture they seek to influence. Most Christian media also reinforce the supposed neutrality of technology, claiming large audiences and converted sinners while ignoring how media promote popular mythologies, articulate an explicit moral order, and influence the way we think about ourselves and interact with the world.

In a prophetic framework, popular media, as culture-forming industries and social institutions, can become sites of struggle, or spaces of action, where individuals demonstrate their resistance toward North America's dominant consciousness. As part of this struggle, prophetic talk would communicate alternative framing stories that question the truth of what is asserted. Prophetic talk would also speak truth to popular media power by asking media owners and operators, for instance, if concentration of ownership is good for the public or how a particular media group or ministry speaks for those without power. In the moment at which the taken-for-granted world that reinforces the cultural status quo is made problematic, and at which its moral contours are illuminated through prophetic talk, popular media can serve as symbols of truth, justice, kindness, and humility.

Glimmers of prophetic talk in popular media appear at times. Among them are news reports that address injustices and serve as instruments not of accommodation but of critique and social change. Documentaries, public opinion columns and journals, *Adbusters*, public broadcasting, and mass-market paperbacks often resonate with a prophetic accent, stir the human conscience, and liberate their viewers or readers from the dominant interpretation. Such media often draw our attention to things in society that stand in the way of justice, peace, and freedom and help us to imagine an alternative, better picture of social reality.

Throughout media history, some newspapers and stations and reporters have refused the arrogance of power and presumption of objectivity and have sought to awaken the public conscience with the vigor of Jeremiah. Pulitzer Prizes are still awarded, by and large, to professionals who distinguish themselves for community service and who shun careerism and mega-dollars. In public broadcasting, the *NewsHour with Jim Lehrer* and National Public Radio's *Morning Edition* and *All Things Considered* frequently probe deeply and sensitively into events. Research centers like the Center for Public Integrity seek to "make institutional power more transparent and accountable."[57] Sometimes local papers rise to the occasion and produce a penetrating, often first-person account of a local problem. In recent years, bloggers and citizen reporters outside the mainstream press have taken on the role of holding popular media institutions accountable to the needs of the community. Some sites develop in direct response to human rights violations or governmental abuses and develop into vibrant communities with alternative visions.[58] And humans can obviously be aided in moral literacy of this kind through drama—whether in film, television, or theater—as much as through news and public affairs.

Prophetic talk about popular media requires us, as part of our own faithful company of critics, to ask tough questions and reframe others. Important questions include the following: What vision prompts my decision to create or consume certain media content? Where in the media do I find clear evidence of the Bible's call for justice and servanthood along with its unmistakable warnings about wealth and greed? What is the ultimate purpose of media in light of what the Bible says about justice and the reconciliation of all things in a hurting world? When I critically examine my own tribe's media ownership and practices, what hidden priorities come to light? Prophets do not hesitate to ask what our media should look like and how they might address the world's greatest needs.

As voiced dissent—whether through critique, creation, or consumption of popular media—prophetic talk lets tribal members channel their dissatisfaction and construct resistance messages that confront North America's dominant framing story. Along the way, the communication channels used may be both informal (e.g., blogs, email, personal websites, conversations with others in one's community) and formal (e.g., publication or appearance in recognized media outlets). Regardless of the channel used, prophetic talk gives tribal members an opportunity for valuable corrective feedback.

Are U2/You Too a Prophet?

Even though U2 does not "explicitly proclaim the Kingdom," explains Eugene Petersen, "they certainly prepare the way for that proclamation. . . . Amos crafted poems, Jeremiah wept sermons, Isaiah alternately rebuked and comforted, Ezekiel did street theater. U2 writes songs and goes on tour, singing them."[59] So, are *you too* a prophet? You may not be in a rock-and-roll band, but if you are willing you can still cultivate your capacity to talk (and listen) prophetically.

In sum, as we survey the practices of Old Testament prophets presented in this chapter, a prophetic profile emerges. As a connected critic, deeply informed by a particular tradition, the prophetic critic is one who (1) becomes inconsolably burdened by humanity's greed and arrogance; (2) in light of the burden, considers humanity's fallen plight and the alienating effects of greed on individuals and institutions; (3) rejects a spirit of acceptance among individuals and institutions toward the culture's dominant messages; and (4) emotionally burns with critical images that shock the complacent out of their numbness toward the effects of the dominant consciousness. We consider each of these characteristics separately in chapters 3 through 6.

3

Becoming Burdened

The creative writing students gathered in a circle to discuss what motivated their work. "For Christians," said one student, "it must be Jesus Christ." Another said, "If it is not functionally him, it is certainly love." Others chimed in with strong agreement. Case closed. Just then, and to others' surprise, Alex confessed that her motivation was closer to rage than anything else. Awkward silence followed. Rage sounded like radical overreaction from a young convert. Maybe a frustrated artist seeking to make a name for herself? At the very least, it seemed to demonstrate a lack of biblical knowledge.

But as Alex explained, her stories were fueled by a specific burden: a deep sense that something was terribly wrong with the world. Not just her job or children. Not just the decreasing rain forest or general lack of peace on the planet or economic crisis, although such things were certainly burdensome and required attention. Instead, she was grieved by the grotesque greed and rampant disregard for others that surrounded her—even when that disregard was her own.

In this chapter we argue that becoming burdened is the source of prophetic talk about popular media. Prophetic criticism begins in one's capacity to grieve about life's unjust realities. Like many burdens, the prophetic burden is heavy and weighs down the prophet, making her life complicated and costly. But the complications and costs of the burden have redemptive value.

Second, we argue that the prophetic burden is something that can grow incrementally over one's lifetime. Growing the burden is important, since the degree to which one grows it faithfully is the degree to which one can talk, listen, and act prophetically. For individuals willing to make the commitment, there are several workouts that can help the burden to grow—for example, participating in media fasts and stewarding one's exposure to media. Immersing oneself in a community in which a prophetic burden is readily and faithfully demonstrated is another way to grow the burden over one's lifetime.

Finally, we explore how critics can use the media to demonstrate the prophetic burden and help us to grasp emotively, or to grieve deeply about, the human condition. Popular media function prophetically to the extent that they offer a deep sense that something is wrong with the world without exploiting individual suffering for commercial gain or entertainment.

The Prophetic Burden

The biblical prophets' concerns were not centered solely on issues of theology. The prophets were also thrust into "orations about widows and orphans, about the corruption of judges and affairs of the marketplace." The world is a beautiful place indeed, full of natural and technological marvels, but the prophets raged "as if the whole world were a slum."[1]

The prophetic burden is an unshakeable sense, sometimes evoking despondency and rage, that something is out-of-whack or seriously wrong with the world. Ancient prophets were deeply burdened that Israel had replaced their covenant with consumption;[2] that they had chosen alienation from God over communion with him: basically, that they had drifted "toward death."[3]

The Hebrew prophets were burdened by rampant greed and arrogance in all its forms. The prophet Jeremiah wails, "From the least to the greatest, all are greedy for gain" (6:13). He chastises the people of Jerusalem, "Like cages full of birds, their houses are full of deceit; they have become rich and powerful, and have grown fat and sleek" (5:27–28). Nahum complains about the uncontrolled onslaught of passion for commercial gain in ancient Assyria's capital city of Nineveh.[4] Jeremiah was stunned by the fierce greed of the false prophets and priests who sought preservation of their own prominence and esteem.[5] Ancient society cherished above all else wisdom, wealth, and might. To the prophets, such infatuation was ludicrous and idolatrous. Assyria, for instance, would be punished for such boasting about their own power.[6]

The events that horrified the Old Testament prophets are still daily occurrences all over the world. There is no cultural setting in which Amos's words, for example, would not resonate today: "Hear this, you who trample the needy and do away with the poor of the land, . . . and cheating with dishonest scales, buying the poor with silver and the needy for a pair of sandals, selling even the sweepings with the wheat" (8:4–6).

Yet to such prophetic descriptions then and now, there often comes a cynical reply: "So what?" To many passive observers of prophetic performance in ancient Israel, prophets were excessive in their fervor. Their emphasis on injustices—whether interpersonal, social, or institutional—seemed overstated, like hysterical reactions to the natural order of things. For ancient observers as well as many observers today, a single act of injustice—whether cheating in business or exploiting the poor—is a minor thing, but for the prophets, and for those developing a prophetic sensibility, it was a tragedy. Few of us get overly excited about inhumane realities surrounding us, but to the prophets "even a minor injustice assumes cosmic proportions."[7]

The prophets were also burdened, therefore, by the fact that their own people did not grieve as they should. The people saw the world as serene; the prophets saw its chaos and confusion.

Jeremiah spoke to "people with glazed eyes that looked and did not see."[8] The people were so dulled by the dominant consciousness and its program of achievable satiation that even with their "best looking they could not see what was there to see."[9] They lacked the capacity to be shocked or dismayed at the horrors of life. The people assumed that their luxuries shielded them from the miseries of the poor, but in fact their luxuries deadened their ability to grieve over the state of the nation.[10]

In addition, the prophets were burdened that their nation's leaders conspired to foster the people's numbness. The kings who sought to maintain control over their kingdoms would do everything but grieve about Israel's rejection of their covenant with God; after all, "weeping is something kings rarely do without losing their thrones."[11] Imperial economics and state religion kept people focused on consumption and satiation so they did not discern misery alive in the heart of God. Even though it is odd to think of God being filled with grief, it is a repeated description in the book of Jeremiah.[12]

It is the prophet's burden that leads her to "feel fiercely."[13] The fierce feelings of the prophetic sensibility can be expressed generally as a passionate love for good and hatred of evil, or specifically as a passionate expression of grief about the cost of selfish ambition. The eighteenth-century Puritan theologian Jonathan Edwards described such passionate expressions as "religious affections." Without religious affections, humans would be inactive. Edwards said these affections were common graces, or capacities, given to all people. It is these affections, these passions, which are the "spring of action," the "things that set us moving in our lives, moving us to engage in activities."[14] In the case of the prophetic burden, one is grieved by humanity's greed, its arrogance, and its selfish ambition and is moved to engage in activities that cultivate justice, mercy, and peace.

Embrace the Negative

The lyrics from "Accentuate the Positive," a popular 1940s North American song, encourage us to emphasize the positive and "latch on" to the affirmative attitudes in life, to keep "gloom" at a "minimum," and get rid of the negative things. There is biblical truth here we might recognize; for example, "Set your minds on things above, not on earthly things" (Col. 3:2), and "whatever is true, whatever is noble, whatever is right, whatever is pure, whatever is lovely, whatever is admirable—if anything is excellent or praiseworthy— think about such things" (Phil. 4:8).

But for the prophets, while accentuating the positive may lessen depression and make us feel better about ourselves and our environment, it will not help to cut through our "comfortable numbness"[15] toward the dominant consciousness. It will not help to confront our accommodating attitude toward the typical consumerist priorities. Instead, what cuts through the numbness is our courageous willingness to embrace the negative or talk about what is wrong with the world.[16] The embrace of all that is wrong with the world brings one face-to-face with all that humanity (and one's self) is capable of. The embrace illuminates in striking ways the consequences of humanity's (and one's own) greed and arrogance.

The prophet can begin to embrace the negative and help others to embrace it through the language of grief: the rhetoric that engages the community in mourning. This rhetoric begins with the public articulation that we are "fearful and ashamed of the future we have chosen" and the past we have neglected.[17] This is not your average "feel-good" message. The language of grief invites the community to a funeral—a funeral where they can mourn over the loss of justice, mercy, and peace. It is a funeral few of us wish to attend, since the funeral is our own.

The language of grief also includes vivid descriptions, "a near play-by-play" of the disaster as it reaches the prophet's front door.[18] With the intensity of a modern-day horror film or disaster movie, the prophet shouts, "Hey, stop and look outside your window and see the horror around you!" The prophet calls for grief, not platitudes or praise, with the hope that God's ache might break through the comfortable numbness.

Not surprisingly, the prophetic voice is often accused of "negativity," of lacking faith, or of allowing death and despair to have the last word. However, grief over sin is not incompatible with obedience to God in praise. Though grieving, the prophet can still rejoice "in all things" (Phil. 4:4); she knows that repentance and transformation are not possible without lament. Therefore, both grief and joy are expressions of prophetic confidence in the sovereignty of God. Suffering and decay require our wise grief, which, in turn, provokes our redemptive action. When grief does not lead to repentance and subsequent good deeds, it merely becomes an end in itself, leading to death.[19] "The riddle and insight of biblical faith is the awareness that only anguish leads to life, only grieving leads to joy, and only embraced endings permit new beginnings."[20]

Christian media are guilty of reinforcing numbness toward the dominant consciousness and reinforcing the false tension between grief and praise. Those responsible for helping to raise issues of justice and righteousness are preoccupied with other, albeit important, aspects of ministry. Despite its many benefits, for instance, the praise and worship movement has shifted attention away from issues of justice and righteousness to "getting our praise on."[21] A recent study of the most frequently used contemporary worship songs in North American churches over the past fifteen years found that less than 10 percent of the total number of songs addressed issues of justice and righteousness. The study's author concludes that even though contemporary worship music (CWM) with themes of justice and righteousness is being produced, it remains "largely ignored in churches that use CWM."[22]

Additionally, messages from the pulpit about becoming deeply burdened by the pain and suffering of others do not pack the pews with new members like "Saddleback Sam," who is self-satisfied, affluent, and comfortable with his life.[23] Neither will people see a book titled *Embrace the Negative* at the local Christian bookstore. Instead, many popular megachurch pastors and media personalities write bestselling books that urge followers to dwell only on positive things and to avoid pondering negative thoughts as a way to become more Christlike. They assume that biblical faithfulness and optimism are synonymous. Furthermore, many televangelists and radio talk show hosts lead audiences to wrongly believe that faith is a ticket to earthly "health and wealth" rather than a call to deny self.[24] Audiences can become so focused on meeting their own needs that they overlook others' needs. We recognize that some Christian authors do call Christians to account for the tendency to elevate oneself over others, but more often than not, tribal books in Christian (and mainstream) retail outlets that emphasize the "power of positive thinking" and other such self-help mantras are the top sellers.[25]

In brief, becoming burdened by *embracing the negative* is the necessary catalyst for criticism and redemptive change.[26] Radical criticism begins with the capacity to grieve because that is the most "visceral announcement that things are not right."[27] Grief is what makes humans capable of shock and outrage with the world around them. Grief can push individuals toward compassionate acts that foster justice and bring about peace. Taking time to cultivate one's prophetic burden is thus a critical first step toward listening, talking, and acting prophetically.

Growing the Burden

Although a burden may have been the operative gift God gave to Jeremiah "before he was born" (Jer. 1:4–5), for most of us it is something developed over a lifetime. Occasionally specific burdens for specific situations come fully developed from God, but few of us wake up suddenly one morning with a proper ability to feel the pain of the human condition. Nor is it something that fully forms after a single mission trip or one-time volunteer experience at a homeless shelter. Even in Jeremiah's case, the prophetic burden was not the same during the time of his youthful call as it would become later in his ministry.

Developing the prophetic burden, which we understand as a "religious affection," is a work Jonathan Edwards compared to building the body's strength over time through rigorous exercises. To be sure, these exercises would include all of the traditional spiritual disciplines—such as solitude, silence, fasting, study, worship, and prayer[28]—but with special emphasis on growing a "fearless heart,"[29] despair-defying faith, and sacrificial love. Such soul-strengthening workouts allow the prophetic voice to effectively "run the race" and "strain" wisely "toward what is ahead" (Phil. 3:13).[30]

We admit that workouts can be painful. It is a risky venture when ligaments and muscles we do not use regularly are worked out rigorously. Muscles we have already developed can also atrophy if not properly maintained. As in a good physical workout, part of the pain comes from identifying areas of weakness and needed growth. Part of the pain also comes through the exercises designed to address those concerns. With this in mind, we offer several workouts that may grow one's prophetic burden. Although designed originally for our students, these workouts may be adopted by churches, families, prayer groups, and others as a way to steward one's affections toward popular media.

Media Fasts. Since media saturation may have a significant numbing effect on the development of prophetic burden, we ask students in one of our classes to take part in a *media fast*. Throughout the semester, students fast for a few days or a week at a time on all kinds of media: everything from television to cell phones, from magazines to movies. We also ask them to take a one-mile walk for ten days straight. The walk is not for exercise, but primarily to experience fifteen to twenty minutes outside of their technological cocoons—so no iPhones are allowed. We then ask them to keep a journal of their experiences during fasts. The experience for many is startling.

First, students underestimate the near omnipresence of media. It is everywhere, and it is difficult to tune out no matter how hard they try. Second, most recognize media's uniform, dominant message: we deserve a comfortable and exciting life. Another overarching, albeit subtle, message is that we should emulate celebrities, sports heroes, and product-rich living. One student wrote in her journal, "I can't believe how many advertisers lead us to believe that shampoo brings orgasms, beer brings sex, and fresh breath brings friends!!" Finally, students could not believe how much time they wasted. Most turned to media out of boredom. They had little capacity to withstand the lure of media distractions that pulled them away from their work, their own art, and their own life's curriculum.

Without much prompting from us, the media fasts helped students explain how oversaturation of popular media lessened their emotional response to such things as violent content and the pain of others and, in some cases, even increased their acceptance of the necessity of violence to solve real-life problems. Media distractions were perpetual and multifaceted, and typically invited them into a reality more stimulating than their own. Over time, students had become desensitized to the kicks in the shins given to them by their dominant dance partner, popular media. Media fasts helped many of the students get acquainted with their addiction to the dance, helped them slow it down, and helped make sure they were the ones leading.[31]

Intentional Media Appointments. A commitment to grow the burden through media fasts allowed many of our students to intentionally step away from the dictates of mass media. Another simple exercise was to watch no television for two weeks unless it was a program chosen ahead of time. The students were not to use any popular electronic medium to alleviate boredom—so, no spur-of-the-moment media encounters. The pre-appointments allowed them to experience greater levels of intentionality and higher levels of academic and artistic productivity. As a result of the media fasts and the new habit of *by appointment only*, many students realized the patterns of (1) boredom and (2) the alleviation of boredom through media—hardly a cycle that breeds redemptive passion for godly service.

A Company of Critics. As observed in chapter 2, the prophetic critic is a connected critic, tied to a community of shared blessings, warnings, memories, and possibilities. On the good side, each tribal community—whether an avid group of *Star Trek* fans or a religious denomination—is a community of discourse that equips members to decipher, discuss, and debate reality with others. On the negative side, tribal communities of discourse can limit how members perceive reality or even confirm members' simplistic or false conclusions.

So, to become better students, in addition to spending more time alone in study, we also study more with students who are serious about learning. To become better athletes, we increase our private time in the gym but also work out with other players pushing themselves to improve. In the same way, to grow the prophetic burden we spend more time in personal reflection about what is wrong with the world but also immerse ourselves in communities in which the prophetic burden is well developed and faithfully expressed. We join that company of critics—even when it includes people who are going to irritate us because of their different political or cultural perspectives. If we cannot physically join them, we can join them virtually by reading their blogs, receiving their newsletters, listening to their music, watching their movies, reading their poetry, or buying their magazines.

We are not regular listeners of hip-hop music, for instance, but we identify a strong prophetic burden in Lauryn Hill's and Tupac Shakur's brutally honest portrayals of the fallen world.[32] We do not subscribe to *Sojourners*—a multidenominational progressive magazine—but reviewing it online once a month calls our attention to relevant social concerns not addressed by other tribal periodicals. We are not Roman Catholic, but reviewing the *U.S. Catholic*—a monthly journal published by the Claretian Missionaries, a Roman Catholic community—brings our attention to issues of justice, peace, and the environment in the United States and across the globe. Such media present invitations to grieve. They address issues that transcend an individual's tribal agendas.

Popular Media and Prophetic Burden

Many of our culture's great dramatists sought to live out their burden through artistic expression. The pioneering genius of Eugene O'Neill was partially launched from the difficulties of having an alcoholic father.[33] Sam Shepard's plays specialize in families broken by alcoholism, many of them drawing from autobiographic material.[34] North American playwright David Mamet's experiences of childhood cruelties and intense (and what some might call emotionally abusive) parental control fueled his thoughts about the ugliness of the human condition and the need to address injustices.[35] Each dramatist was, from an early age, gripped by a sense that something was wrong with the world.

Rampant greed is a common sin addressed in the plays of David Mamet.[36] Mamet's world is one in which greed has run amok and in which society has a single bottom line: "How much money you make."[37] The ethical system that describes the business world in *Glengarry Glen Ross* is "that you can be as predatory as you want within a structured environment,"[38] an environment free from virtues like charity, mercy, and grace. His play *American Buffalo* is an attack on the North American free-enterprise system, sparing no participants on either end of the economic spectrum and pummeling its audience with the message that "all have sinned."[39] His play *Speed-the-Plow* indicts a culture filled with fantasies about power and selfish ambition and criticizes the moviemaking business as the culture's perfect pimp.[40]

Not surprisingly, David Mamet, in ways similar to the Hebrew prophets, is often accused of being hysterical when he focuses on the sins of humanity. But the "heart" of humankind, to Mamet, is "deceitful above all things and desperately wicked" (Jer. 17:9 KJV). This assumption about human nature dictates the contours and parameters of his literary creations and critique. The minor injustices of petty crooks and weasels in *American Buffalo*, or the verbal savagery of a business entrepreneur in *Glengarry Glen Ross*, or the devilish construction of history in *Wag the Dog*, are all symptomatic of the human condition. Such offenses are anything but minor to Mamet; they are tragedies.

Mamet would, however, disassociate himself from the premise that God thrust a burden upon his soul in the same way that God burdened the biblical prophets. Instead, his being bowed and stunned at humanity's basic greed is perhaps traced to his vague assumptions as a child that something was wrong with the way life is lived. To Jeremiah, the prophetic message and passion was the direct result of the command of God.[41] To Mamet, the fierceness of human greed was an early and inescapable conclusion.

Of course, one's burden need not come from stressful childhood experiences or other dysfunctions. Sometimes the burden arises after simply taking stock of one's own surroundings. The lyrics of Christian musician Rob Rock's "Something's Wrong with the World" reads like a modern-day lament by Amos or Jeremiah. With pulsating heavy metal guitar in the background, Rock's lyrics invite us to take a look outside his window to see the beggar on the street shooting intravenous drugs, a rape in the park, child abuse, theft, and other injustices. Rock asks, "Where's the love we need to share? / Where's the hope, we need to care? / Where's the faith in our society?" Rock's lyrics—not unlike Lauryn Hill's and Tupac Shakur's lyrics—invite us to grieve about everyday brutality.[42]

At the same time, the passionate expression of the prophetic burden is not a license for lewdness or an excuse to exploit human pain and suffering for commercial gain or audience entertainment. Many daytime talk shows are like carnival sideshows that use personal tragedy and abnormality as ways to titillate audiences. Some viewers watch reality TV programming to see how characters will react to embarrassing situations and are often gratified by watching the humiliation and misfortunes of others.[43] In contrast, authentic portrayals of prophetic burden will invoke thoughtful reflection on the human condition. The pictures painted are not always appropriate for sanctuary lobbies or restaurant walls, but they will haunt without being gratuitous.

Novelist Kurt Vonnegut wrote advertising copy before he was a bestselling novelist. He learned how advertisers and other dominant systems of society manipulate language to influence human behavior, and he applied those lessons in his novels. Novels such as *Breakfast of Champions* and *Slaughterhouse Five* alone convinced many that "we were headed for a collision with our own egos as we grasped for everything we could buy and consume in the most narcissistic ways." Vonnegut's work demonstrates a prophetic awareness of how a society focused on achievable satiation "co-opts the very souls" of its citizens.[44]

For Vonnegut, the purpose of the arts is to be "the canary in the coal mine." Artists are "useful to society because they are so sensitive . . . super sensitive"; they keel over like canaries in poisoned coal mines long before others realize there is any danger.[45] Put another way, the prophetic critic notices what typically goes unnoticed, such as the patterns of indifference toward injustice. Her ear perceives the silent sigh of the suffering. No wonder many of the Hebrew prophets died prematurely. No wonder their godly passions consumed them. The contemporary prophetic critic is the canary in the coal mine.

What about the "S" Word?

Although the biblical prophet's concern was not centered solely on the development of new theology, we cannot simply reduce them to social critics. The social ills they railed against were happening because the people had broken their relationship with God. In other words, the greed and arrogance that burdened the prophets were symptoms of a deeper human condition; namely, in biblical terminology, humanity's fallenness—aka *sin*. The "S" word.

Some readers may have a problem with giving folks credit for merely pointing out social problems, especially if they do not attribute the cause of those problems to sin. One of our friends was a member of the radical Left in North America in the 1960s before she became a Christian. Like many of the playwrights and artists we mention above, she too knew there was something wrong with the world. "But simply knowing the griefs over greed and expressing them," she explained, "is fruitless per se, and since we did not address any of the root causes of the ills, all we ended up doing was feeling very proud of ourselves for pointing out all the ills and standing against the crummy society that was so awful."

For the Christian prophetic voice, addressing the root cause of sin, as our friend describes above, is necessary. Surely mainstream media hold signs of human fallenness *and* rays of hope, or what Christian theologian Francis A. Schaeffer refers to as the *minor* theme and *major* theme of the Christian faith.[46] As we consume popular media, then, we are bound to observe the minor theme that all people are fallen and displease God with selfish motives and hurtful communication. Popular media products created by individuals outside the Christian tribe are clearly capable of such observation.

For Christians, it is this minor theme that sets the stage for the major theme: that God offers meaning and purpose to life through salvation offered through Jesus Christ. Have you ever walked out of a movie theater deep in thought about the big questions of life: "What is the true meaning of life?" "Why do good things happen to bad people?" A movie may not present the plan of salvation that led someone to faith in Jesus Christ, yet may still be pre-evangelistic in that it asked the big questions that very well may have prepared the way for Christ. It may be our reconstruction of the popular media narrative in later conversations with friends (or strangers) that illuminates basic biblical truths.[47]

Conclusion

In dialogue with her creative writing colleagues, Alex came to realize that her burden was, indeed, a critical blessing. The inner agitation at injustice energized her work. Her understanding of art's purpose identified with Vonnegut's notion. Her shock over the heart's deceitful wickedness[48] persisted while others around her partied. Alex was learning to keel over. Indeed, something smelled ominous in the coal mine.

The prophetic burden, acting as a "religious passion," fights against the erosion of sensitivity caused by cultural greed. The burden helps the prophetic critic to be shocked: not in ways that immobilize but in ways that energize and help her to break through her own (and others') numbness toward the dominant consciousness. This religious passion is available to anyone—not just artists or poets or individuals with special gifts—who willingly commits to workouts that, over time, help to grow one's prophetic burden.

The prophetic burden is closely linked to the plight of humanity. As the prophet considers humanity's plight—that is, the alienating effects of greed and arrogance on interpersonal, social, and institutional arrangements—the prophet deepens her burden and, in so doing, discovers even more opportunities for prophetic talk, listening, and action that provoke individual and social transformation. In chapter 4, we address the comprehensive nature of humanity's plight and trace its spiritual origins. We also consider the ways popular media contribute to and in some cases positively confront humanity's plight.

4

Considering Humanity's Plight

When rapper Ice-T's heavy metal group Body Count released the song "Cop Killer," police organizations and urban teens interpreted the lyrics in different ways. Police groups wanted to ban the song, arguing that it would lead to violence. Fans of the band said it accurately portrayed police behavior in urban North America.

Since songs like "Cop Killer" may encourage some people to act more violently, we are wise to be cautious.[1] But most of us do not imitate in real life the aggression we see or hear in such songs. This is too simplistic a view of the communication process. It also ignores negative social conditions like poverty, racism, and drugs that lead to violence. As "Cop Killer" illustrates, audiences selectively interpret individual media messages to fit their own viewpoints.[2]

Yet at its most significant level, popular media can and do influence a society's perception of events, its attitudes, and its actions. On the one hand, popular media create simple stories and characters with values that most people can relate to. In a priestly sense, these stories reinforce common values and affirm what audiences want to believe about their own tribe's superiority. On the other hand, popular media provide the unfamiliar and innovative, challenging audiences to think outside their tribal boxes and move toward originality and complexity as it relates to their own lives and the world around them.

In this chapter we argue that both tendencies provide a staging ground for prophetic engagement. First, the prophetic critic can draw attention to an audience's desire to see itself favorably along with media's tendency to affirm and in some cases worsen the plight of humanity. This plight, often described as the effect of sin on humanity, is rightly understood as alienation from God, from oneself, from others, and from the environment. These four alienations fundamentally corrupt our ability to communicate in ways that promote peace and justice.

Second, we argue that the prophetic critic can confront popular media's role in affirming and worsening humanity's plight by calling for, and creating, media content and practices that promote mutual benefits and responsibilities among individuals and social institutions. Often, the result of such mutually beneficial relationships is *shalom*—the presence of God's peace and justice in our lives.

The Plight of Humanity

"The ancient masters of religion," explains G. K. Chesterton, "began with the fact of sin"—a fact as "practical as potatoes."[3] But the idea of sin as descriptive of humanity's plight is not popular today.[4] For those in "Generation Me," the idea is simply too negative or old-fashioned.[5] In the field of communication, most communication scholars talk about the problems of noise, bias, or relational conflict, instead of about sin.[6]

But unless we recognize the reality of sin, we wrongly assume that all we need for better communication is a bit more education, money, or practice. In other words, we tend to act as if there is nothing inherently wrong with us.

Alienation from God. Alienation from God is the great alienation that underlies all other human alienations. To Jeremiah, the alienation of Israel from God came in the form of forsaking God, the "spring of living water," and digging their own cisterns, their own water supply (2:13). Forsaking God in this way was denying God as the source of all human gifts, including the gift of communication.

When we break our relationship with God, we listen to our own selfish cravings instead of to God's commands. We pretend to be God, constructing "alternative universes" that allow us to live out our god-like pretensions.[7] One digital game, *Spore*, is symbolic of our "God envy." *Spore* lets players create a "metaverse" where they control the development of a species from its beginnings as a unicellular organism, through development as an intelligent and social creature, to a fully evolved being capable of interstellar space exploration. The game's creators and others describe *Spore* as a "god game."[8]

Additionally, in place of worshiping God we worship false idols, including celebrities and sports figures. Researchers recently identified a new psychiatric condition they call *celebrity worship syndrome*. The syndrome ranges from casual stargazing, to imagining a relationship with a star, to stalker-esque behavior in its most extreme form. About one-third of us have the syndrome to some degree.[9]

At other times we worship ourselves. Narcissistic personality disorder is one of the fastest growing disorders in the country. It is described as "a pervasive pattern of grandiosity, need for admiration, and a lack of empathy."[10] The narcissistic personality is preoccupied with fantasies of unlimited power, brilliance, beauty, and ideal love—characteristics typically attributed to God. The narcissist believes that she is special and thus requires excessive admiration, or worship, from others. The narcissist becomes, in essence, her own "god."

Alienation from Self. Alienation from God is closely related to alienation from self. The foundation of human worth, or the source of self, in the biblical record is the fact that individuals are created in the "image of God" (Gen. 1:27–28) and have the capacity to represent what God is like to the rest of the earthly creation. Without embracing this foundation of individual worth, distorted impressions of the "source of the self" can dominate one's existence.[11] Without allowing such God-given worth to inform human tasks, impressions of inadequacy can take the form of depression or despair, on one hand, or create compensating forms of arrogance or even excessive self-love, on the other hand.

The self-alienating impulses of despair and narcissism are intensified by the cult of celebrity. The average media consumer is dwarfed by the spotlight that is glued always to someone else.[12] In the desire to break free from anonymity, celebrity wannabes willingly degrade themselves for fifteen minutes of fame. On reality television, it has never been easier to "lose one's dignity."[13] Social critic and historian Daniel Boorstin details the "extravagant expectations" kept alive for millions of people by the dominance of image over reality in the electronic age.[14]

Alienation from Others. In addition to oneself, alienations occur with others. Coinhabitants in one's house, neighborhood, or distant continents are image-bearers worthy of dignity and respect. According to the prophetic critic, to forsake such dignity and respect is to choose alienation from others.

The prophet Amos complained about the moral condition of the ten northern tribes of Israel, focusing on their inhumane treatment of the poor and disenfranchised.[15] Outraged by their actions, Amos announces that the "wrath of God" will not be turned back. By "wrath" we do not mean lightning bolts from heaven, although God's wrath in the Bible and through the Middle Ages is often understood through natural demonstrations (such as volcanoes, earthquakes, hurricanes, and the like). In our current context, it is helpful to imagine God's wrath as his willingness to allow his human creation to "lie in the beds they have made"; that is, to suffer the consequences of their alienating choices.[16]

Sometimes we demonstrate alienation from others when we fail to speak out against injustices. Television executives help to cover up an actor's illegal or immoral activity to avoid losing program sponsors. Newspaper editors often refuse to correct stories with unfortunate errors that damage reputations. Public relations specialists put positive spins on their corporate clients' environmental waste or financial irresponsibility. In contrast, the Old Testament prophets were whistle-blowers who told the truth despite harsh consequences. Sometimes it is wise to remain silent, but self-interested or apathetic silence weakens communities and hurts others, especially those who are powerless and exploited.[17]

If not addicted to technology, many of us are so infatuated by it that we neglect to nurture quality relationships with our neighbors.[18] We construct techno-cocoons that allow us to avoid conversing with individuals standing nearby. We send email or instant messages to our friends sitting in the next room or on the couch next to us, or we send text messages while in the middle of conversations with others. Furthermore, many in our faith communities prefer the "convenience" of virtual *koinonia*, or fellowship, over the face-to-face kind. More people tune in, however briefly, to some form of Christian media than actually attend church monthly.[19]

In addition, media institutions can be used to build collective structures that further alienate individuals from self and others. Advertising agencies create false myths about identity, success, and happiness in an effort to build markets for commercial goods. Other agencies deliver campaigns that promote destructive behaviors, such as smoking. Philip Morris's Marlboro brand started in the 1920s as a fashionable woman's cigarette. Back then, the ads equated smoking with emancipation and a sense of freedom, attempting to appeal to women who had just won the right to vote. Later, Marlboro associated its product with powerful images of an active, rugged man roping a calf, building a fence, or riding a horse over snow-covered landscapes.

Moreover, news and other television programming persistently pound us with violent images that indirectly isolate us from others. In local news, the concept "if it bleeds, it leads" influences what makes it on air. "As for putting in even six minutes of hope, of pride, of dignity" on the news—it is much more difficult to sell.[20]

Young television watchers will see around one hundred thousand depictions of violent actions, including eight thousand murders, before they enter college.[21]

What is the significance of all the violence? The sheer quantity promotes fear and distrust of neighbors along with the idea that aggressive behavior is normal. Heavy television viewers (those who watch four or more hours per day) believe the world is a more dangerous place than light television viewers; heavy viewers are also more likely to believe in certain cultural stereotypes.[22] A number of long-term studies demonstrate how repeated exposure to violent images during one's youth develops a set of values and response options that make real-life aggression more acceptable in later life.[23]

Whenever people use communication merely to advance personal or institutional agendas, they practice *symbolic dominance*.[24] Through the use of verbal and nonverbal symbols, they manipulate others, forcing their symbolic reality on weaker people groups. "Wherever the few have power to control the many," such domination exists.[25]

In recent decades, North American media ownership has been contracting rather than expanding. This means that fewer companies own more types of media businesses, and a small number of very large companies dictate what we see. Consequently, despite positive advances over the last century in minority media ownership, the number of independent and diverse voices in mainstream media is limited.[26] Meanwhile, mainstream media represent the interests of the dominant culture and directly or indirectly suppress groups along the margins. Not surprisingly, scores of media studies continue to document stereotypical representation of such groups in mainstream media.[27]

In television drama, stereotyped characters, whether ethnic types (Arab terrorist, black street thug) or individual conventional types (the evil land developer, dumb blonde), give writers the luxury of not having to devote expensive storytelling time to explaining the motivations of minor characters. Yet this narrative luxury comes with a price, often reinforcing the rationale behind relational alienation. The fact that the stereotype works for efficient storytelling in the minds of the audience confirms the residing and often deepseated belief in the stereotype's validity.[28] Gender relations is another arena for symbolic domination. In many tribes, men gain power simply because of their gender, not because they are more talented than women.[29] Gender stereotypes in popular media are pervasive and alluring, tapping into deep collective fantasies. The ideal man in most commercial ads is virile and strong, unrestrained and unattached. The ideal woman, in return, is submissive and committed solely to her dominant male partner. While some ads demonstrate the *countertype*—for example, women as executive or as superheroes with extraordinary powers—the majority of ads perpetuate gender stereotypes.[30]

Considering the pervasiveness of gender stereotypes, it is not surprising to find that they influence Christian perspectives. John Eldredge, well-known Christian author, counselor, and lecturer, for example, drew on such stereotypes to construct his ideal of masculinity in his bestselling *Wild at Heart*. Eldredge cast "men as warriors wielding swords not plowshares, and not ambassadors for Christ carrying on a ministry of reconciliation (2 Cor. 5:17–20),"[31] explains communication scholar and author William D. Romanowski. Women are cast as vulnerable, voluptuous seductresses, an image that "hardly diverges from that of the makers of the Barbie Doll or the franchisers of Hooters restaurants."[32] Despite the many benefits of his work, the extent to which Eldredge relied upon the world of western novels and action-adventure movies to construct "an authentically biblical" masculinity is problematic.[33]

Alienation from the Environment. Finally, alienation from our ecological environment is rooted in the same human condition that leads to the destructive habit of forsaking God. To take for granted and thereby disregard the earth as a garden requiring human stewardship is to forget the command to "work it and take care of it" (Gen. 2:15). To exploit the earth for profit is a desecration of God's creation and shows disregard for our responsibility as human stewards.[34]

Alienation from the environment is evidenced in the mountains of high-tech trash and "e-waste." Space debris such as discarded rocket boosters and communication satellites litter the galaxy.[35] Discarded PCs and computer wires with flame-retardant insulation are burned away in toxic fires that dot the city dumps and marketplaces in third-world countries. The fires not only darken the sunlit marketplaces, but fill the throat and lungs of the young men who understand that the key to making money in this scrap metal business is speed, not safety.[36]

Of course, continued disregard of ecological balance threatens humanity's biological existence, as the evening news constantly reminds us. The continued focus of the prophetic witness as it relates to the environment is not tied to any particular political platform or tribal agenda, but to the interconnectedness of ecological alienation to alienation from God, from oneself, and from others.[37]

In sum, many scholars suggest that we can become excellent communicators simply by working harder. Unfortunately, it is not that easy. We need to drink, as Jeremiah suggested, from the "spring of living water." Unless we recognize the alienating effects of sin on human communication, we will continue to critique, create, and consume popular media in ways that impede "mutually-benefitting, community-creating relationships."[38]

Confronting Humanity's Plight

Although we cannot blame popular media for humanity's plight, we can hold them partially accountable for the alienation and oppression they reinforce. If we look only to our own personal communication and comfort, we are not being obedient caretakers of the created order. Developing a prophetic sensibility as symbolic caretakers requires that we confront and offer imaginative alternatives to the symbolic domination present in both private and public communities. This means that we must learn to observe and listen in more prophetically sensitive ways.

Confronting Symbolic Dominance. Stereotyping or demonizing particular groups is an extension of humanity's fallen nature, or alienation from God.[39] Adam blamed Eve. Eve blamed the serpent. Likewise, we all look for "scapegoats to make us feel better about ourselves. As the media oversimplify reality and feed existing stereotypes, they satisfy our desire to confirm that we are members of a superior tribe."[40]

Since stereotypes describe individuals with collective rather than unique characteristics, they can make us lose sight of individual identity and worth. Confronting stereotypes, then, is about preserving human dignity, not supporting a particular lifestyle or political agenda. It is easy for us to be sensitive to stereotypes against our own tribe while ignoring, or even subtly reinforcing, stereotypes against other tribes. But confronting stereotypes about all groups is critical since stereotypes often lead to hatred, violence, and even state-sponsored genocide.

Scholarly research and conversations in families, businesses, churches, and other social institutions that call attention to stereotypical representations of all kinds in popular media offer a prophetic corrective to symbolic domination. Most popular texts in media and culture chronicle the volumes of important research in this area. Such research demonstrates the lack of representation and misrepresentation of certain groups, particularly African American, Native American, Asian, Arabic, Latino, and gay and lesbian cultures. People of faith—Jews, Christians, and Muslims—are also frequent targets of stereotypes. The research in these areas also demonstrates the harmful consequences of stereotyping. For instance, a significant body of research links gender stereotyping of young women and men in the media with common mental health problems including eating disorders, anxiety, and depression.[41]

Certain nonprofit watchdog and advocacy organizations such as Commercial Alert, Center for Media Literacy, Free Press, and Citizens for Media Literacy monitor bias, free speech, violence, deceptive advertisements, and the excesses of commercialism in popular media. Other groups rigorously combat stereotypical media portrayals of specific groups, such as African Americans (National Association for the Advancement of Colored People), Hispanics (National Hispanic Media Coalition), and Jews (Jewish Defense League). Still others, like Women in Media and News, seek to increase women's presence and work against gender-based stereotyping in popular media.

While some critics draw attention to harmful media stereotypes, others point to alternative, positive portrayals of marginalized groups. One historically stereotyped group is people with physical disabilities. Media often portray the disabled as villains, or as depressed and bitter because others will not accept them as full persons.[42] *Sue Thomas: F.B.Eye*, which appeared on PAX-TV, challenged such stereotypical representations. The show was based on the real-life story of the first deaf woman to do surveillance for the Federal Bureau of Investigation. The producers cast a deaf actress for the lead role and focused on her deafness in only a few of the show's episodes. Their portrayal of Sue did not patronize, victimize, or demonize people with disabilities. Rather, it depicted people with disabilities as normal people in normal situations.[43] Most other minority or marginalized groups described in this chapter use popular media to demonstrate and promote positive portrayals of their own group.[44]

Promoting Peace and Justice. Public journalism might best be imagined as a *conversational* model of journalistic practice concerned about peace and justice. Modern journalism draws a distinct line between reporter detachment and community involvement. In contrast, public journalism—driven by citizen forums and even talk shows—blurs this line. Similar to the prophetic blessing that seeks to bless the community at large, public (or civic) journalism encourages reporters to move beyond the limited modern mission of simply "telling the news" to a broader mission of "helping public life go well."[45]

Behind public journalism is the realization that many citizens feel alienated from participating meaningfully in public life. According to media scholar Richard Campbell and his colleagues, this alienation arises from "watching passively as the political process plays out in the news media." The process stars, among others, "politicians who run for office, the spin doctors who manage the campaigns, and the reporters who dig for dirt in 'every nook and cranny.'" Along the way, "readers and viewers serve as spectators, watching a play that does not seem to involve them."[46]

Like the Old Testament prophets, public journalists move from being detached outsiders to reporting on events as intimate participants in public life. They move beyond only describing what is going wrong to also imagining how things could go right. They move beyond seeing fellow community members as mere consumers of news to seeing them as "potential actors" in arriving at solutions to common problems.[47] A number of midsized daily papers in the 1980s and 1990s—for example, *The Charlotte Observer*, *The Wichita Eagle*, and *The Virginian-Pilot*—experimented with public journalism. By 2000, although exact numbers are difficult to calculate, well over a hundred newspapers practiced some form of public journalism, many partnering with local television and public radio stations.[48]

The goal of public journalism is to help communities ultimately transform themselves into more just and cohesive entities.[49] While the modern, mainstream newsroom adage "if it bleeds, it leads" may attract audiences and increase revenue, it may also give a false impression of a community to its members. Civic-minded journalism does not disallow the coverage of crime or violence, but it does demand a context to help audiences decide if they need to take action.

Consider the classic case of Wounded Knee. On February 27, 1973, about two hundred Native Americans seized the small town of Wounded Knee on the Pine Ridge Sioux Indian Reservation in South Dakota. Tensions had begun just three weeks earlier, when Indians clashed with police while protesting the light prison sentence for a white man who killed an Indian. The siege eventually turned violent. The coverage lasted for ten weeks. It was the first time in broadcast history that every national news show covered the same story five days a week. We did not get this kind of coverage again until the Gulf War and the O. J. Simpson trial. Ninety-three percent of the population claimed to follow the story of Wounded Knee through television.[50]

If we look at the ten weeks of media coverage, we find that nearly all of it was sensationalistic, focusing on the battle action without getting to the real issues underneath. Many reports were also filled with clichés, insensitive language, and stereotypes. A small number of reporters at each network, however, broke through the battle action with substantive accounts of the event. For example, one reporter from NBC described the trail of broken treaties that reduced the vast Indian territory to a few small tracts. A reporter from CBS understood that the American Indian movement really sought a revolution in attitudes of the Indians toward themselves. Another reporter from ABC laid vivid hold on life on the Pine Ridge Reservation itself by "getting inside the Indians and looking at what was happening through their eyes." These three standouts sought to replace harmful images with healing images. They brought a sympathetic manner of understanding to the controversy as a way to foster peace and neighborliness.[51]

Granted, it is difficult to portray the kind of complexity and historical nuance involved in Wounded Knee and other similar incidents of cultural upheaval in interesting ways. It involves ethnography; that is, reporters must be fluent in the languages, know the history of the people and their ethnic tensions, and so forth. News outlets focused on reducing production costs and increasing ratings by leading with what bleeds will probably not decide on such reporting. But Wounded Knee is a clear example of journalism committed to justice and peace. Such efforts attempt to recover lost or silenced voices and can serve as a model for reporting on other kinds of social tensions or disasters—from race relations to floods, famine to wars—that appear on the local, national, and international levels.

Finally, confrontation of popular media may come in the form of peace journalism. Peace journalism is a paradigm shift with prophetic overtones. It offers an alternative frame for reporting news about conflict, especially as it relates to war. It is provocative because it proposes that most war journalism, while claiming to be neutral and objective, is actually biased in favor of war. How so? Traditional war journalism is modeled after sports journalism with a focus on "winning in a zero-sum game"—the side with the fewest dead bodies wins. Participants are portrayed as "pugilists." What is newsworthy is based on "who outsmarts the other, and who maintains his original position."[52]

In response, peace journalism asks us to imagine war coverage that sidesteps the adage "if it bleeds, it leads." Instead, reporters take an interpretative approach and concentrate on stories that highlight peace initiatives rather than bloody combat. Similar to public journalism, peace journalism focuses on the societal structures in which the conflict occurs. Editors and reporters make conscious choices that create opportunities for viewers to imagine, and even value, nonviolent responses to conflict.[53] Expensive to produce? Definitely. Entertaining? Probably not.

Critical Consumption. Most of us are not professional researchers, and few of us report on wars. Yet through our critical consumption (and nonconsumption) of certain popular media messages, we can prophetically confront what we know to be unjust in society.

Sometimes we can make a conscious choice not to purchase products that rely on stereotypes, no matter how good a deal we could get. For instance, many ads for men's personal care products celebrate machismo and womanizing. The Degree for Men deodorant ads featured G.I. Joe action dolls for men afraid to take risks. They also feature a "Mama's Boy" doll, complete with an uncut umbilical cord and manicured fingernails. Other spots feature his equally emasculated friends: "The Wuss" and "The Suck-Up." The question for men watching the commercials is, "Are you man enough to wear Degree for Men?"[54] "Come on," says one critic, "why don't they just come out and say you are gay if you do not use Degree? I'm sure that's what the ad agency was thinking."[55]

What about those North American icons of ideal manhood and womanhood, G.I. Joe and Barbie? Next time you decide to buy one of these dolls for Christmas, consider the biceps of the original G.I. Joe doll from the 1960s. If Joe's biceps from the 1960s were scaled to actual human dimensions, they would be about twelve inches in circumference, similar to an ordinary man's biceps. The biceps of some real-life athletes measure nearly twenty inches. Now compare the G.I. Joe doll from the 1960s to the 1997 G.I. Joe Extreme, which "had a biceps circumference of more than 26 inches, almost the size of a small man's waist."[56]

And what about Barbie? The average woman is five feet four inches tall, with measurements of 37–29–40. The majority of women in North America wear size twelve or larger. But if a Barbie doll were scaled to human dimensions, she would be slightly over seven feet tall with measurements of 40–22–36. It would be difficult, if not downright impossible, for her to stand up straight. Such images of men and women can distort reality for children and may lead to negative body images later in life.[57]

At other times, prophetic resistance against symbolic domination may come in the form of what news we read or what entertainment we consume. We may decide to purchase alternative newspapers that challenge taken-for-granted assumptions about commercialism, justice, and social reform as reported in mainstream press outlets. Groups like the Association of Alternative Newsweeklies provide access to sources that "produce high-quality journalism that offers a valuable alternative to the mainstream media in their area."[58] We may also decide to read minority newspapers or magazines that provide in-depth reporting on issues and concerns important to such groups that mainstream reporters frequently oversimplify.[59] We may even decide to attend plays, see movies, and watch shows on cable networks that present unconventional views of life in minority communities.[60]

And even if we do not conduct research about stereotypes, we can certainly read books and articles that report on such portrayals and carry on conversations about them in our churches, schools, and business. We may visit websites sponsored by organizations devoted to combating symbolic domination, receive their newsletters, purchase recommended materials, and if the mood strikes, participate in a chat room. For those with ears to listen or eyes to see, opportunities to develop a prophetic sensibility abound.

Conclusion

Songs like Ice-T's "Cop Killer" renew long-standing debates over the negative effects of popular media. This chapter, however, was not about settling those debates. Our focus, instead, was how such songs may worsen, or intensify, humanity's plight—which is the object of the prophetic burden—and how such songs and other images that injure groups and individuals present creative opportunities for prophetic confrontation.

Given the breadth and depth of humanity's alienation, the prophetic critic is impatient with, and even agitated by, excuses that seek to justify the current state of affairs. The prophetic communicator will not allow the masses—whatever their economic class, race, gender, or religion—to shift responsibility for self-destructive behavior by pointing only to other tribes' institutions or their leaders. In chapter 5, we take up common justifications used by individuals and institutions that reinforce the dominant consciousness' stranglehold on culture, and we explore prophetic responses to each.

5

Rejecting a Spirit of Acceptance

In Oliver Stone's now-classic film *Wall Street*, Gordon Gekko defends himself as a liberator of companies, not a destroyer. According to Gekko,

> Greed—for lack of a better word—is good. Greed is right. Greed works. Greed clarifies, cuts through, and captures the essence of the evolutionary spirit. Greed, in all of its forms—greed for life, for money, for love, knowledge—has marked the upward surge of mankind. And greed—you mark my words—will not only save Teldar Paper, but that other malfunctioning corporation called the USA.[1]

At one level, Gekko demonstrates how our selfish satisfaction of personal aspirations can become the ultimate goal in life. At another level, Gekko illustrates how every cultural system has built-in justifications that are used to attract supporters and reinforce the system's continued dominance. For Gekko, greed's offspring—efficiency, human progress, and salvation—demonstrate the wisdom and superiority of North American capitalism and consumer life. But to the prophetic critic, such rationales are intolerable excuses that ultimately promote a "spirit of acceptance" of unjust and destructive conditions.[2]

In this chapter we argue that individuals and institutions use several key justifications to support North America's dominant consciousness. In their priestly role, popular media package and deliver these justifications to the public with commonly repeated symbols and phrases that nearly everyone can understand. Those who criticize these justifications are regularly dismissed or rejected, but more often their criticism is absorbed by the system and repackaged for mass consumption.

Second, throughout this chapter we demonstrate how the prophetic critic, in the tradition of the Old Testament prophets, comes against the justifications used by the "kings and priests" to affirm the superiority of the presiding cultural system.[3] The prophetic critic also comes against his own tribe when it embraces similar justifications as a way to legitimize the superiority of its own agenda while excusing the unjust treatment of tribes it considers inferior. The prophetic critic is an iconoclast, or one who seeks to intensify individual and institutional responsibility by challenging what is apparently "holy, revered, and awesome" within the dominant culture.[4]

Justifying the "Story of Stuff"

All dominant framing stories, whether they are Christianity, Islam, Marxism, Freudian theory, or consumerism, require *justification systems*. By justification system, we mean the sum total of rationales available as evidence that the system is good and should remain dominant. Justifications can be legitimate and ethical, but they can also be illegitimate and vile.[5]

The justification system supporting North America's dominant consciousness works to sustain our blessed assurance that owning stuff is good.[6] The sum total of rationales available in our culture work to build our confidence in consumption as a way of life: "We need things consumed, burned up, replaced and discarded at an ever-accelerating rate."[7]

Additionally, our confidence in consumption as a way of life is based on our belief in the program of "achievable satiation"[8]; that is, our belief that consumer life can deliver on its promises by always satisfying our hungers, whatever their type, size, or propriety. In popular media we find easily accessible evidence supporting these promises, dominated by the broad category labeled *proof of progress and efficiency*.

Proof of Progress and Efficiency. Proof of progress is no further away than the rote retelling of the most recent technological hurdle scaled: from the first manufactured automobile, to the first talking motion picture, to the first computer small enough to fit on our lap. When computer processing speed doubles every eighteen months, we marvel at our culture's ability to make our lives more efficient. Commercial ads rely on proof of progress language such as "fastest," "easiest," and "best deal on the planet" to stir consumer frenzy and reinforce our belief in the system's superiority.[9]

In addition, the dominant system's ability to satisfy our desires for immediate gratification is further proof of its preeminence. As the system rewards our extravagant demands with immediate supply, our identification with its power to deliver us from boredom is strengthened.[10] "No money down," "Get it now," and "Why wait?" are common mantras of commercial advertising that reinforce our obsession with efficiency and immediacy, very often measured in the seconds required to deliver the satisfaction.

Immediate gratification is so foundational to North America's dominant framing story that it is often portrayed as something we are entitled to as citizens.[11] From a very early age, a variety of groups—including advertisers, retailers, overindulgent parents, and schools—socialize children as consumers to believe that it is their right to have all their expectations met. Consequently, children increasingly expect more at increasingly younger ages. By adulthood, these extravagant expectations regularly develop into full-blown aspirations for a number of big-ticket material goods as a source of personal satisfaction.[12]

Bigger Is Better. Moreover, bigger is usually, if not always, better in North America's dominant framing story—extra proof of progress. Bigger homes, cars, and paychecks express a higher level of success and influence, while small indicates a lower level. *Bigger is better* also saturates human relationships, devastatingly infected by the restless desire to perpetually trade up—always in the market for better neighbors, better friends, and better romantic partners.

In all its forms, popular media reinforce *bigger is better*: the idea that size truly does matter. Big box office receipts define a movie's success and determine if a sequel is made. In television and radio, larger ratings equal larger audiences, which equal larger advertising revenue. The cost of print ads in newspapers and magazines is determined significantly by the ad's actual size. And advertisers draw on our national obsession with size by announcing that for just a few pennies extra, our meal can grow from regular to "supersized," "biggie," or "extra value."

The *bigger is better* mantra undergirds many Christian ministries as well. Christian broadcast and print media gauge effectiveness based on audience size or readership. A local church's impact is frequently determined by the size of its congregation or the number of ministries it provides. The largest and fastest-growing churches in North America, where all of one's theological needs can be met in a single stop, appeal to the shopping-mall generation. In consumer culture, the easiest thing to measure is size. While it is difficult to quantify things like exceptional creativity, spiritual growth, or prophetic faithfulness, it is easy to count the people in the stackable chairs.[13]

At other times we see the consumer mindset at work in our never-ending search for a better, more efficient, more satisfying church experience—a wise and necessary trade-up to meet our personal desires and lifestyle choices. As national pollster George Barna reported, "One out of every seven adults changes churches, and one of six attends two or more churches on a rotating basis."[14] The consumer mentality, suggested Barna, is one common explanation for our church-hopping. "People are staying put in their faith," but there is less concern about "brand loyalty" to specific churches than there used to be.[15] As another critic observed, it seems as if religion has become "just another product in the broader marketplace of goods and services."[16] Thus, even in tough economic times, when we buy less and buy smaller, our enthusiastic consumerist habits can appear in less overtly economic areas of our lives.

Evangelical Christian churches throughout North America feed the consumer mentality by offering "service menus" designed to accommodate worshipers' divergent musical tastes and to attract the "unchurched."[17] But in an effort to appeal to religious consumers and grow brand loyalty, "some churches become like 'Saint Happy's: The Worship Place,' where the slogan is 'Have It Thy Way' while selecting from the overhead menu their preferences for 'Liturgy Lite' or 'Kiddy Kristianity.'"[18] Menu approaches tend to "dumb down" worship and can foster an individualistic religion of self-fulfillment.[19]

In brief, North America's dominant framing story is supported by a system that constantly produces proof of its superiority in solving problems and satisfying hungers. These proofs affect every aspect of our lives, from interpersonal to institutional arrangements. Priestly popular media deliver such proof in readily available forms, confirming and exploiting what our culture wants to believe about its own superiority. Armed with our collection of proofs, we cannot help but be optimistic about our culture's strength and the possibilities for our personal success. But proof of progress in all its forms clears the way for an "official religion of optimism,"[20] replacing dependence on a transcendent God with an optimistic dependence on the efficient system of consumerism and the all-powerful self.

North America's Official Religion of Optimism

North America's official religion of optimism can be likened to temple worship during Solomon's reign. Years earlier, Moses's alternative vision confronted the static god of the Egyptians with a "free" God, one unrestrained by the wishes or authority of the Pharaoh.[21] But in the generations after the temple is constructed, the ruling powers slowly but surely allow their perception of God to evolve from a "free," sovereign Lord to one who is "on call," with access to him controlled by the royal court.[22] Although begun by King David, this radical shift stabilizes under Solomon's reign. Eventually, God is used by both religious and political leaders to officially "sponsor," or give sanction to, the nation's ideology.[23]

Just as occurred in Solomon's day, North America's dominant framing story places God "on call" to help "maintain our standard of living" and satisfy our personal desires, thus "ensuring his own place in his palace."[24] God becomes a consumer-friendly deity who serves our cultural system and our personal desires, often at the expense of others. In so doing, we do not serve God.

The religion of optimism's basic principle—supported by a never-ending stream of proof of progress data—is the unbridled belief that everything always has, always does, and always will continue to get better and better, forever and ever, amen. "Recessions may come and go, but consumption is eternal."[25]

This optimism also includes an inability to recognize the reality of limitations on anything—growth, potential, money, or resources. Within the religion of optimism, God would not allow economic collapse, climate change, or drought to destroy our way of life—as if God never allowed his people to suffer, become poor, or die! If for some inexplicable reason our way of life *is* derailed, or evidence of our vulnerability is brought to our attention, it is only a temporary setback—just another problem to be overcome through the modern miracle of technological advancement.

In Christian communities, the religion of optimism is sometimes reinforced by visual symbols used during worship. For instance, in 2008, with three hybrid sport-utility vehicles on the altar and auto workers in the pews, one of Detroit's largest churches prayed for Congress to bail out the struggling auto industry in the midst of a national economic crisis. The preacher closed his sermon by leading the congregation in the gospel song "We're Gonna Make It," as hundreds of auto industry workers gathered around the altar to have their foreheads anointed with consecrated oil. "I pray in good times and in bad times," said the preacher, "but I pray these days because it's something that directly affects our lives."[26]

Although the church was not promoting car worship, it may be difficult for some to shake a "Golden Calf vibe" (see Exod. 32) after hearing this story. With the icon of North American ingenuity, freedom, and individuality on the altar, church leaders invite God to partner with them so they can maintain their current standard of living. As one union executive told the congregation, "We have done all we can do in this union, so I'm going to turn it over to the Lord."[27]

The religion of optimism finds more deliberate expression in prosperity theology. The "prosperity now" message—sometimes referred to as the "name it, claim it" message—is embraced by many widely known television preachers. It teaches that all people need to do is state what they want and it will be done. Viewers are urged to name and claim money and prosperity, almost with a sense of entitlement. One prosperity preacher who reaches millions with his cable television show urges followers to recite a list of things that belong to them: "I want my money—God has my money—and, God, I want my money now . . . I am a money machine—money comes to me—I want the money that belongs to me."[28]

Proponents of the prosperity message equate the "abundant life" (John 10:10) as set forth in the New Testament with pursuit of the "good life" as defined by North America's dominant framing story. Indeed, prosperity ministries begin with a biblical truth: namely, that Jesus came to set us free from the burden of the law and give us abundant life. Sin, death, sickness, and poverty are certainly parts of humanity's plight. However, the emphasis in prosperity theology is most often on deliverance from the curse of poverty, with far less attention paid to the rest of humanity's plight.[29]

In short, the religion of optimism birthed by North America's dominant framing story suggests that God's main job is to help satisfy our hungers, no matter what kind or how small they may be. Along the way, the continuing ascension of self-interest and self-gratification promotes idolatry on at least two fronts: idolatry of technology and its almost messianic power to deliver us from evil, and, perhaps more importantly, idolatry of the self, or self-deification.[30]

When it comes to self-deification, no one makes the claim that she is "God incarnate" unless she is having a psychotic episode. But instead of defining God as "irreducible"—that is, the ultimate being beyond which there is nothing—our God, however subtly, "becomes Consumption."[31] Consumption consistently elevates self-regard over other-regard and ultimately places oneself on the throne above all else. God becomes not the sovereign Lord of all creation, but the loving (that is to say submissive) partner in one's sense of entitlement to achievable satiation.[32]

Not surprisingly, given the system's tendency to promote self-deification, mainstream religion is often transformed into a narcissistic, therapeutic enterprise by individuals who lack allegiance to religious institutions or communities.[33] Instead of hungering for social justice, many people hunger for "the feeling, the momentary illusion, of personal well-being, health, and psychic security."[34] Concepts like growth and self-awareness become ends in themselves, divorced from broader individual and social responsibilities. In the words of influential Protestant moralist Harry Emerson Fosdick, the foundation of modern religion is faith in "man's personality, with all its possibilities and power."[35]

Intensifying Responsibility

Prophetic criticism, fueled by a prophetic burden and focused on humanity's plight, is "intent on intensifying responsibility" and is "impatient of excuses" that justify the program of achievable satiation.[36] Such criticism asks for a reexamination of everything, from the seemingly mundane to the most cherished. By its very nature, prophetic criticism cannot resist the temptation to look under the rock and press for disquieting perspectives that upset our comforting reliance on "proof of progress and efficiency."[37]

Becoming Aware. In 1955, economist Victor Lebow offered the following formulation of North America's dominant framing story: "Our enormously productive economy . . . demands that we make consumption our way of life, that we convert the buying and use of goods into rituals, that we seek our spiritual satisfaction, our ego satisfaction, in consumption."[38] Whether intended as prescription or critique, Lebow's remarks make clear the underlying logic for our dominant framing story: the transformation of everything, including spirituality, into commodities for sale.[39]

Perhaps the most fundamental way to intensify responsibility is through simple awareness of the dominant consciousness' underlying logic. For instance, consumer culture, explains Georgetown University professor Vincent Miller, "trains us to substitute consumption for other practices," including spiritual practices. The moment of consumer choice can become so seductive that it may disconnect us from "traditional practices of commitment, such as joining a community or organizing for change." So instead of joining a community, we come to believe that reading a book on racism or listening to ethnic music are just as effective as direct involvement. Indeed, books and music can help one's prophetic burden to grow, as explained in chapter 3, but they should never be a substitute for more direct involvement or engagement.[40]

We also need awareness of the underlying similarities between consumer desire and religious desire. Both types of desire are built on the same basic principle: that material objects can*not* satisfy human longing. Religious desire says that nothing apart from God—whether material "stuff" or other human beings or ideas—can fully satisfy human longing. Consumer desire redirects this in a different way: the endless seeking of fulfillment in more and more material stuff. Since material objects can only satisfy temporarily, we need to keep consuming to remain satisfied. Thus, in consumer desire, extended satisfaction is always one purchase away.[41]

The endless seduction of new consumer desire, spread across an unlimited range of available products, can work against the life of spiritual devotion. Instead of experiencing restlessness as a discomfort, or as a reason to change the way we live, we experience it as pleasure. St. Augustine (AD 354–430) hints at this when he gives the example of someone in a foreign country on a journey home: "They face the danger not only of being so beguiled by the beauties of the foreign land as to forget their goal of returning home, but also of getting caught up in the delights of the journey and the actual traveling."[42]

Similarly, Thomas Aquinas (1225–74) spoke of human desire for temporal things: before they are "possessed, they are highly regarded and thought satisfying; but after they are possessed, they are found to be neither so great as thought nor sufficient to satisfy our desires, and so our desires are not satisfied but move on to something else."[43] In other words, we do not regret our restless desires but only their fulfillment. The pleasure typically comes in desiring the things we want, not in actually possessing them.

To borrow St. Augustine's language, seduction through material stuff tempts us to become entangled in the "love of lower things," causing our pursuit of higher things to be "impeded and sometimes even diverted." Rather than turning our hearts toward what can truly fulfill us, we squander our love on the never-ending pursuit of insignificant objects.[44]

Finally, we need to be aware of the way consumer culture deals with criticism directed against its underlying logic. Doubters are regularly marginalized or dismissed outright as pessimists who assault the "American way of life" and ruin the positivity necessary for cultural vibrancy.

But more often, challenges are absorbed by the system and repackaged for mass consumption. Consumer culture appears capable of selling anything, including the criticism of its most vocal opponents—regardless of how right or wrong, wise or foolish, their criticism might be. So, as Vincent Miller observes, for the 150th anniversary of Karl Marx's *Communist Manifesto*, bookstores across the country placed reprinted copies of Marx's anticapitalist criticism next to cash registers as a way to "tempt impulse purchases." Or consider Kurt Cobain, the late lead singer of *Nirvana*, whose critiques of consumer culture proved enormously market-able. *Nirvana*'s popularity, suggests one scholar, was not because listeners failed to grasp Cobain's irony. "Far from it; they could not get enough of it. What could be more deliciously ironic than mindlessly moshing to a song about the mindlessness of popular music fans?"[45]

To sum up, an ounce of awareness may be worth a pound of cure when it comes to confronting our dominant culture's justifica-tion systems. But given the system's ability to withstand critique, engaging consumer culture wisely involves more than politicians or preachers telling people what to do; a healthy self-analysis is also required. Self-analysis forces us to consider that as citizens of the richest, most technologically advanced nation on earth, "we ourselves might sometimes be the prospering wicked," the false idolaters, and the oppressors "of whom the Hebrew prophets spoke."[46]

Challenging the Sacred. As Abraham Joshua Heschel observes, the Old Testament prophets were *iconoclasts*: individuals who came against what was apparently "holy, revered, and awesome" in their culture. "Beliefs cherished as certainties" and "institutions endowed with supreme sanctity" drew heavy fire because they pro-vided justification systems that reinforced the people's numbness toward the effects of the dominant framing story.[47]

When we endow our most cherished institutions with "supreme sanctity," they often become security blankets.[48] Jeremiah tells the people that the "city of God" will be destroyed because they turned their temple into their source of spiritual confidence. What response does he get? "This is the temple of the Lord, the temple of the Lord, the temple of the Lord!" (7:4). This confession centers on the belief that God had taken up permanent residence in the temple and that no one, including Jeremiah, could challenge their way of life as long as they repeated their confession often enough.

Prophetic voices call for healthy reexamination of ruling powers and institutions. Such voices point out that God's purposes do not inevitably coincide with whatever a nation's (or tribe's) leaders or its institutions decide to do. Instead of cursing the enemies of Israel as the kings and priests did, the prophets condemned their own nation and its leaders. They rightly understood how both kings and priests used God to "bless," or give sanction to, their self-serving agendas.

So, rather than thinking of "God Bless America" as a theological command, the prophetic critic might see it as a political saying that transfers allegiance to our leaders instead of God. In many cases, the phrase is used to sanction a leader's decisions after the fact—no matter how contradictory to biblical truth the decisions may be—and surround their actions with a "biblical-sounding aura."[49]

For such reasons, President Barack Obama's former pastor, Reverend Jeremiah Wright, said, "God Bless America. No, no, no, God damn America."[50] As uncomfortable as it may be for some to hear this, it calls attention to the way that tribes and their leaders reduce religious expression to self-serving statements that ultimately justify the wisdom of a chosen course of action or our dominant culture's superiority. To dismiss Reverend Wright outright, based on his conclusions about the government's role in the spread of HIV/AIDS or its responsibility for September 11, misses an important point: North America "acts like she is God and she is supreme."[51]

Arguably, Dr. Martin Luther King Jr. embodied the very best of the African American prophetic tradition. King courageously condemned North America for the sin of racism while calling on North America to become the beloved community. We are quick, however, to romanticize King based on his hope-filled rhetoric while ignoring his more scathing prophetic witness. For instance, King once described the war in Vietnam as a "demonic destructive suction tube," calling the U.S. "the greatest purveyor of violence in the world today."[52] In his 1968 call for a Poor People's Campaign, King offered a warning that is echoed by Reverend Jeremiah Wright's more recent damning of North America: "America is going to hell if we don't use her vast resources to end poverty and make it possible for all of God's children to have the basic necessities of life."[53]

Whether North America at the time King spoke was the "greatest purveyor of violence" is debatable. Also, we may be going to hell as a nation, but not only because of our racism and disregard of the poor. But to dismiss King for these reasons again misses an important point. As a prophetic voice, King challenged institutions and leaders—both political and religious—who confused the will of the people for the will of God, or who branded God (or Christianity) as a "wholly owned subsidiary"[54] of a particular political party, religious denomination, or nation. (Much of the protest music of the 1960s offered similar challenges to these leaders and institutions.[55]) In any case, when our first response to such criticism is defensiveness, we fail to see the prophetic invitation to repent of very real sins. This is exactly what the audience of the Old Testament prophets did. They found themselves habitually defensive, not open to hearing truth.

Not only do we endow religious and political institutions and leaders with supreme sanctity, but we do it with instruments of mass media as well. Mainstream and tribal media professionals and consumers both embrace the "mythos of the communication revolution,"[56] optimistically associating North America's rapid industrial expansion and technological development with the "will of God." In so doing, however, they place a naïve hope in the power of technology to improve society.

Confronting Media Idolatry. Throughout media history, humankind has practiced *media idolatry*—a cherished belief that the "latest media can solve practically all of our social and individual problems."[57] All new electronic media—from the telegraph to the internet—produce mystical promises of some kind, including universal communication, the spread of democracy worldwide, and even worldwide peace.[58] Few of the grand promises associated with new media, however, are ever fully realized.

Optimism about the powers of technology must be tempered by the all-encompassing effects of humanity's plight, as described in

chapter 4. Popular media, no matter how comfortable and convenient they make our lives, no matter what advances they promise,
do not have the power to save us from ourselves. Media technologies
are part of several social institutions driven mainly by commercial
gain, which regularly corrupts even the best of intentions. As long
as we idolize technological advancement and hold it up as proof of
our system's superiority, we fail to see the difficulty of transforming
the media and ignore the root causes of our plight.

Many Christian tribes, especially those described as Proclaimers in chapter 1, tend toward technological idolatry, or at the very
least, toward the extreme veneration of technology. Many believe
that God gave media to the church so it could communicate the
gospel around the world. Media are therefore invested with almost
messianic promises of universal communication, as a way to usher
in the second coming of Christ. Accordingly, the hope is that the
church will seize control of the latest technologies for the glory of
God. Needless to say, Christians have been pioneers in adapting
every kind of new media for evangelistic purposes.[59]

In the electronic era, the rhetoric surrounding television captures
clearly Proclaimers' extreme veneration of technology. For instance, in
the 1950s, it was said that television allowed Billy Graham to "preach
to more people in one night on TV than perhaps [the apostle] Paul did
in his whole lifetime."[60] In the 1970s and 1980s, Proclaimers pushed
forward with satellite technology. As televangelist Jimmy Swaggart
said of such technology, "For the first time in history God has given
a handful of men the opportunity to reach tens of millions with the
gospel of Christ."[61] One former director of the National Religious
Broadcasters argued that satellite and cable television would offer
"a revolutionary new form of the worshipping, witnessing church
that existed twenty centuries ago." He also wondered whether the
angel mentioned in Revelation 14:6 was a communications satellite
used by God to fulfill the prophecy of the last days.[62]

North American evangelicals' overemphasis on Jesus Christ's
Great Commission (Matt. 28:19) as the main goal in the use of
Christian media—along with their veneration of technology—makes

personal religious conversion the "alpha and omega of all Christian media activity in the world."[63] As such, it also means that there is little room for the idea that media might be prophetic or devoted to social injustices or wider societal concerns. Instead, the measuring stick for "good Christian media" becomes how clearly the particular work points others to salvation in Christ, not how well it is written, produced, or delivered. Proclaimers shift the burden of proof to anyone not using mass media for overtly evangelistic purposes.[64]

At other times, since the media goal is winning souls, there is a tendency to communicate the gospel with slickly designed show-business performances that play on emotions and fears. "With the overarching demand of the Great Commission looming over every evangelical enterprise, it is very easy to go for ratings instead of rationality, quantity rather than quality."[65]

The problem, of course, is not that popular media should never be used for evangelism. Nor do we suggest that evangelism is a secondary communication function of the church. Rather, the point is that the overemphasis on the Great Commission as the goal of media use disregards the biblical wisdom of communication beyond the evangelistic sales event.[66] Beginning with the Great Commission incorrectly assumes that the only way to faithfully engage popular media is with preaching and teaching. But God gave communication not only for preaching the gospel; God also intended it for forming and informing culture in ways that promote *shalom*. Within a cultural view of communication, everything Christians do in communication, whether or not the gospel is directly proclaimed, is "implicitly evangelistic as a witness to the lordship of Jesus Christ."[67]

Reconnecting with Tradition. North America's official religion of optimism embodies the enticing idea that self—and not others— defines our past, present, and future. It therefore denies adherence to any tradition that calls individuals to reflect on the past and to cultivate memory. Quite simply, a collective memory announcing that we are accountable to others, including God, for how we treat others—not just how we treat ourselves—works against the ascension of self-interest and immediate gratification at the heart of North America's dominant framing story.[68]

In response, prophetically reflective media voices beg for an alternative consciousness "devoted to the pathos and passion of covenanting."[69] This prophetic passion finds footing in the biblical assertion that individual identity is understood only within the context of group and communal identity.

A passion for covenanting, however, seems out of place in a culture of polarization, in which mainstream and tribal media regularly promote ideological divisions rather than collective memory. As described in chapter 1, most media criticism today is faddish. Instead of being grounded in anything meaningful, it is often driven by the latest hot-button issue or a particular tribal leader's personal agenda.

The prophets avoided faddish critique by situating their message within a particular tradition. They simply reminded the people of their past covenant with God and called them to make good on their promises. The prophets' criticism arose out of the tribe's collective past, since the past provided a moral frame of reference for the present. To the classical Hebrew prophet, nothing seemed worthy of preservation in the current societal system apart from a restored memory of the covenantal bond ensuring justice.

Tradition countervoices today can help to keep alive tribal tradition as a frame of moral reference. We do not mean *tradition* as in "outdated rules, meaningless habits, or petty moralisms" that sustain oppressive power structures, but *tradition* as in the "accumulated wisdom and the resulting disciplines, customs, and beliefs that a people carries from person to person through generational time—all of it nurtured as a living dialogue that includes the remembered 'voices' of the past."[70] When viewed this way, tradition involves personal responsibility. Community members are responsible for seriously engaging what is passed down: for interpreting, applying it to the present moment, and preserving it for the next generation.

One example of a tradition countervoice is Emergent Village. This web-based group promotes a "conversational friendship" that cuts across tribal divides in an effort to strengthen shared faith and mutual commitments to care for one another.[71] Through a variety of web sources and face-to-face cohort meetings around the United States, this global network binds believers together by drawing on core religious values and practices that arise from a common biblical heritage. As part of their effort to define the church and its communication activities in the world, Emergent Village avoids the latest fads by appealing to deeply biblical, ancient traditions.[72]

Tradition countervoices may also exist in more traditional communal media institutions, such as religious publications and denominational presses. Instead of delivering trendy content in an effort to attract new audiences, such institutions can foster "communion and discernment that help the tribe to locate itself at the intersection of tribal tradition and the public interest."[73] Such efforts will strengthen tribal interdependence, but also serve a prophetic role for their readers by helping them to see mainstream culture—and their own tribe—critically through the lens of biblical faith. For without "a shared religious language and common core labels, tribal media cannot sustain significant prophetic conversation."[74] They will lose their own special perspective on the world around them.

Finally, tradition countervoices can intensify responsibility by cultivating a mindset and habit of gratitude. Quentin J. Schultze asserts that "tradition-specific discourse flows largely from gratitude, which is ultimately thankfulness for the creation" and recognition of service to others. The habit of gratitude, commanded by the apostle Paul,[75] admonished by the psalmists,[76] and even the custom of Jesus Christ,[77] requires focused attention on the contributions of others. When we listen to and practice the message of gratitude, we plant "our self-identities and intimacies in the wisdom of revealed truth" rather than in the consumption of material things. These "roots grant us a sense of responsibility for things greater than our own survival and higher than our own self-interest."[78] These roots also reinforce that an encounter with tradition requires an encounter not just with ideas, but with specific practices.[79]

Information and entertainment-based media can help to promote a mindset and habit of gratitude. For instance, several networks aired post-9/11 reports expressing gratitude to response teams and others who put responsibility toward others above personal safety. In cooperation with the Newspaper in Education Institute, *The Washington Times* sponsored a page dedicated to cultivating the spirit of gratitude in children. Television talk-show host Oprah Winfrey promotes her gratitude to writers through Oprah's Book Club, which introduces millions to her favorite authors.[80] Mainstream media regularly promote the *science of gratitude* as a source of emotional, physical, and spiritual health,[81] and Christian media are awash in materials that help believers to cultivate gratitude. Academic research demonstrates that gratitude is just one of several pro-social behaviors that audiences can learn to express by observing positive role models in popular media.[82]

Conclusion

Although excessive consumption is widespread, most of us are not sociopathic yuppies like *Wall Street*'s Gordon Gekko. Yet we often unintentionally accept the values and justifications of the dominant culture. We inadvertently allow them to shape our own personal justification systems—whether at home, at work, or at church—in ways that interfere with *shalom*. Unless we attend to deeper cultural justifications, we may miss the most profound challenge of North America's dominant framing story.

The characteristic style of the prophet's spirit of non-acceptance is fueled by agitation and anguish over the existing unjust patterns, policies, and justifications of a society. We should not, however, be readily put off by the prophet's strident language or seemingly heavy-handedness. As the next chapter demonstrates, the outcries of the prophets were often a form of shock therapy, which was intended to jolt the complacent out of their numbness toward the dulling effects of the dominant consciousness.

6

Shocking the Complacent

Imagine that one Sunday morning your pastor begins his sermon wearing waist-high waders, then walks to a large steel-cased cooler and opens it. Before you see what he pulls out, you can smell it: the overwhelming odor of cow manure fills the sanctuary. Several congregants let out sounds protesting the stench.

Then your pastor pulls up handfuls of the excrement—yes, dung—and starts walking down toward the front pew. More yelps from the congregation. Has he lost his mind?!? How could he do this in such a sacred place?!? The pastor comments that he is handling what many people feel like inside and think they could never mention to anyone, let alone talk about in public.[1]

Several minutes later, still not used to the sanctuary stench and still somewhat stunned, you hear the pastor describe that this kind of pulpit stunt was not absolutely foreign to the prophets. In fact, Ezekiel used animal excrement to make a slightly different, although equally provocative, point.[2]

Unpleasant? Yes. Dramatic? Yes. Prophetic? Absolutely. Prophets through the centuries regularly said and did outlandish things to provoke their audiences out of a sinful stupor.

In this chapter, we argue that the Hebrew prophets' no-holds-barred confrontations were a form of *shock therapy* designed to shock the complacent kings, priests, and people out of their destructive habits. From the haunting perspective of the Old Testament's dominant framing story, the Hebrew prophets prodded their audiences toward reconciliation with God through graphic images, R-rated monologues, and outrageous street theater. Yet the prophets were not exhibitionists who shocked for shock's sake; rather, they were faithful truthtellers whose communication unapologetically demonstrated the depths of Israel's own disregard for peace and justice.

Secondly, we argue that faithful critics, consumers, and creators of popular media today must develop a sensitivity and openness to media that shocks complacent individuals and institutions out of their self-serving agendas. This requires a courageous willingness to view popular media through the lens of the Old Testament's dominant framing story instead of relying on our own tribe's taken-for-granted assumptions about what is sacred or moral content. We recognize that this may cause conflict for some. But the kind of criticism that cuts through our numbness toward the effects of North America's dominant consciousness is often edgy, uncomfortable, and, as the pastor's example at the beginning of this chapter demonstrates, perhaps even disgusting.

Critical Images that Burn

A basic overarching story, or framing story, guided the prophets' confrontations. All framing stories include a main storyline with several acts. For instance, as explained in chapter 1, North America's dominant framing story, consumerism, is characterized by the sacred cycle of acquisition, consumption, and disposal. Israel's framing story consisted of three very different acts: first, God's *covenant* with Israel; second, Israel's *rebellion* against God's covenant; and third, God's urging *reconciliation* with his chosen people.

Israel's "three-act play" of covenant, rebellion, and reconciliation is depicted throughout the Old Testament with several key metaphors, such as a bride unfaithful to her groom and a spoiled child spurning his benevolent parent. The major dramatic question is whether the marital partner or the wayward child will survive by turning in the nick of time toward redemptive life. Such word-pictures carried the whole "structure of meaning" for the community.[3] They were familiar images that provided easily referenced frameworks for passion, purpose, and goodness.

As one might expect, the prophets' communication was strongly critical of Israel's rebellious second act. The prophets were deeply burdened by Israel's numbness toward their own plight, and so they "bubbled forth" with passion and fire.[4] The prophets desperately wanted their thick-headed fellow community members to see themselves as the adulterous partner or the spoiled child headed toward death and destruction. Not surprisingly, the critical images used by the prophets were intended to critically "burn" rather than pleasantly "shine."[5] They were purposely neither fanciful nor elegant. There was no time for such frivolities.

Like all artists interested in engaging their audience, the prophets also wanted their audience to be affected. Brian Swarts writes that prophetic criticism, like good art, "unveils truths about our world around us, by bringing us face-to-face with realities we normally let pass unnoticed or purposefully choose to avoid."[6] The prophets hoped for an extravagant effect in the case of Israel. Israel's idolatries had become a wicked scandal that caused the heavens to "shudder with great horror" (Jer. 2:11–12). The prophets, quite simply, desired that their audience notice the reality of their plight and share in heaven's horror.

The Anatomy of Shock

The prophets were well aware of the human tendency to resist change, especially the kind of change preceded by admissions of weakness, guilt, or shame. The prophets also knew what was necessary to bring about the willingness to change. Long before contemporary discussions of "emotional invasions of value programs,"[7] the prophets understood that the possibility of change is linked to the "emotional extremities of life."[8] Put another way, the prophets recognized that often we need more than knowledge about right and wrong; we need an emotional jolt!

Shock brings individuals into contact quickly with the "emotional extremities" of life. Typically the most immediate way to be shocked is visually: an image so overpowering that the process of categorizing it is difficult yet memorable, even to the point of provoking action.[9] Shock also comes from things communicated verbally. Consider the very personal moment when someone hears a medical doctor's diagnosis, especially if it is an unanticipated terminal diagnosis. Other times, provocative similes or metaphors evoke powerful images, or word-pictures, that stay with us for days, months, and even years.

The shock we experience, whether from visual or verbal stimuli, comes from some kind of penetrating and unexpected revelation. To shock means to strike against; a shock is a clash encounter of some kind that shakes us. Shocking images and descriptions strike against or collide with our taken-for-granted social, religious, and political norms—norms that are often used to justify our personal or institutional agendas. In many instances, shocking stimuli bring us face-to-face with unnoticed or purposefully avoided realities in our lives or the lives of others.

In the prophetic context, the experience of shock provides favorable conditions for grief. And without grief, there is no repentance, or change, that leads to reconciliation. In the case of the doctor's diagnosis, for instance, the patient hearing the diagnosis of a shorter life expectancy than she had assumed is shocked, then grieved over the loss of time suddenly taken away from her forty years of plans and dreams. The grief then leads to a radical shift in her approach to everything, including her relations with loved ones and promises once made but long forgotten.

The prophets spoke to a generation—much like ours today—
that was hard of hearing, numb to their bad choices, and no longer
able to see their sin. The prophets lamented over Israel's blind-
ness to their own cruelty and hypocrisy.[10] They were amazed by
the people's bold assumption that despite their sin, God was not
angry with them.[11]

Southern writer Flannery O'Connor, herself a premier example
of a prophetic critic, describes her commitment to what we here
call *prophetic shock therapy*, explaining that she hopes to shock
her audience to make her vision clear because "to the hard of
hearing you shout, and for the almost blind you draw large and
startling figures."[12] The prophets did both: they unapologetically
used language and images (figures) audiences considered offensive,
foolish, and even profane as a way to deliver unexpected "emotional
jolts" and to stimulate their "moral imagination."[13]

Prophetic Shock Therapy

The classical prophet's program of shock relied on both direct and
indirect communication strategies. The most *direct communication strategy* was pronouncement, or explicit warning and call to
repentance—stop, drop to your knees, repent, and be reconciled![14]
For instance, in Jeremiah 26, the prophet simply tells the community that God left their city and that their false sense of security
betrays them and commands them to repent. Jonah's message to
the people of Nineveh follows a similar direct communication
approach.[15]

Indirect communication strategies were equally powerful modes
in prophetic shock therapy. Sometimes the prophets told brief,
succinct stories to illustrate a moral lesson. For instance, God sent
the prophet Nathan to bring forth a truth already known by King
David.[16] Nathan does not tell the king directly that he is aware of
his adulterous affair and successful plot to kill his lover's husband.
Instead, he tells David a story that addresses his treachery indirectly. As the story unfolds, it sounds like a literal news event; it

describes the actions of a rich man in David's kingdom who steals a poor man's lamb. In the end, however, the prophet informs David that he is the heartless thief. Nathan's narrative setup does more than "catch the conscience of the king"[17]; it provokes a shock in David's self-justification system and radically changes his life and that of the nation.

If not telling stories, the prophets used startling word-pictures and graphic imagery to confront Israel's alienation from God. In chapter 23, Ezekiel describes Judah's idolatry, or worship of other gods, through metaphors of prostitution and sexual immorality. He depicts the spiritual prostitution of both Jerusalem and Samaria, describing them as two sisters chasing after various lovers in Assyria, Egypt, and Babylon, lovers with genitals "like those of donkeys," and genital emissions "like those of horses" (v. 20). Ezekiel shocks the citizens of Jerusalem and Samaria by making them see who they have become. His descriptions in chapter 16 are, in fact, "so gross and shocking" that Jewish public worship "avoids the passage."[18]

When not shocking with language, the prophets' shock therapy relied on symbolic actions—or "rhetorical non-verbal communication"—as a medium for their message.[19] Nearly a millennium before the Old Testament, prophets were using symbolic *sign-acts*, including dramatic performances, object lessons, and living parables designed to "visualize a message and in the process to enhance its persuasive force" for the audience.[20] In one ancient Near Eastern text, a prophet from Mari devoured a raw lamb to announce an imminent danger that could devour the land.[21]

In the Old Testament we find similarly provocative symbolic acts. Isaiah removes his clothing and sandals and walks around naked for three years as a demonstration of what the king of Assyria would do to the Egyptians and the Ethiopians (Isa. 20:2). Jeremiah preaches first in a loincloth and then in a wooden collar to demonstrate, in part, how God would ruin the pride of Judah (Jer. 13:1; 27:2). In the case of Hosea, the prophet marries an adulterous woman, Gomer (Hos. 1:1–3); Gomer repeatedly leaves her husband for other lovers, only to return to Hosea and be reconciled. Hosea's living parable—or object lesson embodied over an adult lifetime—demonstrates the agonies and ecstasies of the marriage bond between the living God and his adulterous, wayward people.

Ezekiel uses more symbolic actions than any other prophet. His life and actions are part of his prophetic message. He speaks the word of the Lord and also dramatizes the divine plan in creative, sometimes profane, ways.[22]

In one instance, the Lord commands Ezekiel to bake bread made of wheat and barley, beans and lentils, millet and spelt and to use, as the baking fuel, human excrement. That's right: human dung. Ezekiel's usage of the excrement is symbolic of Israel's being forced at God's hand to eat defiled food in a foreign land (4:13). Ezekiel protests, "I have never defiled myself" (v. 14), and the Lord relents, allowing Ezekiel to bake his bread with cow manure instead of human excrement as fuel (v. 15). We can imagine a good many citizens of Jerusalem walking several blocks out of their way to avoid exposing their children to such an untidy dramatic display.

Another indirect communication strategy that the prophets used to provoke audiences' moral imagination was satire. This was not the kind of satirical humor one hears in many stand-up comic routines today, however. Probably no one laughed right away—they were too offended or shocked to find anything funny. Laughter in the Old Testament is primarily focused on God's scoffing laugh. Through the prophets and psalmists, God laughs mockingly at the pretensions and arrogance of his human creatures.[23]

For instance, Hosea makes fun of the high priest and the people of the Northern Kingdom worshiping carved wooden phallic (penis-shaped) symbols: "They consult a wooden idol and are answered by a stick of wood" (4:12). In his disgust, Hosea satirizes Israel's wayward devotion that has led them to the preposterousness of listening to a phallic stick.[24] The prophet Elijah satirically ridicules Baal and his priests at Mount Carmel,[25] prodding them to call out to Baal more vigorously since he may be preoccupied with his own needs, "perhaps bathroom occupied."[26] Amos,[27] Jeremiah,[28] and Habakkuk[29] offer equally scathing satirical jabs intended to get a rise out of their audiences.

In the sixth century, Saint Symeon, sometimes known as the "holy fool," spent twenty-nine years living in a cave near the Dead Sea. He was not known for any strange behavior until he entered the Syrian town of Emesa. Once inside the city he found a dead dog at the city dump, tied its leg to a rope around his waist, and dragged it through town to make a point about how rich people carry the same loads. The next morning he entered the church, blew out the candles, and threw nuts at the women. On his way out, he overturned the tables of the pastry chefs.[30] This sequence of events bears an obvious relationship to the New Testament accounts of Jesus's entry into Jerusalem (Matt. 21:12).[31]

This was merely the first act of many satirical, symbolic acts for Symeon. In the streets he developed a theatrical limp, and on solemn fasting days he feasted loudly and ate vast amounts of beans, with predictable results. During his lifetime, Simeon was regarded as an unholy scandal. His behavior, however, invokes images of a number of Old Testament figures who behaved strangely. In the life of Symeon the holy fool, the Old Testament model for outlandish behavior remains intact. He embodies the notion "that if the truth is worth telling, it is worth making a fool of yourself to tell."[32]

In short, the prophet's pronouncements and pleas—whether packaged in straightforward sermons or street theater—pushed the people to see a three-act pattern to their lives and community. This pattern remains today: you were married to God, bound to him in covenant, you have wandered from his care in rebellion, and God is persistently inviting you to return to his arms. To perceive such purposeful pattern in life provides "tremendous moral power."[33]

Prophetic Shock Therapy and Popular Media

Shock art is not new. Even a cursory review of art history demonstrates a host of artists who have shocked their audiences. Surrealists, minimalists, and artists in the 1980s and 1990s who used cheap, sentimental objects all pushed audiences to reconsider preconceived notions of art's function and purpose. This list is by no means exhaustive; rather, the point is that prominent art throughout the century has often shocked audiences.[34]

While some shock art is created to shock the public for the artist's personal gain, some is designed to directly confront individual and institutional injustices. For instance, Spanish painter Francisco Goya's work responded emotionally to his country's many troubles, including poverty and the excesses of regal settings. His work is often described as shocking and disturbing. In 1796, Goya's series of eighty prints titled *Los Caprichos*—which the artist explained did not aim to mock anyone in particular— was a scathing commentary against social, political, and religious hypocrisy.[35] Goya drew inspiration from what he described as "the innumerable foibles and follies to be found in any civilized society, and from the common prejudices and deceitful practices which custom, ignorance, or self-interest have made usual . . . and which, at the same time, stimulate the artist's imagination."[36]

Some shock art points directly to social injustices in the world caused by humanity's rebellion against God. Simply look at the horrors of some traditional paintings on this theme: Michelangelo's (1475–1564) *The Last Judgment* (in the Sistine Chapel) or Hieronymus Bosch's (c. 1450–1516) *The Garden of Early Delights*. Bosch's painting depicts a world where humans suffer the chilling consequences of their bad choices. In a single, dense scene, the viewer witnesses the burning of cities, war, torture, mutated animals feeding on human flesh, and nude figures attempting to cover their genitals. This art certainly convicts, but before it convicts it shocks.[37]

There are contemporary values and practices associated with North America's dominant framing story that warrant prophetic shock therapy. The wild prophetic mockery of "Reverend Billy" and the "Church of Stop Shopping" is part direct pronouncement, part street theater. The "Rev" (who is not a real Reverend and does not represent any religion) irreverently lampoons our culture's shopping lusts and the belief in "salvation" through consumerism. The church's simple "statement of belief" is that "consumerism is overwhelming our lives."[38] Whether pronouncing doom in New York's Times Square, in local shopping malls, on television, or on film, the "Rev" is usually backed by the "Stop Shopping Gospel Choir," whose "soaring harmonies [are] lovely enough to convert even the most jaded consumer into a stop shopping true believer."[39]

Or consider pop singer Peter Gabriel's compelling track, "Big Time." The song mocks the significance that our culture places on hitting the big time. In the "big city," sings Gabriel, there is so much stuff we can own; and we can pray to our "big god" while kneeling in our big places of worship. In the video, Gabriel appears to be in a robot-like haze as he pokes fun at the bigger is better mantra, even enlarging his mouth to insure that his oversized words come out right. In the song's chorus, the audience is invited to witness its own ridiculous devotion to proof of progress and conspicuous consumption as the song's title phrase is repeated over and over again.[40]

Steve Taylor's song "Cash Cow (A Rock Opera in Three Small Acts)" echoes Gabriel's prophetic tone toward North America's dominant framing story, described earlier in chapter 5 as the "story of stuff." Taylor's song mocks the prowling "golden Cash Cow"—that is, the golden calf of Exodus 32, essentially now all grown up—and our culture's addiction to material goods. The Cash Cow roams the local shopping mall looking for "proud mortals" to devour—telling them that he loves them, and that he is willing to offer them "good credit" so they can purchase all the creature comforts they deserve. The music video includes grotesque clay-animated characters with deformed, expressionless faces. Taylor's lyrics, performed over ominous Gregorian-like chants at times, confronts our dominant culture's justification systems.[41]

Alex Shakar's novel *The Savage Girl* creatively confronts the cornerstone of consumer culture: discontentment. In his story, the "trend spotters" take the protagonist, Ursula, through a supermarket, and Chas, Ursula's boss, tells her that every consumer product has a *paradessence*, or a paradoxical essence: two desires that it promises to satisfy simultaneously. So, the paradessence of coffee is stimulation and relaxation; ice cream connotes eroticism and innocence. Through paradessence, commodities deliver satisfaction but simultaneously promote our discontentment, making further consumption a necessity.[42] Ursula later learns more about the rules of consumer desire and exploitative commercial advertising while trying to market a brand new product: diet water, or "Litewater."[43]

The popular animated sitcom *The Simpsons* is not simply a cartoon, but a series known for its self-reflexive, biting critique of the very consumer culture it simultaneously promotes. Episodes frequently highlight the values and contradictions of consumerism. One episode, "Simpson's Spin-off Showcase," critiques the compulsive behavior that drives consumer society and leads to addictions that often cause us to overlook society's ills. Another episode, "The Itchy & Scratchy & Poochie Show," begins its usual satirical commentary by mocking how the conspicuous consumption of lavish goods to attain social status dominates North American life.

Additionally, main characters in *The Simpsons* are iconic figures who represent the values of consumer culture. The father, Homer Simpson, for instance, represents the consumption-addicted hedonist who is governed by an urge for immediate self-satisfaction. His consumer obsession, naturally, is developed mainly by watching commercial television.[44] Also, capitalism is shown as destructive and cruel through Mr. Burns (Homer's boss). And Indian immigrant owner of Kwik-E-Mart, Apu, is presented as almost "fully American" through his incorporation into mainstream consumer culture.[45]

Shock Therapy for Sacred Cows. The targets of prophetic shock therapy include not only the cash cows of mainstream culture but also sacred cows within the Christian tribe. *The Wittenburg Door* (intentionally misspelled), a humor magazine started in 1971 by youth workers, is especially effective when it aims at criticism

against church foibles and "sacred" Christian culture.[46] The magazine's editors describe their satire as "lining up 100 sacred cows
and shooting them all with a machine gun. Whichever one yelps
the loudest, you shoot 10 more times."[47]

The editors roast greedy TV evangelists, churches with silly advertisements, and cheap merchandise ("Jesus Junk") sold by Christian
retailers. They even sponsor a "loser of the month." Reading their
magazine is an excellent exercise in reading with a prophetic eye,
being sensitive to the possibility that the sacred cow being shot is the
one in our own backyard. On some evangelical college campuses,
The Door is the "most stolen" periodical. "What does that say about
other evangelical publications stocked in their reading rooms?"[48]

Another sacred cow deserving of prophetic shock therapy is
contemporary Christian music. Fans of "Christian" music often
complain that certain "Christian" bands do not mention Jesus
enough in their "Christian" songs. After all, how else would we
identify them? In response, a Christian rock band named All Star
United recorded "Smash Hit" in 1997, mocking the Christian music
industry's obsession with branding; that is, associating Jesus's
name with any movement or music in order to gain support from
Christian audiences. Ironically, the song was a hit on Christian
radio on the basis of its chorus, which described "this Jesus thing,"
or branding, as a "smash hit!"[49]

Bands like All Star United follow in the tradition of Christian
musicians and artists like Larry Norman, The Seventy Sevens, and
Michael Knott, to name a few, "who refuse to toe the line and do
what is expected of them" by Christian audiences.[50] They confront
the church and Christian popular media by using unconventional
images and language. One does not need to enjoy the musical style
of the Christian goth band Dead Artist Syndrome to appreciate
their prophetically irreverent humor. For instance, in one song,
after pledging their love to Jesus, the band tells Jesus that they
simply don't understand why his wife (the church) wears excessive
makeup, fights all the time, and in a world characterized by "black
and gray" argues for "shades of white."[51]

In addition, decades before Peter Gabriel and Steve Taylor confronted our culture's cash cows or *The Wittenburg Door* and All Star United appeared on the scene, North American novelist Flannery O'Connor took prophetic aim at our culture's dominant justification systems. O'Connor was also quick to recognize the negative influence of consumer culture on North American Christianity and to hold Christians responsible for unfaithful tribal practices.

In her first novel, *Wise Blood* (originally published in 1952), O'Connor critiqued contemporary North America through Taulkinham, a fictional city whose people worship only their own desires as reflected in North America's new god: consumerism.[52] A flashy Christian evangelist, Onnie Jay Holy, promotes his church of cheap grace where potential members can join for a dollar: "It's based on your own personal interpitation [sic] of the Bible, friends," Holy says. "You can sit at home and interpit [sic] your own Bible however you feel in your heart it ought to be interpited [sic]."[53]

The protagonist, named Hazel Motes,[54] preaches on the street for a "Church Without Christ"[55] in order to escape his misguided Christian upbringing and to embrace a life of sin like everyone else. Through a near-death experience, Hazel's "wise blood" (hence the title) teaches him that how he lives and what he believes does matter, and that this is not a world where anything goes.

Hazel needed an emotional jolt to knock him out of sin's complacency and the numbness toward ultimate realities in life. As Old Testament scholar Walter Brueggemann explains, the dominant consciousness—in biblical times and still today—leads people to numbness about death. It is the task of prophetic voices, therefore, "to bring people to engage their experiences of suffering to death."[56] Often the reality of death is the very shock therapy O'Connor used to awaken her characters, and her readers, to their jeopardy.

Horror as Shock Therapy. As a form of shock therapy that awakens people to the reality of death, horror films have a unique prophetic quality often overlooked by tribal media. Horror films can function both as a threat and a catharsis by confronting us with our fear of death and loss.

First, we agree that many horror films are excessive in their exploitation of sex and violence. But horror is a broad category that involves everything from soft horror, like *Scream* or *The Others*, to hard horror, like the infamous *Texas Chainsaw Massacre*. Evil in the world is real. Therefore, to the extent horror movies deal with evil, whether supernatural or natural, we need to be wise and discerning. St. Augustine complained of the characters and settings still living in his memory from the profane plays he attended years before his conversion.[57] Some horror films—like some films in every genre—are thus best left unseen.

But in a prophetic sense, true horror treats evil as evil. True horror, like true prophetic expression, seeks to represent evil in all its ugliness, without holding back. It also reminds us of the craftiness and subtleties of evil: good people have the capacity for great acts of evil, and evil often seduces us, slowly but surely, by presenting itself in attractive forms.

Bram Stoker's classic Victorian tale of *Dracula* is a great reminder of the seduction of evil. To perceive Count Dracula—who is profoundly charming, and easily allowed into one's town, one's home, and one's bloodstream—as the embodiment of the biblical perspective of evil is to witness the prophetic power of Stoker's work. It is also a reminder of the necessity of the Bible's admonition to "put on the whole armor of God" (Eph. 6:10–20), to escape "corrupting influences of this corrupt generation" (Acts 2:40), and "to abstain from sinful desires, which wage war against your soul" (1 Pet. 2:11).

True horror further shocks us out of complacency, away from the idea that everything is okay around us. It carries us to the brink of our limitations as humans and forces us to confront the disorder and confusion in the world around us. Theatrical devices of horror—suddenness and surprise that invoke the threat of danger—challenge our belief that we are "in control." We think we control things with our advanced technology and efficient systems, but we do not. Horror often deals with things beyond our control, thereby keeping us humble and opening up for us the possibility of the transcendent.[58]

Finally, true horror allows for an "experience of grace." It suggests that we too are disturbed and distorted; we too fear death; we too become monstrous in our longing for power and prestige. "Looking at our deformed selves in the exaggerated characters on screen, we experience a cathartic release (Thank God that isn't me!) or a genuine moment of self-knowledge (Oh, God, I need help!) which reminds us of the two-way movement of grace: grace for ourselves, grace for others." In the hands of the Christian, horror films can become an "invitation to redemption."[59]

The Faithful Practice of Shock Therapy

The possibility of prophetic shock therapy is not a justification to consume or create anything under the guise of redemptive shock. Even truthfulness as the ultimate intention cannot stand without the quality of loving regard for one's neighbor. The prophets' communication was not driven by animosity toward their community or condescension toward foreigners or enemies of Israel, but by a deep sense of compassion and concern for humanity's plight. Several guidelines can help us discern when shock is faithfully prophetic.

First, faithful prophetic critics recognize that prophetic shock value is never an end in itself. As suggested throughout this chapter, prophetic shock therapy is not just a crude instrument for self-expression or personal notoriety. It is always an instrument serving the greater end of alleviating human brokenness.

Many shock artists today, however, operate under a different assumption. Radio "shock jock" Howard Stern, for instance, provokes by parading sexual brashness and brazen crudeness. In MTV's shock show *Jackass*, people perform dangerous and disgusting stunts, including self-mutilation and public defecation. Still other radio jocks use shocking language to stereotype groups of people and offer up easy scapegoats to life's most complex problems. Beyond self-promotion, the predominant purpose of shock in these cases is to feed the audience's addiction to the titillation of the shock itself.

Secondly, faithful shock therapists avoid unethical humor. This might come in the form of sarcasm and cynicism. The intent of sarcasm is to wound. Don Rickles, a comedian whose career spans several decades, built his career around sarcasm. Rickles developed sarcasm as a surefire but often humiliating way to stop his hecklers. As Rickles's act evolved, the humiliating, cynical insults of certain audience members eventually became the routine everyone paid to see.

Neither is prophetic shock therapy an excuse for cynicism. Cynicism denies the possibility that anything will get better and rarely appears to motivate either the cynic or his target toward justice. Along these lines, we applaud documentary filmmaker Michael Moore's role as social critic and his burden for the poor and oppressed; his critique of the powers-that-be is often compelling. Yet we have difficulty with the cynicism that dominates many of his documentaries. Some of Moore's comic cynicism in films like *Roger and Me, Bowling for Columbine,* and *Farenheit 9/11* subtly amplifies a viewer's sense of moral superiority as Moore focuses on the responsibility of the elite and powerful for social ills. By blaming corporate villains and greedy politicians, the viewer is thus allowed to escape from her or his own responsibility. In essence, Moore gives viewers "a moral safety and security that requires no action or participation." Not surprisingly, while many of his films are financial successes, "they appear to have very limited effect in accomplishing their rhetorical aims and purposes."[60]

Thirdly, faithful shock therapists know what shocks their audiences. In our increasingly coarsened, media-saturated culture, the possibility of experiencing *shock fatigue* is significant. Many audiences have high shock thresholds, leaving them not only more hardened, but also more skeptical about the possibility of prophetic shock therapy. As shock therapists, our first response may be to escalate the level of shock, to be even more outlandish or extreme than originally planned so we can produce the same effect. But such extremes usually backfire.

Depending on the audience and the setting, a single shocking image, word, or dramatic scene may be more provocative or more jolting than a dozen images, words, or scenes. Consequently, shock therapy is used wisely and sparingly and only after careful audience analysis: Who is my audience? In what setting or location will they receive my message? What common experiences do they have? What image, word, or scene might be shocking for *this* community? Will my shock therapy penetrate what I perceive to be this community's sinful stupor, or will it simply promote my personal notoriety?

Tony Campolo, influential evangelist and social justice activist, repeatedly makes a memorable and provocative point about mainstream Christians' numbness toward humanity's plight. After telling his mainly Christian audience that while they were "sleeping last night, thirty-five thousand children died, either of starvation or diseases related to malnutrition," Campolo stuns the listeners by saying, "What's worse is that most of you don't give a shit!" Following the requisite gasps and a necessary dramatic pause, Dr. Campolo drives home his main point: "What's worse than *that* is that you're more upset with the fact that I said 'shit' than that thirty-five thousand children died last night. And that's what's wrong with your Christianity."[61]

Campolo might have used another, more extreme, four-letter word, but with what effect? Also, his chosen expletive was surely not uncommon to his audience in everyday usage. Many Christian students watch as many PG-13 and R-rated movies that include such language as non-Christian students. But given the context—a chapel service at a conservative Christian college—and his audience's expectations, a single shocking word was sufficient to produce the desired emotional jolt.

Finally, faithful shock therapists require accountability to a community dedicated to both priestly and prophetic sensibilities. Even when the distinction between faithful and unfaithful (or exploitative) shock therapy is understood, questions about appropriateness, censorship, and honesty are raised when mature

Christians create shocking media, or media that offends personal sensitivities or accepted social and religious norms.

For example, consider the work of Christian artist Edward Knipper. Paintings such as *The Stoning of Stephen*, *The Dying of St. Stephen*, and *Isaiah in the Temple*, to name a few, portray nudity and a level of what Knipper calls "physicality" that may shock audiences but whose deeper intention, in part, is to confront our tendency to minimize the "messy" realities of the physical world in the name of progress.[62] Or consider the plays of Christian playwright Paul Nicholas Mason, *The Discipline Committee* and the award-winning *Sister Camille's Kaleidoscopic Cabaret*.[63] Mason's penetrating analysis of the human capacity for cruelty includes some profane language and R-rated scenarios that shock audiences. But the profane material contributes to the story line's truthfulness and penetrates audiences' defenses toward sensitive issues all too often ignored by the church.[64]

Praying for wisdom in the creative process is a necessary starting point for Christians. Educating audiences on the prophetic possibilities of popular media is also necessary. But prayer and education are only the beginning. To promote faithful media stewardship, prophetic shock therapy—before and after the fact—must be shared with a company of critics for processing and discernment. This means a humble willingness to process the critique of others, either inside or outside the tribe, who question our tactics. In so doing, we are reminded, just like Elijah was reminded, that bearing witness to the truth, even in ways that provoke shock and anger, never leaves the prophet completely alone.[65] To the extent that Knippers, Mason, and the rest of us in our informal and formal communication channels demonstrate such accountability, we practice faithful shock therapy.

Conclusion

The steel-cased cooler was closed, and the pastor continued with his sermon. The stench eventually left the sanctuary, actually much faster than it left the minds of the congregants. Church members were shocked into the new and holy idea that their sanctuary location in one sense was a safer place than ever before. They learned that jolts of self-repulsion—feeling like excrement—should not keep them from doing the group work of worship, confession, and thanksgiving.

Perhaps it takes more than we realized to recognize the necessity of repenting of attitudes, habits, or direction in life. If Israel sometimes responded angrily, defensively, or indifferently to the capital-P Prophets, we can readily expect the same. We can also begin to note that when we are angry, defensive, or indifferent, it might be a hint that the prophet is directing his or her charges against us.

In our next chapter, we discuss how popular media technology, and not just the content it delivers, presents opportunities for prophetic criticism. As human creations, technology reflects human values and biases that are foundational for our understanding of self and society. As such, media technologies themselves can become sites of struggle against our culture's dominant consciousness.

7

Promoting Prophetic Critique of Technology

A Case Study

Jacob Bronowski tells the story of the Sherpas in his book *Science and Human Values*.[1] The Sherpas know intimately the face of Mount Everest, but only as seen from their home valley. Sometime when climbers show them a different side of the mountain, they refuse at first to believe. How could it possibly be the same mountain from a different angle? But they are moved emotionally, and their disbelief eventually turns to amazement at the revelation that their time-worn mountain can open to them in a new way.

So it is with most Christian media use and criticism, driven both by belief and disbelief, the familiar and unfamiliar. With several notable exceptions,[2] most Christian critics (as explained in chapter 1) focus only on one side of the mountain. On this side, popular media *content* matters most when it comes to influencing our culture. They think that media technologies (or channels that carry communication) are neutral—albeit powerful—channels of communication that simply transmit news and entertainment to eager audiences.

But from the other side of the mountain, media technologies are seen as more than just neutral. Rather, they are value-laden human constructions that send their own messages in addition to the actual news or entertainment they carry. Each technology influences the way people think about themselves and interact with others and institutions in society. On this new side of the mountain, technology, as well as content, is a cultural creation and therefore falls within the prophetic critic's scope of analysis.

Early on we explained that faithful media criticism requires attention to content, institutions, and technology, since each forms and informs culture. In the first six chapters, we focused primarily on popular media content. Along the way, we addressed how certain social institutions surrounding popular media—for example, churches, schools, commercial advertising, businesses, and government—influence the way messages are constructed and eventually interpreted by audiences. We occasionally highlighted how certain media technologies, in addition to the actual messages they deliver, influence human interaction and contribute to humanity's plight (see chapter 4). Now, before concluding, we demonstrate in greater detail another way that faithful media stewards might critique and engage the technology used to produce and distribute the popular media content we consume.

As demonstrated in chapter 1, technology *is* culture. Just as popular media content reflects the values of its writers and producers, so too do popular media technologies themselves reflect the values of their human creators. Each communication technology has values—or things it considers valuable—apart from the messages it sends that influence individuals and societies. Also, each technology—whether radio, film, or computers—has its own unique language that gives distinct shape and bias to its messages. As such, a particular technology's values and biases present additional opportunities for faithful critique and media stewardship.

So, in approaching any popular media technology critically, we need to ask some basic questions: What values and biases are inherent in each medium? How do such values and biases affect one's relationship with God, with oneself, with others, and with the environment?[3] These questions allow us to critique popular media in fresh ways, recognizing the significant relationship between the content we consume and the delivery systems that bring it to us.

In this chapter, television is our medium of choice. As a way to spark imagination and encourage additional analysis of technology beyond these pages, we demonstrate how television's inherent values and biases ultimately interact with the messages it sends, and how understanding its unique technological properties help us to make better, more discerning choices about which content to consume.

Television

Although each medium needs to be understood and critiqued, we chose television to answer the guiding questions above for several reasons. First, television continues to be the most influential popular media in the United States more than sixty years since it first became commercially viable. Second, in recent years, smaller, more portable, and less expensive video equipment has led to an explosion in new programming by mainstream and independent producers. Third, despite ever-increasing picture quality and media convergence—or the appearance of older media on the new media channels—television retains its key values and distinguishing properties.[4] Finally, as the reigning champion among evangelical media, television is an excellent candidate for analysis and critique.[5]

When it comes to television's inherent biases, television values images over words and encourages us to think that seeing—more than reading or hearing—is believing.[6] It also can weaken our imagination or imaginative capacities. Unlike books, television does the imaginative work for us: it pictures the castle, shows us the landscape, and draws the detailed contours of the protagonist's face. Over time, under the guise of the least effort principle, we may come to accept and even prefer the imagination of others over our own.[7]

Furthermore, television for the most part is *visually hyperactive*: it values the dramatic cut and short commercial over the long-term event.[8] Television thus values interruption rather than continuity or sustained reflection, such as that found in a Mozart symphony.[9] Imagine an orchestra stopping every seven minutes so the conductor can pitch his sponsors' latest products!

Also, as we watch television, our attention is attracted to the images on the screen more than to others in the room. The bursts of color ignited with every scene change and camera angle change draw the attention of the viewer much like the flames of a campfire draw the visual focus of those gathered around it. But unlike the campfire, there is typically no conversation around the television by its viewers. Faces are glued to the screen and drawn away from family members and friends.

Finally, television encourages physical inactivity. As we watch and enjoy our favorite sporting event, for instance, we are discouraged from practicing the sport we are watching. Television's very popularity is built upon the vicarious experiences it offers, from sports teams to soap operas. The phrase *couch potato* refers to individuals who spend too much time in sedentary activities, such as watching television or playing computer games.

Hence, the values inherent in television include image over word, visual interruption, interpersonal distraction, and physical inactivity. Over time, these values can subtly influence our interactions with others, including our desire for face-to-face interaction in community and the world around us.[10]

In addition, as explained in chapter 1, each technology has its own unique language, or its own unique way of capturing and presenting reality. Television's unique language, or iconography, includes at least two properties that are specific to this medium: intimacy and immediacy.[11] Intimacy and immediacy illustrate television's inherent biases in capturing and presenting reality, and also how these biases shape the Christian message just as they have formed the contours of commercial television.

Intimacy. Television is inherently an intimate medium. Compared with other dramatic media, television emphasizes intimacy and accentuates characters and personalities over ideas and propositions.[12] In fact, the face is the image that television captures best. It fits the size of the TV screen and overcomes issues related to picture resolution. Most fine details on television are lost—even with a high-definition quality picture.[13] Television is a relatively tiny box into which people are crowded and must live, unlike film, which gives us a view of the wider world. With its huge screen, film is perfectly suited for Civil War epics, panoramas, the sea, and so forth.

The small screen's constraints force producers to develop the drama by concentrating on characters' faces and trusting them to unfold the beauty and depth of the human personality in all its complexities. A television actor's facial expressions are as important as the dialogue in interpreting the actor's character. Television's visual scale grants a level of privacy unavailable elsewhere and thereby demands a believable performance. Vivid and highly professional acting over the history of television accounts for nearly all those series most highly rated for quality—*Hill Street Blues*, *M*A*S*H*, *The West Wing*, *Law and Order*, and *The Sopranos*, to name a few.

Not surprisingly, given television's emphasis on characters' faces, it often creates the illusion of face-to-face interaction between individual viewers and people on the screen. Because of the close-ups of faces and private content, many viewers feel they have a personal relationship with certain characters—a phenomenon researchers refer to as *para-social interaction* (PSI).[14] On the positive side, the illusion of intimacy makes for good television by providing characters that audiences can connect with along the dramatic journey. On the negative side, it leads some to find interaction with real-life characters less rewarding than interaction with television personas. It further accounts for powerful personality cults that form around mainstream celebrities.

The same effect occurs among audiences of various Christian programs. Thanks to television's inherent intimacy, even when it is not intended, viewers often feel as if they know Joel, Joyce, Kenneth, Pat, Robert, Charles, and T. D. (Do you recognize any of these personalities?) Tribal media personalities may not seek to promote their own personality cults, but their use of the medium counteracts even their best of intentions.

Immediacy. Television is inherently an immediate communication technology. Some of the most powerful moments in television programming have been live transmissions—the funeral of assassinated President John F. Kennedy, the moonwalk, O. J. Simpson's trial, 9/11, the Iraq War, Barack Obama's inauguration, to name just a few.

Partly due to the multi-camera setup and the instantaneous switching capacity from one angle to another, television captures immediacy and eventfulness; its portrayal of reality often coincides with a particular event's origination. John F. Kennedy's burial did not take place in Arlington Cemetery alone, but in the living rooms, bus terminals, and town squares of the world. Because of television, his "casket did not ride down Pennsylvania Avenue only. It rode down Main Street."[15] Television made the land mines in Iraq explode in our own backyards. And because of television, we were at ground zero for 9/11 as helpless victims jumped from the smoke-filled Twin Towers.[16] Television has the tremendous advantage of enabling us to participate in events as they occur. As one critic explained, each shot provides the viewer with a "God's eye view" that is always front and center.[17]

Sometimes television's immediacy is used purposefully to increase viewership: Princess Diana's royal wedding or a "very special live episode" of our favorite show during sweeps week. Celebrities and activist groups alike regularly leverage live media coverage of staged events not only to spread the word about their causes but to connect immediately and emotionally with potential supporters. Similarly, in the hands of certain religious communicators, immediacy can narrowly serve personal or tribal agendas.

Television creates a sense of visual immediacy even when—much like intimacy—it is not intended, communicating televangelists as powerbrokers over empires, for example, and audiences as members of their worldwide congregations.

These brief examples of some of television's technological properties illustrate the potency of technological biases. These biases place limits on television's symbolic capacity, or the way it captures and presents reality to its audiences. Audiences, for better or worse, are affected by these biases as they interpret content and assign meaning to certain events. The challenge for faithful critics, then, is to respond creatively and imaginatively to a medium's inherent biases, or its symbolic limitations, in ways that promote peace and justice.

Prophetic Possibilities of Television

What are some of the prophetic possibilities of television in light of the way two of its medium-specific properties discussed above (intimacy and immediacy) shape the content it delivers? How can critique of these medium-specific properties promote what we described earlier in chapter 2 as moral literacy? In other words, how can prophetic critique call popular media technologies to their appropriate role in opening windows on the moral landscape, in ways that promote *shalom*?

Intimacy. Television's bias toward intimacy shapes the content it delivers and the stories it tells. Television's inherent capacity to exhibit intimacy can foster the development of artificial personas based on stereotypes and superficial markers like physical attraction, sex appeal, and popularity. And television's capacity to penetrate deeply the privacy of human character promotes the presumption of real-life intimacy—or para-social relationships—that can slowly erode the mystery of humanity and its messiness in the three-dimensional world. (This capacity to penetrate privacy is exaggerated in reality TV programming.)

In contrast, Scripture sheds light on the innumerable dimensions and complexities of humanity—the whole person, the full person (not just the public image), the responsible moral agent (not just the passive victim acted upon by others), the creative image-bearer of God who lives in a dependent relationship with him and who was created for relationships with other human beings (not just the lone-wolf individualist who can make it on his or her own). So no matter how much we like or are attracted to a character's persona, "we ought to be shrewd enough to ask what the character represents before we pledge our political, moral and artistic allegiance."[18] What drives our favorite characters? What do they care about? Why should we care? If we do not ask such questions, we may end up reinforcing the cultural values symbolically represented in a particular character's on-screen persona.

In one sense, then, television can redeem its peculiar capacity for intimacy when its writers and producers seriously wrestle with our humanity and the complexities of life. For instance, occasionally programs portray human beings as responsible moral agents (as opposed to passive and autonomous ones) and portray the complications of choosing between righteousness and evil, with people held morally accountable for the alternatives selected. Even as the programs could be criticized fairly on other grounds, characters in shows such as *The Shield*, *The Closer*, and *Desperate Housewives* demonstrate moral agency. Dismissing such programs based on the big three immoralities—sex, violence, profanity—misses these shows' underlying moral agency.

Other television shows confront ultimate human problems—not just *this* war, but "why any war?"; not just *this* loneliness, but "why any loneliness in the midst of multitudes?" For example, *M*A*S*H**, one of North America's longest running shows, raised the permanent questions about life's logic and God's involvement. Shows like *Lost* offer a model for how permanent questions of human existence can be explored in ways that move beyond the cult of persona. Through its large cast of characters, the show regularly deals with complex themes including redemption, an ordered universe, and the sins of the fathers, "all with an untidy approach that fits the messy subject matter." Along the way, "no easy answers are offered. Characters take one step forward and two steps back as they try to grasp their purpose and overcome personal weaknesses."[19] Similar themes and multidimensional messiness are identified in Home Box Office's (HBO) highly acclaimed series *The Sopranos*.[20]

Likewise, *Joan of Arcadia* presented imaginative portrayals of life's permanent questions beyond dominant cultural values such as youth, beauty, and appearance. Joan is a struggling teenage girl who sees and speaks with God, who appears to her in different forms. No single religion is emphasized, and God quotes Bob Dylan and the Beatles. Complex story lines span multiple episodes, promoting the positive outcomes of wise choices and demonstrating the painful consequences of poor choices. Christian critics on both the Left and Right panned the show, citing its New Age, feminist, modernist, and humanist overtones, without considering its prophetic possibilities. As series creator Barbara Hall explained, the show "asks questions that people ask in their own lives and it doesn't try to provide answers. It just opens up the discussion." The resistance from the network early on, explains Hall, "was the fear that the show was going to try to preach,"[21] or morally pound its audience, a common complaint against much Christian media today.

Still other mainstream programs wrestle with humanness by portraying the injustices and hardships of human life in a fallen world. Shows such as *Law & Order* seriously probe issues about authority, punishment, racism, and gender domination. A revolving cast of characters often becomes an instance of what Jean Paul Sartre called the "universal singular": that is, a particular embodiment of broad historical struggles and achievements.[22] *NYPD Blue*, a favorite of critics until it waned toward predictability in its later years, also presented truthful representation of serious, often uncomfortable, issues.

Immediacy. Given television's emphasis on simultaneity, or the self-contained here-and-now, faithful critics should ask, "What view of history emerges from television? How does it treat human society in space and time?"

With the exception of occasional miniseries or made-for-television movies, each episode on television tends to be ahistorical: unconcerned with or unrelated to history. Classic shows like *Little House on the Prairie*, which still runs in syndication today, and more recent shows like *Mad Men, Life on Mars, Christy, Dr. Quinn, Medicine Woman*, and *China Beach* are situated somewhere in a historical period, yet seldom connect their story lines to the larger historical context. Put another way, television can insulate audiences from the broader scope of history.

In contrast, as Protestant reformer John Calvin put it, God is constantly vigilant, efficacious, operative, continually engaged, and edging history toward a purposeful climax.[23] He controls history in his providence. Thus, however obscurely seen, nothing is aimless or circular. In this view, things do not merely happen; they are brought about and shaped by the God who resides at the center of a meaningful universe. Likewise, the prophets grounded their critique in a purposive view of history.

Programs that present humanity's historical understanding of itself and invoke remembrance about the ties between the past and present respond to television's capacity for immediacy and open windows on the moral landscape. They introduce more complexity into our conversations about morality by showing how human fallenness is both judged and overcome. NBC's nine-and-a-half-hour docudrama, *Holocaust*, reenacted a historic event through the story of two German families from 1935 to 1945. Critics scorned NBC for exploiting such serious material for commercial gain, and the enormous complexity of the moral issues was inevitably trivialized. Despite its shortcomings, however, *Holocaust* raised the consciousness of millions about the insidiousness of anti-Semitism by embedding its own events and characters within the flow of history. More recently, HBO's *Band of Brothers*, a ten-part miniseries set in World War II, revolved around the life of E Company of the 2nd Battalion, 506th Parachute Infantry Regiment. The series follows a single company from basic training to the airborne landings at Normandy through the defeat of Hitler's Nazi Germany.[24]

In contrast to *Holocaust* and *Band of Brothers*, however, programs in which things simply remain the same in the end are weak examples of purposive history. Continuity in television occurs when writers and producers creatively develop character and plot from day to day (as in the miniseries listed above) or from week to week (as in serialized television). Some shows take advantage of continuity by portraying changes in characters, settings, and plot over time.[25] Viewers of shows such as *CSI* and *ER* are treated to remarkable continuity; they are immersed in the ongoing stories and become connected over time to the psychological changes taking place among key characters.

Although television offers the potential for continuity and development within serialized (weekly) television, such potential is warped when characters remain unchanged, as is the case with so many sitcoms. *All in the Family* took viewers through more than a decade in the lives of the Bunker and Spivak families. Archie essentially held his place in history, unable to learn and grow. Few sitcoms represent this idea better than *Seinfeld*, a show unapologetically "about nothing." After nine years of doing nothing, the show could only end the way it did: with Jerry, George, Elaine, and Kramer sentenced to jail for violating a Good Samaritan law. The last conversation in the final episode repeats the very first conversation from the pilot episode, discussing the positioning of a button on George's shirt. The characters were essentially the same in the end as they were in the beginning, unable to change.

It is difficult to dismiss a show outright, of course, even when it warps purposive history and reinforces television's bias toward immediacy. As popular media critics convincingly demonstrate, even shows like *All in the Family* and *Seinfeld*, despite their obvious limitations, can be interpreted redemptively or in ways that illuminate the moral landscape. For instance, Archie Bunker can be interpreted—and rightly so—as an icon of white racist attitudes in North America. Archie's character is not celebrated by the show's producers, but repeatedly mocked. Along the way, the audience is invited to confront their own stereotypes and ignorance.[26] The show, then, can be seen as a subtle form of prophetic mockery.

Similarly, upon closer inspection, *Seinfeld* is not without some redeeming qualities. The show, like Seinfeld's comedy routines, was intelligently written and prophetically addressed many things. Not the least was its overarching focus on the nature of humanity. Adept at allowing the audience to still love its characters and without a heavy hand, the show's tone could be partially described as *self-mockery*, something we would describe again as *prophetic self-mockery* (see chapter 6). Instead of glorifying the self-indulgent cloister of characters that made up the show, as with Archie Bunker, the laughable situations gave us prophetic peeks at our laughably pathetic, narcissistic selves. Essentially, no one ever really got away with anything. A lie told in one episode would return to haunt in another. Although disappointing for a large percentage of the show's fans, the series ended with Jerry, Elaine, Kramer, and George being arrested for their sin of omission.

Interpreting popular television texts, therefore, is a multilayered and complex process. In most cases, a show is not all good or all bad. Numerous books on television criticism demonstrate this with great detail and nuance.[27] Additionally, several books by Christian authors explore positive messages that appear in some of the most unlikely places, from *The Simpsons* to *The Sopranos*.[28] Their criticism is exegetical or hermeneutical, as described in chapter 1. They begin with the text, or the media content, and perform close readings by explaining its context and identifying a dominant reading or interpretation. Such interpretation yields much insightful analysis, and we rely on it in many places throughout this book.

In contrast, we began our case study in this chapter with the media technology itself and worked our way forward, instead of beginning with a particular media text as most Christian critics of popular media do. This distinct approach should not be lost on the reader. Our goal was to demonstrate that technology itself, which is a value-laden cultural creation full of inherent biases, might open fresh angles of analysis and new perspectives on the moral landscape perpetuated by mainstream television. This approach in no way intends to replace the valuable work of critics doing close readings of particular programs; rather, it intends to work alongside such analyses to provide a fuller view of the critic's cultural task.

Such an approach adds practical benefits as well. In the case of intimacy, for instance, we can select programs that merely entertain us or confirm what we already know to be true, or we can choose programs that push us out of our comfort zone to consider serious issues of injustice that stand in the way of *shalom*. In the case of immediacy, understanding continuity can help us decide whether to invest our time only in a typical sitcom series, in which things regularly revert to the same state of affairs, or to commit our time to programs that explore deeply the lives of their characters.

Conclusion

Back on Mount Everest with the Sherpas: what you once perhaps took for granted now appears fresh. What was once unfamiliar now appears familiar, even if you cannot yet fully grasp its splendor. In any case, it is clear that things are not always as they appear. Tired from the journey? Perhaps. Intrigued enough to keep exploring? We hope so.

The goal of our brief expedition together in this chapter was not to exhaust every nook or cranny of television's technological landscape. In actuality, we only scratched the surface of one particular medium. But if our bird's-eye view of both sides of the mountain planted a seed compelling enough to convince you to take further expeditions on your own, then our journey, at least for the time being, was a success. To the extent that we understand the inherent potential and limits of any particular technology, we open up its prophetic possibilities—whether as critics, consumers, or creators.

Conclusion

Considering the Downs and Ups
of Prophetic Media Criticism

Our brief pilgrimage together is coming to a close, but we hope the journey toward faithful prophetic criticism will continue. We suspect that our readers experienced a combination of newly formed questions and some glimpses at prophetic possibilities in their own lives as critics, creators, and consumers of popular media.

As we argued throughout, the challenge for Christians is to become aware of and cultivate a small-p prophetic sensibility. All Christians are not only part of the "*priest*hood of believers,"[1] but the *prophet*hood of all believers as well.[2] As part of this Christian vocation, all believers, regardless of skill or position, are called to be everyday prophets—to serve as vibrant, truthbearing witnesses who courageously confront individual complacency and institutional self-righteousness. "We might not like it," one observer says, "but we are prophetic communicators of the bad news as well as priestly communicators of the good news."[3] Both voices are sorely needed today just as they have been throughout history.

Most tribal media, however—along with Christian critics and users of popular media—lean toward priestly confirmation rather than prophetic illumination. Instead of speaking prophetically, tribes on the Left and Right practice their own brand of tribal correctness by "preaching to the choir" and telling already-loyal audiences what they want to hear. And rather than seek out media that introduce discomfort and provoke change, we prefer programs or magazines that confirm our tribe's position (or perceived superiority) over another. The results of such practices are as inevitable as they are disappointing: fragmentation, ideological division, and local rather than unified effort.

When cultivated wisely, prophetic talk (and listening) that confronts North America's dominant consciousness can offer a prophetic blessing for one's own community and society at large. Yet critics who courageously take up this challenge assume certain risks. Prophetic criticism from one tribe often looks like disloyalty or liberal or conservative propaganda to another. Even individuals who fairly criticize their own tribal media often become victims of harsh and unfair condemnation. Telling people what they do not want but need to hear is never easy.

As we bring to a close our conversations in this volume, we offer a brief listing of what we call *vocational hazards* for prophetically incorrect voices to ponder. After presenting these hazards, we offer several responses to these hazards as a way to encourage prophetically incorrect voices in their vocational pursuits.

Being Aware of Vocational Hazards

We identify the following hazards associated with cultivating a prophetic voice:

Depression and Despair. The prophetic communicator, like the "weeping prophet" Jeremiah, is often very sensitive, feeling deeply about the sufferings of his or her fellow community members.[4] As explained earlier (see chapter 3), living with an unshakeable but jarring sense that something is wrong with the world, and with a willingness to do something about it, often comes with a price.

Granted, some despair and depression can come with the prophetic territory.[5] Ideally the prophetic burden, that sense that something is wrong, fuels the prophet's continued passion for and commitment to God's redemptive plan for humanity.[6] It can, however, also lead to depression or even, as happened with Elijah, to unbearable extremes fluctuating between severe depression and elation.[7] If despair or depression becomes the dominant spirit of our prophetic voices, then the promises of hope and the restoration of justice may be muted.

Arrogance. If left on their own, and especially if they have a following, some prophetic voices can assume they have superior insight and understanding. This assumption can lead to the distortions of condescension and arrogance. Forgetting that leaders are servants first in the kingdom of God, prophetic leaders can fall into arrogant posturing and can lord their position and authoritative voice over the people they should be humbly serving.[8]

In extreme cases, such arrogance can lead to manipulation or even cruelty. False prophets who claim "unique insight from God" often arrogantly insulate themselves from criticism by falsely aligning themselves with Jesus and the prophets. As "God's men and women," they feel they are "above reproach." In the Bible, however, there are no examples of arrogant capital-P Prophets.

Ruthless Truthfulness. People may say something truthful, but their tones and their intentions can make it a lie. This is why the apostle Paul admonishes his readers to "speak the truth in love" (Eph. 4:15). Evidently, it is possible to "speak the truth" with hate, condescension, or mean-spiritedness, or to speak it for manipulative reasons. Sometimes we use the truth as a shield to cover our cruelty, with no intention of doing anything but hurting someone. Then it becomes too convenient to self-righteously proclaim, "Well, I was telling the truth."

In popular media, consider how news coverage can sometimes become ruthless with the truth: for example, invasive, intimate close-ups of people grieving in their weakest moments, or photos of dead bodies, or photos of victims leaping from burning buildings. Being first on the scene with breaking news regularly trumps loving regard or respect for one's neighbor. Without permission, intimate spaces are violated and the most vulnerable exposed—all in the name of speaking the truth or righting some wrong. This is ruthless and rotten truthtelling.

Harmful Images. In some ways, being open to the prophetic potential of popular media can become a lame excuse for prematurely exposing oneself to media better left unseen. For a variety of reasons, pornographic, excessively violent images, and hate blogs are better left unseen and unread.[9] The prophetic sensibility is not without freedom, to be sure, but it is also not without discipline.

All things are "permissible, but not everything is beneficial," explains the apostle Paul.[10] Prophetic voices must therefore be graciously serious about the two distinctions: what is permissible, as opposed to what is beneficial. This should guide their consciences in choosing their mass media consumption as well as their critiques and artistic creativity. The apostle Paul's distinction between the two is that the permissible things, like most kinds of media engagement, can become addictive. Paul's commitment is that he will not be "mastered by anything," (1 Cor. 6:12). As Christians concerned with cultivating our prophetic voice, we must share Paul's commitment to freedom.

Tunnel Vision. Sometimes prophetic critics develop tunnel vision. They become so consumed by a single issue of injustice that they lose sight of a host of issues deserving of prophetic criticism. With tunnel vision one can assume that everyone else should be equally impassioned about the same justice issue. A justice issue might be as large as a continent or as small as a slum lord's unrepentant heart.

One's prophetic passion about a particular injustice is a practical sign that *that individual* should confront it. Certainly we can encourage others to join our cause, whether it is working against abortion or racism or pornography, but we should not make the mistake of thinking that those who are not passionate about the same justice issue are less concerned for the needs of others. Many prophetic voices from all tribes—both inside and outside the church—are needed to confront obstacles to peace and justice.

Managing Vocational Hazards

The vocational hazards above can be viewed as temptations. Fortunately, there are ways to deal with every temptation.[11] The following are important reminders for those who faithfully seek to cultivate the prophetic sensibility and avoid some of the temptations listed above.

Faithful Choices Matter. Sometimes the critic's depression and despair arise from a perception that words and actions make little difference when it comes to serving justice, mercy, and peace. However, the prophetic communicator must "keep alive the notion that history is incomplete, that the world is unfinished, that the future is open-ended and that what we think and what we do can make a difference."[12] Without such hope, the prophetic work cannot proceed.[13]

To faithfully deal with feelings of depression and despair, or at least to keep them from immobilizing one's passion for prophetic criticism,[14] we suggest that the critic remember that faithful choices do matter, that "every deed counts," and that "every word has power."[15] In so doing, the critic lines herself up with the testimony of Jesus and the apostles, Moses and the prophets. The apostle Paul tells his readers that "whatever you do, whether in word or deed, do it all in the name of the Lord Jesus" (Col. 3:17). The last word of the preacher in Ecclesiastes is that "God will bring every deed into judgment, including every hidden deed" (12:14). These Scriptures certainly encompass our engagement with popular media as critics, creators, and consumers.[16]

Practicing the Presence of God. Furthermore, cultivating a prophetic sensibility is an invitation to do the disciplined work of keeping hope alive in intentional ways. The work of prayer is one such daily act. Prayer, for the prophetic communicator, is always an expression of hope.[17] When the prophetic critic is persistent in prayer, she is "practicing the presence of God," as Brother Lawrence used to say.[18] Practicing the presence of God helps the prophetic communicator to be hopeful courageous.[19]

In practicing the presence of God, we suggest that Christians who want to cultivate their prophetic sensibility regularly think through what it means to represent and serve God in any particular moment. To begin, pick three to four times per day at random and ask what demonstrating prophetic talk and prophetic listening might mean in a particular moment, whether in conversation with a friend or watching your favorite program. Media fasts and intentional appointments with media described in chapter 3 are also ways to practice the presence of God.[20]

We also recommend taking seriously the admonition of the apostle Paul to "let the word of Christ richly dwell in your heart as you teach and admonish one another with all wisdom" (Col. 3:16). "Teaching and admonishing" one another hints at the possibilities of the prophethood of all believers. Letting God's word richly indwell us as a daily habit might mean memorizing the words of Jesus or the prophets or others throughout history, or the words of those in popular media whose prophetic proclamations resonate with scriptural truths. Begin with the texts that strike you, that provide the shocking jolt mentioned in chapter 6. Choose a memorization schedule—one verse or phrase per day or week or month—but keep track of the verses that move you.[21]

Community Accountability. As has been noted in previous chapters, we strongly encourage the prophetic communicator to be receptive to critique from his community. Opening up to the possibility of critique requires relationships within a community in which discerning conversations, questions, and even rebukes can actually happen without the threat of loss of relationship. Such a community environment helps to guard against some of the other vocational hazards: being ruthless with truth, being overly presumptuous or arrogant, and being judgmental, for instance.

The impulse of some artistic, passionate, and outspoken members of a church—those, perhaps, with heightened prophetic sensibilities—is to withdraw from the community of believers who might not faithfully support their art or adequately appreciate their outcries over injustice. They may feel freer in their isolation, but only for a while. Why? In their seclusion, they end up surrounding themselves only with others who agree with them. As such, they abandon the more complex, demanding, and often frustrating environment of the larger community. Yet sometimes the frustration within the community is the very thing that energizes and refines the prophetic sensibility.

Not Everything Is Prophetic. It is simply too presumptuous to label one's own criticism, creation, or consumption of popular media as *prophetic*. In other words, saying something like, "I am a prophetic critic and therefore what I create, consume, or critique has prophetic overtones," will not justify anything in the name of speaking the truth in love. As explained in chapter 2, capital-P Prophets were not self-appointed. Thus, in general, small-p prophets should not be self-appointed either.[22]

For instance, Abraham Joshua Heschel never described himself as a prophet; it was left for Martin Luther King Jr. to say that of him.[23] The Christian theologian Reinhold Niebuhr never described his work as "prophetic," but in the funeral eulogy for Niebuhr, one of Niebuhr's close friends described him as one with prophetic characteristics.[24]

Essentially, the old proverb applies here: "Let another praise you and not your own mouth" (Prov. 27:2). We might call our contribution to a debate or conversation as speaking truth to power, or we might consider the lyrics of a song, or poem, or play we write as driven by a deep burden for humanity's plight, but we should let others assign the label *prophetic* to our work.

Loving Your Neighbor. Consistent with the idea of the prophetic blessing that seeks to address ideological divides, we also suggest that the prophetic communicator make a full-time commitment to loving his or her neighbor as well as loving his or her enemies—whether they are inside or outside the tribe. This will mean a conscious willingness to develop empathetic concern for others. Empathy—or "prophetically thinking empathy"—means "never losing sight of the humanity of others."[25] As explained in chapter 2, compassion related to humanity's plight is the essential fuel of prophetic passion.

Loving your neighbor and your enemy also means being immersed in the biblical wisdom of "being no respecter of persons."[26] The Bible's first description of God's impartiality (Deut. 10:17) tells of his benevolence for all, a benevolence displayed in his defense of just causes—irrespective of gender, marital status, or national boundaries.[27]

At a very practical level, this can play out for prophetic critics by intentionally and regularly engaging popular media from cultures other than their own: films and novels that assist them in seeing and loving beyond themselves. It might also involve a willingness to learn another generation's music until it is understood. It could mean monthly reading of newspaper commentary and magazine articles from continents and religious perspectives not affirming our own. All of these could be exercises in remembering the impartiality of God, helping us to overcome our desire to see only our own lifestyle choices and self-justifications confirmed in the media we critique and consume.

Keeping the Conversations Alive

Certainly this project is an introduction and not the final word on prophetic engagement with popular media. No single volume can fully address the depth and nuance of prophetic criticism of popular media, as readers who took the time to peruse our endnotes hopefully discovered.

Our goal was not to exhaust every possible prophetic moment in popular media, but to start the conversation in some places and keep it alive in others. We hope that our readers have already started the process of finding better examples, closer to home, that resonate with prophetic possibilities. We hope that some of these examples include case studies—or more elaborately detailed investigations—of individuals whose communication, whether appearing in formal or informal media channels, fits the chapter emphases in this book.[28]

Additionally, one need not be Christian to recognize the wisdom and benefits of voices devoted to promoting peace, justice, and freedom around the globe. Many faith traditions have their own brand of prophetically incorrect criticism that stewards an alternative consciousness and challenges North America's dominant consciousness. To the extent that such voices promote *shalom*, they should be embraced.

As we emphasized throughout, prophetic talk about popular media is open to anyone who is willing to make a commitment to steward his or her affections toward popular media—whether a book, a film, a website, a television show, or a painting—and regularly ask important questions: What does it confirm or provoke for me? Defy or confront? How is it consistent with the great biblical prophetic values of peace, justice, and righteousness? Again, our answers, as well as the process in finding them, are a crucial aspect of prophetic engagement.

Our general vocation and curriculum for life—to learn and practice faithfully loving God and neighbor[29]—is often so woefully lacking in dynamism that it does not inform or inspire us to faithfulness in our popular media practices. A main reason for this lack of dynamism, as suggested throughout this book, is our accepting attitude toward, and immersion in, the typical North American consumerist priorities. A significant emphasis throughout this book, therefore, has been to awaken readers to the dulling and often numbing effects of America's dominant consciousness and its ethos of consumerism on our prophetic sensibilities.

Toward that end, we have labored to inspire our readers toward a prophetic sensibility in all that they do, whether consuming, creating, or critiquing popular media. We need spiritual discernment to see beyond the big three moral issues—sex, violence, and profanity—to recognize how popular media mythologies reinforce North America's dominant framing story by idolizing consumption and preaching worldly success. C. S. Lewis once suggested in *The Screwtape Letters* that the biggest threat to Western Christians might be a "bourgeois mind," not sexual promiscuity.[30] If Lewis is right, then prophetic voices that ask the tough questions and challenge our own desires for popularity and material success are desperately needed.

Notes

Acknowledgments

1. The portions we use in chapter 2 and chapter 7 originally appeared in Quentin J. Schultze, ed., *American Evangelicals and the Mass Media* (Grand Rapids: Zondervan, 1990), 331–56, reprinted with permission from the copyright holder, Quentin J. Schultze.

Foreword

1. Søren Kierkegaard, *Provocations: Spiritual Writings of Kierkegaard*, ed. Charles E. Moore (Farmington, PA: Plough, 1999), 227.
2. Ibid., 226.
3. Ibid., 227.
4. Nicholas Wolterstorff, *Divine Discourse: Philosophical Reflections on the Claim that God Speaks* (Cambridge: Cambridge University Press, 1995).
5. See Susannah Heschel, "Abraham Joshua Heschel," http://home.versatel.nl/ heschel/Susannah.htm, para. 25.
6. Ibid., para. 1.
7. Matthew Mikalatos, "'Interview': Superman," *The Wittenburg Door*, May/ June 2007, 36–37.
8. J. Richard Middleton, "Curiosity Killed the Cat (Or, the Outrageous Hope of Reformational Scholarship and Practice)," *Perspectives* 32, no. 4 (December 1998): i–iv.
9. Evan Drake Howard, "Reflections on the Lectionary," *The Christian Century*, June 17, 2008, 21.
10. Václav Havel, *The Art of the Impossible: Politics as Morality in Practice, Speeches and Writings, 1990–1996* (New York: Fromm International, 1998), 57.

11. Kenneth R. Chase, "Christian Discourse in a Nietzschean Age: Mapping a Theological Location for Persuasion" (paper, annual convention of the National Communication Association, New York, November 12, 1998).

12. Brian Friel, *Translations: A Play* (New York: Samuel French, 1981), 50.

13. Ibid., 51.

14. Kierkegaard, *Provocations*, 227.

Preface

1. For elaboration on Nietzsche's life and work as they relate to communications, see Clifford G. Christians, "Friedrich Nietzsche: Becoming an *Übermensch*," in *Ethical Communication: Moral Stances in Human Dialogue*, ed. Clifford G. Christians and John C. Merrill (Columbia, MO: University of Missouri Press, 2009), ch. 8.

2. Friedrich Nietzsche, *The Birth of Tragedy* (1872), trans. Walter Kaufmann (New York: Vintage Books, 1967), preface; see also Friedrich Nietzsche, *Beyond Good and Evil* (1886), trans. Walter Kaufmann (New York: Random House, 1966).

3. Friedrich Nietzsche, *The Will to Power: Attempt at a Revaluation of All Values* (1901; rev. ed. 1906), trans. Walter Kaufmann and R. J. Hollingdale (New York: Random House, 1967), 1–2.

4. Walter Kaufmann, *Nietzsche: Philosopher, Psychologist, Antichrist* (New York: Vintage Books, 1968), 130.

5. Friedrich Nietzsche, *On the Genealogy of Morals* (1887), trans. Walter Kaufmann and R. J. Hollingdale (New York: Random House, 1967).

6. Nietzsche, *Birth of Tragedy*, 31–32.

7. Ibid., 5, 24.

8. For a description of relativism today as the legacy of Nietzsche and his circle, see Clifford G. Christians, "Ethical Theory in Communications Research," *Journalism Studies* 6, no. 1 (February 2005): 3–14.

9. Nietzsche, *Beyond Good and Evil*.

10. Zygmunt Bauman, *Postmodern Ethics* (Oxford, UK: Blackwell, 1993), 178–79.

11. Robert C. Miner, *Truth in the Making: Creative Knowledge in Theology and Philosophy* (New York: Routledge, 2004).

12. "Alternative consciousness" is a phrase Woods and Patton use throughout the book. It comes from Walter Brueggemann, *Prophetic Imagination*, 2nd ed. (Minneapolis: Fortress, 2001), 13.

13. The concept of a created order is developed here following Oliver O'Donovan, *Resurrection and the Moral Order*, 2nd ed. (Leicester, UK: Apollos, 1994), chs. 1–3.

14. See Paul Tillich, *Theology of Culture*, ed. R. C. Kimball (New York: Oxford University Press, 1959); Paul Tillich, *What Is Religion?* trans. J. L. Adams (New York: Harper & Row, 1969); and Paul Tillich, *My Search for Absolutes* (New York: Simon & Schuster, 1967).

15. For elaboration see Arthur Holmes, *All Truth Is God's Truth* (Grand Rapids: Eerdmans, 1977).

16. Paul Ricœur, "Ethics and Culture: Habermas and Gadamer in Dialogue," *Philosophy Today* 17 (1973): 153–65.

17. Heinz Bluhm, "The Young Nietzsche and the Secular City," *MLN* 84, no. 5 (1969): 726.

18. Richard J. Mouw argues that there are "proper grounds" for commonness with "those who reject the biblical message." The idea of common grace, along with natural law, are two of our crucial resources. See his *He Shines in All That's Fair: Culture and Common Grace* (Grand Rapids: Eerdmans, 2001), ch. 6, and *Uncommon Decency: Christian Civility in an Uncivil World* (Downers Grove, IL: InterVarsity, 1992).

19. Ricœur, "Ethics and Culture: Habermas and Gadamer in Dialogue."

20. For an elaboration of this kind of scholarship, see John G. Stackhouse Jr., *Humble Apologetics: Defending the Faith Today* (New York: Oxford University Press, 2002).

Introduction

1. In 2 Pet. 1:20–21, Peter speaks of the capital-P Prophet: "Above all, you must understand that no prophecy of Scripture came about by the prophet's own interpretation. For prophecy never had its origin in the will of man, but men spoke from God as they were carried along by the Holy Spirit."

2. We borrow this small-p/capital-P description from Os Guinness, *Prophetic Untimeliness: A Challenge to the Idol of Relevance* (Grand Rapids: Baker Books, 2003), 21. The prophetic tradition stems from classical Hebrew prophets. So when we speak about prophets in the West, we are not speaking of Islamic prophets, but of Amos, Jeremiah, Ezekiel, and so on.

3. Tracey Mark Stout, "Would That All Were Prophets," in *Prophetic Ethics*, ed. Robert B. Kruschwitz (Waco: Baylor University Press, 2003), 15.

4. We adapt the concept of "resistance thinking" from Christian apologist C. S. Lewis, who introduced the idea in an essay titled "Christian Apologetics," in *God in the Dock: Essays on Theology and Ethics*, ed. Walter Hooper (Grand Rapids: Eerdmans, 1994), 89–103. Lewis suggests the idea of the Christian faith as a "resisting material" and demonstrates how Christians might communicate against modernity and the fiction of progress by practicing an alternative and latent form of argument. This essay on "Bulverism" and "Before We Can Communicate" in the same collection are wonderful introductions to Lewis's ideas on communication. (We would like to thank Terry Lindvall, Virginia Wesleyan College, for his help with this note.)

5. See 1 Cor. 14:1–3; Craig S. Keener, *The IVP Bible Background Commentary: New Testament* (Downers Grove, IL: InterVarsity, 1993), 480.

6. John White, *The Golden Cow: Materialism in the Twentieth-Century Church* (Downers Grove, IL: InterVarsity, 1979), 11. See also Matt. 17:1–3.

7. As the chief prophet, Jesus is the embodiment of the hopeful longing for peace and justice. See Isa. 53 and Phil. 2.

8. For instance, in the New International Version of the Old Testament, there are 394 pages recording the Hebrew Prophets (Isaiah to Malachi), which is more than the pages dedicated to the Gospels and Acts of the Apostles (197 pages) and the Epistles (148 pages) combined. For discussion of Jesus as prophetic critic, see chapters 5 and 6 of Walter Brueggemann, *Prophetic Imagination*, 2nd ed. (Minneapolis: Fortress, 2001), 81–113; Michael Walzer, *The Company of Critics: Social Criticism and Political Commitment in the Twentieth Century* (New York: Basic, 2002), 14–15; Robert J. Wicks, *Handbook of Spirituality for Ministers: Perspectives for the 21st Century* (Mahwah, NJ: Paulist Press, 2000), 331–32; Daniel L. Migliore, *Faith Seeking Understanding: An Introduction to Christian Theology* (Grand Rapids: Eerdmans, 2004), 176.

9. James Darsey, *The Prophetic Tradition and Radical Rhetoric in America* (New York: New York University Press, 1997). Sacvan Bercovitch's now-classic *The American Jeremiad* (Madison: University of Wisconsin Press, 1978) identified the American jeremiad as its own rhetorical genre. For other works that consider the rhetorical form and style of the prophets and prophecy, see Margaret D. Zulick, "Prophecy and Providence: The Anxiety over Prophetic Authority," *Journal of Communication and Religion* 26 (2003): 195–207; "The Normative, the Proper, and the Sublime: Notes on the Use of Figure and Emotion in Prophetic Argument," *Argumentation* 12 (1998): 481–92; and "The Agon of Jeremiah: On the Dialogic Invention of Prophetic Ethos," *Quarterly Journal of Speech* 78 (1992): 125–48.

10. Neal Riemer, *The Future of the Democratic Revolution: Toward a More Prophetic Politics* (New York: Praeger, 1984); Jim Wallis, *The Soul of Politics: A Practical and Prophetic Vision for Change* (New York: New Press, 1994); William Cranston, *Prophetic Politics: Critical Interpretations of the Revolutionary Impulse* (New York: Simon and Schuster, 1972); David S. Gutterman, *Prophetic Politics: Christian Social Movements and American Democracy* (Ithaca, NY: Cornell University Press, 2005); Bryan Garsten, *Saving Persuasion: A Defense of Rhetoric and Judgment* (Cambridge, MA: Harvard University Press, 2006); Gary M. Simpson, *Critical Social Theory: Prophetic Reason, Civil Society, and Christian Imagination* (Minneapolis: Fortress, 2002).

11. Marvin A. McMickle, *Where Have All the Prophets Gone? Reclaiming Prophetic Preaching in America* (Cleveland: Pilgrim, 2006); Linda L. Clader, *Voicing the Vision: Imagination and Prophetic Preaching* (Harrisburg, PA: Morehouse, 2004); Elizabeth Achtemeir, *Preaching from the Minor Prophets* (Grand Rapids: Eerdmans, 1998); James Ward and Christine Ward, *Preaching from the Prophets* (Nashville: Abingdon, 1995); Warren Steward, *Interpreting God's Word in Black Preaching* (Valley Forge, PA: Judson, 1984).

12. Grace Emmerson, ed., *Prophets and Poets: A Companion to the Prophetic Books of the Old Testament* (Nashville: Abingdon, 1997); Nick Halpern, *Everyday and Prophetic: The Poetry of Lowell, Ammons, Merrill, and Rich* (Madison: University of Wisconsin Press, 2003); Mabel Driscoll Bailey, *Maxwell Anderson: The Playwright as Prophet* (New York: Abelard-Schuman, 1957); Raewynne J. Whiteley and Beth Maynard, *Get up off Your Knees: Preaching the U2 Catalog* (Cambridge, MA: Cowley, 2003); Christian Scharen, *One Step Closer: Why U2 Matters to Those Seeking God* (Cambridge, MA: Cowley, 2003).

13. See Jacques Ellul, *The Presence of the Kingdom* (Colorado Springs: Helmer and Howard, 1989); and *Propaganda: The Formation of Men's Attitudes* (New York: Knopf, 1971). Clifford G. Christians discusses the possibilities of media's "prophetic witness" and explores the "prophetic task" of communication technologies. See "Technology and Triadic Theories of Mediation," in *Rethinking Media, Religion and Culture*, ed. Stewart M. Hoover (Thousand Oaks, CA: Sage, 1997); and "Redemptive Media as the Evangelical's Cultural Task," in *American Evangelicals and the Mass Media*, ed. Quentin J. Schultze (Grand Rapids: Zondervan, 1990), 331–56. In addition, scholars from critical and cultural studies motivated by a concern for equality, human dignity, and social justice as it relates to popular media demonstrate prophetic sensitivities and represent what Quentin J. Schultze in *Christianity and the Mass Media in America: Toward a Democratic Accommodation* (East Lansing, MI: Michigan State University Press, 2003) describes as "prophetic discourse" (339). For

instance, see Stuart Hall, *Cultural Representations and Signifying Practices* (Thousand Oaks, CA: Sage, 1997); Robert McChesney, *Rich Media, Poor Democracy* (New York: New Press, 1999); Lawrence Lessig, *Free Culture: How Big Media Uses Technology and the Law to Lock Down Culture and Control Creativity* (New York: Penguin, 2004). Thus, the "prophetic" as an organizing concept for media criticism would allow media institutions and practices to be evaluated in terms of whether they tend to "catalyze or inhibit the development of such prophetic capabilities" (Kevin Healey, "For a Political Economy of the Prophetic: An Integral Model of Media Institutions and Spiritual Development" [paper, annual convention of the National Communication Association, Chicago, November, 18, 2007], 2).

14. Abraham Joshua Heschel, *The Prophets*, vol. 1 (New York: Harper, 1962), 5.

15. Ibid.

16. See Ezek. 23.

17. See also Amos 8:4–6; Isa. 3:15; 10:1–2, 59:8–9, 14–15, and Martin Buber, *The Prophetic Faith* (New York: Collier Books, 1985).

18. John Van Dyk, "The Christian School: A Prophetic Voice," *Christian Educators Journal* (February 2008): 13.

19. Gleaves Whitney, Heritage Foundation Lecture #651, "Recovering Rhetoric: How Ideas, Language, and Leadership Can Triumph in Most-Modern Politics," January 14, 2000, www.heritage.org/Research/PoliticalPhilosophy/hl651.cfm.

20. The apostle Paul describes the importance of our God-given critical faculty when he encourages us to "take captive every thought to make it obedient to Christ" (2 Cor. 10:5).

21. Andy Crouch, *Culture Making: Recovering Our Creative Calling* (Downers Grove, IL: InterVarsity, 2008) makes the point that we should also become producers, or creators, of culture as well. The notion of prophetic discourse as edifying, then, includes a movement toward production, not just criticism, of popular media.

22. See 1 Cor. 6:12.

23. As Kenneth A. Myers observes in *All God's Children and Blue Suede Shoes* (Wheaton: Crossway, 1989), "The main question raised by popular culture concerns the most edifying way to spend one's time" (53).

24. Scholars who study media's unique DNA, or characteristic predispositions, align with the media ecology tradition. Media ecology refers to the study of how media affects "human perception, understanding, feeling, and value; and how our interaction with media facilitates or impedes our chances of survival" (Neil Postman, "The Reformed English Curriculum," in *High School 1980: The Shape of the Future in American Secondary Education*, ed. A. C. Eurich [New York: Pitman, 1970], 161). As explained on the Media Ecology Association's official website, it is sometimes referred to as technological determinism, McLuhan Studies, Orality-Literacy Studies, or American Cultural Studies, to name a few terms (see Media Ecology Association, "What is Media Ecology?" www.media-ecology.org/media_ecology/index .html, paras. 2 & 3), and is represented by such works as Harold A. Innis, *The Bias of Communication* (Toronto: University of Toronto Press, 1964); Marshall McLuhan, *The Medium Is the Message* (New York: Bantam, 1967); and Walter J. Ong, *Orality and Literacy: The Technologizing of the Word* (New York: Routledge, 1982), to name a few. This topic is taken up in greater detail in chapter 1.

25. These helpful questions appear in Bill Strom, *More Than Talk: Communication Studies and the Christian Faith*, 2nd ed. (Dubuque, IA: Kendall/Hunt, 2003), 303.

26. We use the term *tribe* anthropologically to refer to cultures or especially sub-cultures. In one sense, evangelicals are a tribe within Christianity; other Christian tribes might include Roman Catholics and mainline Protestants. In another sense, evangelicals themselves are divided into tribes, including denominations.

27. Most books on media criticism teach students how to apply different theories to popular media content: semiotic theory, sociological theory, psychoanalytic theory, and so forth. The goal is to move individuals and critics away from what others have written and to help them find their own, unique voice as they analyze particular media content, or what academics call "texts." See, for example, Arthur A. Berger, *Media Analysis Techniques*, 3rd ed. (Thousand Oaks, CA: Sage, 2004), ix.

28. Maurice Friedman, *Abraham Joshua Heschel and Elie Wiesel: You Are My Witnesses* (New York: Farrar, Straus & Giroux, 1987), vii.

29. Robert McAfee Brown, *Saying Yes and Saying No: On Rendering to God and Caesar* (Philadelphia: Westminster, 1986), 46.

30. See Col. 3:17.

31. John Peck, *What the Bible Teaches about the Holy Spirit* (Wheaton: Tyndale, 1979), 26.

32. Gabriel Fackre's description of the prophetic voice and ministry of Reinhold Niebuhr, a great friend of Abraham Joshua Heschel, provides a good example. See *The Promise of Reinhold Niebuhr* (Philadelphia: J. B. Lippincott, 1970), 88–90.

Chapter 1

1. John W. Vest, "The Prophetic Pathos of *Crash*," *Sightings*, March 23, 2006, http://divinity.uchicago.edu/martycenter/publications/sightings/archive_2006/0323 .shtml, paras. 8 & 9.

2. Christianity Today Movies.com, "The 10 Most Redeeming Films of 2005," www .christianitytoday.com/movies/commentaries/tenredeemingfilmsof2005.html.

3. We borrow the terms *dominant consciousness* and *alternative consciousness* from Walter Brueggemann, *Prophetic Imagination* (Philadelphia: Fortress, 1978), 13. Brueggemann later writes of the "dominant narrative account of reality," which appears to be synonymous with his concept of dominant consciousness. *The Word Militant: Preaching a Decentering Word* (Minneapolis: Fortress, 2007), 18.

4. Justice, mercy, and faithfulness are the three categories Jesus described as the "more important matters of the law" (Matt. 23:23).

5. Aristotle, *Poetics*, trans. Ingram Bywater (New York: Random House, 1954).

6. William D. Romanowski, *Eyes Wide Open: Looking for God in Popular Culture*, exp. ed. (Grand Rapids: Brazos, 2007), 70. Others refer to the rags-to-riches myth as the myth of material success: "If you work hard, play by all the rules you will achieve wealth, power, and/or fame" (Jack Nachbar and Kevin Lause, *Popular Culture: An Introductory Text* [Bowling Green, OH: Popular Press, 1992], 82–86). See also Claudia Springer, *James Dean Transfigured: The Many Faces of Rebel Iconography* (Austin: University of Texas Press, 2007).

7. Quentin J. Schultze, *Communicating for Life: Christian Stewardship in Community and Media* (Grand Rapids: Baker Academic, 2000), 125.

8. Ibid., 124–25.

9. George Barna, The Barna Update, "Barna Identifies Seven Paradoxes Regarding America's Faith," www.barna.org/barna-update/article/5-barna-update/87

-barna-identifies-seven-paradoxes-regarding-americas-faith, para. 18; see also "More People Use Christian Media Than Attend Church," www.barna.org/FlexPage.aspx ?Page=BarnaUpdate&BarnaUpdateID=184. According to Kathy Bruner, "About 45% of all American adults watch some type of 'Christian' TV monthly, about the same percentage of the population that attend church services. That figure includes Roman Catholic, mainline Protestant and evangelical programs via broadcast, cable, and satellite. It also includes those who tune in only briefly because they happen to be tuning across the channel. When all Christian media—radio, television, web and publications—are included, the figure rises to 67%, suggesting that more people tune in, however briefly, to some form of 'Christian' media than actually attend church monthly" ("Thinking Outside the Tribal TV Box," in *Understanding Evangelical Media: The Changing Face of Christian Communication*, ed. Quentin J. Schultze and Robert H. Woods Jr. [Downers Grove, IL: InterVarsity, 2008], 47).

10. Romanowski, *Eyes Wide Open*, 176–78, 70.

11. Gregor T. Goethals, *The Television Ritual: Worship at the Video Altar* (Boston: Beacon, 1981).

12. Jacques Ellul, *Propaganda: The Formation of Men's Attitudes* (New York: Knopf, 1971).

13. In *The Powers That Be: Theology for a New Millennium* (New York: Doubleday, 1998), Walter Wink explains how "principalities and powers" include more than "disembodied spirits inhabiting the air," but also "institutions, structures, and systems" (24). Powers are not just physical (see Eph. 3:10; 6:12); they are earthly and institutional as well (Col. 1:15–20). Accordingly, institutions such as a local hardware store or the Chrysler Corporation have "spirituality" (24).

14. Todd Friesen, review of *Everything Must Change: Jesus, Global Crises, and a Revolution of Hope*, by Brian McLaren, *The Christian Century*, April 22, 2008, 37–39.

15. Richard Covington, "David Mamet: The Salon Interview," *Salon*, October 1997, www.salon.com/feature/1997/10/cov_si_24mamet.html, para. 15 (accessed August 2008); see also James B. Twitchell, *Lead Us into Temptation: The Triumph of American Materialism* (New York: Columbia University Press, 1999), 196.

16. Brian McLaren identifies four closely linked crises: (1) a prosperity crisis caused by our unsustainable consumption of the world's resources and our massive production of waste; (2) an equity crisis that creates a chasm between the world's poor majority and its wealthy minority; (3) a security crisis in which groups and nations increasingly resort to violence; and (4) a spirituality crisis caused by the failure of the world's religions, particularly Christianity, to confront and engage global dysfunctions (*Everything Must Change: Jesus, Global Crises, and a Revolution of Hope* [Nashville: Thomas Nelson, 2008]).

17. Brueggemann, *Prophetic Imagination*, 42–43.

18. Romanowski, *Eyes Wide Open*, 67.

19. Christopher Lasch, *Culture of Narcissism: American Life in an Age of Diminishing Expectations* (New York: Warner Books, 1979), 22.

20. Brueggemann, *Prophetic Imagination*, 43.

21. William F. Fore, *Mythmakers: Gospel, Culture, and the Media* (New York: Friendship, 1990), 53–54.

22. Discover Card Brighter by Discover, "Nation of Consumers Commercial," www .poetv.com/video.php?vid=41357 (accessed October 2008). The ad also tells consumers

that there is a time to spend and a time to save. Discover's ad is the equivalent of the "drink responsibly" commercials. We appreciate their nod toward fiscal responsibility, but at the same time, the ad clearly reinforces America's ethos of consumerism, assimilating negative arguments against it. Discover simply suggests ways to minimize one's risks or practice better consumerism.

23. Bill Strom, *More Than Talk: Communication Studies and the Christian Faith*, 2nd ed. (Dubuque, IA: Kendall/Hunt, 2003), 263.

24. Ibid.

25. Nachbar and Lause, *Popular Culture*, 5.

26. Richard Campbell, *Media and Culture: An Introduction to Mass Communication*, 3rd ed. rev. (New York: St. Martin's Press, 2003), 17.

27. Fore, *Mythmakers*, 207; see also Stanley Hauerwas and William Willimon, *Resident Aliens: Life in the Christian Colony* (Nashville: Abingdon, 1989).

28. John Van Dyk, "The Christian School: A Prophetic Voice," *Christian Educators Journal* (February 2008): 12.

29. See Rodney Clapp, "The Theology of Consumption and the Consumption of Theology," in *The Consuming Passion: Christianity and the Consumer Culture*, ed. Rodney Clapp (Downers Grove, IL: InterVarsity, 1998), 169–204. Clapp explains that "Christians were in a remarkable number of cases architects of twentieth-century consumer culture" (181).

30. As mentioned previously, *alternative consciousness* comes from Walter Brueggemann, *Prophetic Imagination*, 13. Brueggemann's concluding chapter in the second edition of the same book summarizes the workings of the prophetic imagination as it relates to the possibility of contemporary Christian ministry (*Prophetic Imagination*, 2nd ed. [Minneapolis: Fortress, 2001]).

31. See John 17:14–16.

32. Angela Ann Zukowski, "Evangelization as Communication," in *The Church and Communication*, ed. Patrick Granfield (Kansas City, MO: Sheed and Ward, 1994), 169.

33. See Matt. 28:18 for a statement of the Great Commission. The adoption of new technologies includes, but is not limited to, book publishing, religious newspapers, radio, television, satellite technology, and the internet. See, for example, Quentin J. Schultze, "Keeping the Faith: American Evangelicals and the Media," in *American Evangelicals and the Mass Media*, ed. Quentin J. Schultze (Grand Rapids: Zondervan, 1990), 23–46, and *Redeeming Television: How TV Changes Christians—How Christians Can Change TV* (Downers Grove, IL: InterVarsity, 1992); Henry Smith Stroupe, *The Religious Press in the South Atlantic States, 1802–1865: An Annotated Bibliography with Historical Introduction and Notes* (Durham, NC: Duke University Press, 1956).

34. See Mark Fackler, "Religious Watchdog Groups and Primetime Television," in *Channels of Belief: Religion and American Commercial Television*, ed. John P. Ferré (Ames, IA: Iowa State University Press, 1990), 99–116. Organizations such as the American Family Association give Christians instructions, for example, on "How to Boycott" *Walt Disney* pictures; Tim Wildmon, "Why American Families Should Boycott Disney: How We are Financing Disney's Depravity," www.afa.net/disney/disney.pdf. They also encourage letter-writing campaigns, protests, and boycotts aimed at producers, distributors, and corporate sponsors that program obscene content. Martin Scorcese's *Last Temptation of Christ* was targeted by evangelical and Catholic

groups as blasphemous (Michael Medved, "The Last Temptation of Hollywood," *Christianity Today*, March 8, 1993, 26–30, InfoTrac database).

35. See Schultze and Woods, *Understanding Evangelical Media*.

36. Quentin J. Schultze, *Christianity and the Mass Media in America: Toward a Democratic Accommodation* (East Lansing, MI: Michigan State University Press, 2003), 201.

37. Some Proclaimers simply say that all R-rated movies should be avoided. Focus on the Family gives a five-star movie rating based on a film's family-friendliness; that is, the number of offensive words and scenes of violence and sexuality present in the film. The *American Family Association Journal*'s "3–strikes and you're out" rule explains, "watch a program once that offends your family's Christian values, with profanity, crude language, etc., turn it off. Then discuss why you did so. If you watch it again in 2 weeks and it has to be turned off again, that's strike 2. When it gets to strike 3, it's permanently turned off" (*American Family Association Journal*, www.afajournal.org).

38. See Andrew M. Greeley, *God in Popular Culture* (Chicago: Thomas Moore, 1988); Richard J. Mouw, *Consulting the Faithful: What Christian Intellectuals Can Learn from Popular Religion* (Grand Rapids: Eerdmans, 1994). A number of popular books expand on the ways Christians have tried to understand and make use of popular culture and media: for example, William D. Romanowski, *Pop Culture Wars: Religion and the Role of Entertainment in American Life* (Downers Grove, IL: InterVarsity, 1996); Craig Detweiler and Barry Taylor, *A Matrix of Meanings: Finding God in Pop Culture* (Grand Rapids: Baker Academic, 2003); Colleen McDannell, *Material Christianity: Religion and Popular Culture in America* (New Haven: Yale University Press, 1995); Rodney Clapp, *Border Crossings: Christian Trespasses on Popular Culture and Public Affairs* (Grand Rapids: Brazos, 2000); John Wiley Nelson, *Your God Is Alive and Well and Appearing in Popular Culture* (Philadelphia: Westminster, 1976); Richard J. Mouw, *He Shines in All That's Fair: Culture and Common Grace* (Grand Rapids: Eerdmans, 2001); Steve Turner, *Imagine: A Vision for Christians in the Arts* (Downers Grove, IL: InterVarsity, 2001); and Kenneth A. Myers, *All God's Children and Blue Suede Shoes: Christians and Popular Culture* (Westchester, IL: Crossway, 1989).

39. Zukowski, "Evangelization as Communication," 170.

40. For some it also means redeeming media technologies themselves since such technologies are human constructions that support the dominant cultural system. For example, Clifford G. Christians, "Redemptive Media as the Evangelical's Cultural Task," in *American Evangelicals and the Mass Media*, 331; Quentin J. Schultze, *Habits of the High Tech Heart: Living Virtuously in the Information Age* (Grand Rapids: Baker Academic, 2002); Robert S. Fortner, *Communication, Media, and Identity: A Christian Theory of Communication* (Lanham, MD: Rowan and Littlefield, 2007).

41. Schultze, *Christianity and the Mass Media in America*, 199.

42. Ibid., 200–201.

43. Grace Emmerson, ed., *Prophets and Poets: A Companion to the Prophetic Books of the Old Testament* (Nashville: Abingdon, 1997), 16. Similarly, in measuring art on the basis of the personal worthiness or holiness of its creators, Proclaimers tend to overestimate the godliness of the godly. Some drift toward a snobbery in which high church music and certain forms of classical music are considered truer expressions of biblical theology; see Frank Gaebelin, *The Christian, the Arts, and the Truth* (Portland, OR: Multnomah, 1985).

44. See Vincent E. Bacote, *The Sprit in Public Theology: Appropriating the Legacy of Abraham Kuyper* (Grand Rapids: Baker Academic, 2005); Albert M. Wolters, *Creation Regained: Biblical Basics for a Reformational Worldview* (Grand Rapids: Eerdmans, 1985).

45. Schultze, *Redeeming Television*, 31–33.

46. Ibid.

47. An example of the notion of technology's supposed neutrality is stated by Oxford University's R. A. Buchanan, assessing that "technology is essentially amoral, a thing apart from values, an instrument which can be used for good or ill" (*Technology and Social Progress* [Oxford: Pergamon, 1965], 163).

48. See Stephen V. Monsma, ed., *Responsible Technology: A Christian Perspective* (Grand Rapids: Eerdmans, 1986), 41.

49. Scholars working in the media ecology tradition study the inherent values and biases in all communication technologies—from the alphabet to the personal computer—and explain how such biases "change our brains, alter our lives, and shape our faith, all without our permission or knowledge" (Shane Hipps, *Flickering Pixels: How Technology Shapes Your Faith* [Grand Rapids: Zondervan, 2009], 14). Several foundational and frequently referenced works in this line of scholarship include Harold Innis, *The Bias of Communication* (Toronto: University of Toronto Press, 1951), and *Empire and Communications* (Toronto: University of Toronto Press, 1972); Marshall McLuhan, *Understanding Media: The Extensions of Man* (New York: McGraw-Hill, 1964); Elizabeth Eisenstein, *The Printing Press as an Agent of Change* (Cambridge: Cambridge University Press, 1980); Walter J. Ong, *Orality and Literacy: The Technologizing of the Word* (New York: Routledge, 1982); Daniel J. Czitrom, *Media and the American Mind: From Morse to McLuhan* (Chapel Hill: University of North Carolina Press, 1982); Eric Havelock, *The Literature Revolution in Greece and Its Cultural Consequences* (Princeton: Princeton University Press, 1987); Neil Postman, *Technopoly: The Surrender of Culture to Technology* (New York: Vintage Books, 1993), and *Amusing Ourselves to Death* (New York: Penguin, 1985); Barry Sanders and Ivan Illich, *ABC: Alphabetization of the Popular Mind* (New York: Vintage Books, 1989); Lewis Mumford, *Technics and Civilization* (New York: Harcourt, Brace, and World, 1963); Daniel J. Boorstin, *The Image: A Guide to Pseudo-Events in America* (New York: Vintage Books, 1992); and Langdon Winner, *The Whale and the Reactor: A Search for Limits in an Age of High Technology* (Chicago: University of Chicago Press, 1988). More recent books within this tradition written for a general audience include Nicholas Carr, *The Big Switch: Rewiring the World, from Edison to Google* (New York: W. W. Norton, 2008) and Thomas de Zengotita, *Mediated: How the Media Shapes Your World and the Way You Live in It* (New York: Bloomsbury, 2005). For books in media ecology written from a Christian perspective, see Shane Hipps, *The Hidden Power of Electronic Culture: How Media Shapes Faith, the Gospel, and Church* (Grand Rapids: Zondervan, 2006); Quentin J. Schultze, *Habits of the High-Tech Heart: Living Virtuously in the Information Age*; Tex Sample, *The Spectacle of Worship in a Wired World: Electronic Culture and the Gathered People of God* (Nashville: Abingdon, 1998). French scholar Jacques Ellul provides some of the earliest and most influential work on the philosophy of technology and technological culture from a Christian perspective. See Jacques Ellul, *Presence of the Kingdom*, 2nd ed. (Colorado Springs: Helmers and Howard, 1989), and *The Technological Society* (New York: Vintage Books, 1964). American Jesuit

Walter J. Ong is another early and influential Christian thinker in this area. See Walter J. Ong, "Worship at the End of the Age of Literacy" in *Faith and Contexts*, vol. 1., *Selected Essays and Studies, 1952–1991*, ed. Thomas J. Farrell and Paul A. Soukup (Atlanta: Scholars Press, 1992), 175–88, and "Communications Media and the State of Theology" in *Faith and Contexts*, 154–74.

50. Bill Gates, interviewed in "After the Media Class," *New Perspectives Quarterly* 12, no. 2 (Spring 1995): 51. In an interview with *Time* magazine, Gates commented about the apparent inefficiency of religion: "Just in terms of allocation of time resources, religion is not very efficient. . . . There's a lot more I could be doing on a Sunday morning." Bill Gates qtd. in Walter Isaacson, "In Search of the Real Bill Gates," *Time*, January 13, 1997, 51.

51. Similar lists of inherent values are available for every communication technology. See McLuhan, *Understanding Media*, or Ong, *Orality and Literacy*, for example.

52. Schultze, *Habits of the High Tech Heart*, 21.

53. For instance, heavy users prefer yes-no responses, demand brevity in conversations, and see interaction with others as a way to gather information. See Jeremy Rifkin, *Time Wars: The Primary Conflict In Human History* (New York: Henry Holt, 1987), 17. To support the claim that heavy computer use influences interpersonal interaction, Rifkin relies on clinical case studies with "computer compulsives," or people who spend an unhealthy amount of time with computers. One need not be a computer compulsive, however, to demonstrate some of the same tendencies as computer compulsives, albeit in less extreme forms and with fewer disruptions to one's everyday life. See, for example, Nicholas Carr, "Is Google Making Us Stupid?" *The Atlantic*, July/August 2008, www.theatlantic.com/doc/200807/google.

54. Benjamin Barber, "Jihad vs. McWorld," *Atlantic Monthly* 269, no. 3 (March 1992): 53. This sense of diminishing community is consistent with the isolation and psychological/social detachments associated with communities formed by writing and later print. Joshua Meyrowitz lamented on this paradoxical loss of community even before the growth of computer-mediated communication in his book *No Sense of Place: The Impact of Electronic Media on Social Behavior* (New York: Oxford University Press, 1985); see also Robert D. Putnam, *Bowling Alone: The Collapse and Revival of American Community* (New York: Simon & Schuster, 2001).

55. Paddy Chayefsky, *Television Plays* (New York: Simon and Schuster, 1955), 176–78.

56. Nicholas Wolterstorff, *Reason within the Bounds of Religion*, 2nd ed. (Grand Rapids: Eerdmans, 1984), 15–21.

57. Terry Mattingly, "Preaching to a Tempting Choir," *On Religion*, July 23, 2008, www.tmatt.net/2008/07/23/preaching-to-a-tempting-choir/, para. 4 (accessed July 2008).

58. Ibid., para. 5.

59. George Barna, *What Americans Believe* (Ventura, CA: Regal Books, 1992), 127–46; "Half of All Americans Read Christian Books and One-Third Buy Them," January 27, 2003, www.barna.org (accessed April 2006).

60. "Nearly half are born again (43%), or believe in a literal interpretation of the Bible (38%)" (Bruner, "Thinking Outside the Tribal TV Box," 52).

61. Only about 5 percent of editors say that they publish content aimed to persuade nonbelievers (Ken Waters, "Vibrant But Invisible: A Study of Contemporary Religious Periodicals," *Journalism & Mass Communication Quarterly* [Fall 2001]: 313).

62. Without viewer donations, most Christian radio and television ministries could not survive (Larry Martz, *Ministry of Greed: The Inside Story of the Televangelists and Their Holy Wars* [New York: Weidenfeld and Nicolson, 1988], 42–58).

63. Marvin A. McMickle, *Where Have All the Prophets Gone? Reclaiming Prophetic Preaching in America* (Cleveland: Pilgrim, 2005). See also Stewart M. Hoover, *Mass Media Religion: The Social Sources of the Electronic Church* (Thousand Oaks, CA: Sage, 1988), 178. For historical perspective on conservative Protestantism's changing attitudes toward political involvement, see Alan Wolfe, *The Transformation of American Religion* (New York: Free Press, 2003), 111–17; Jim Wallis, *The Great Awakening: Reviving Faith and Politics in a Post-Religious Right America* (New York: HarperOne, 2008), and *God's Politics: Why the Right Gets It Wrong and the Left Doesn't Get It* (New York: HarperOne, 2006).

64. Jerry Falwell, "Global Warming Fooling the Faithful," WorldNetDaily .com Commentary, February 24, 2007, www.worldnetdaily.com/news/article.asp ?ARTICLE_ID=54413.

65. Ray Richmond, "Thinking Outside the Box," *The Hollywood Reporter*, October 12, 2006, S-1.

66. Michael Longinow, "Is Your Jesus a Republican or Democrat?" in *Understanding Evangelical Media: The Changing Face of Christian Communication*, ed. Quentin J. Schultze and Robert H. Woods Jr. (Downers Grove, IL: InterVarsity, 2008), 73.

67. See, for instance, David Abrahamson, *Magazine-Made America: The Cultural Transformation of the Postwar Periodical* (Cresskill, NJ: Hampton, 1996); Charles P. Daly, Patrick Henry, and Ellen Ryder, *The Magazine Publishing Industry* (Boston: Allyn and Bacon, 1997); and Carolyn Kitch, *Pages from the Past: History and Memory in American Magazines* (Chapel Hill: University of North Carolina Press, 2005).

68. Fleming Rutledge, in describing this tribal divide, asserts, "American Christians of both the Right and Left find it difficult to read Scripture from the perspective of communities other than our own" ("When God Disturbs the Peace," *Christianity Today*, June 2008, para. 2, www.christianitytoday.com/ct/2008/june/13.30.html).

69. "Pope Warns Against 'Prophetic Actions,'" *The Christian Century*, May 20, 2008, 17.

70. Mattingly, "Preaching to a Tempting Choir," paras. 13–15.

71. Julian N. Hartt, *A Christian Critique of American Culture* (New York: Harper & Row, 1967), 405–6.

72. Patrick O'Heffernan, "The L.A. Riots: A Story Made for and by TV," *Television Quarterly* 26, no. 1 (1992): 5, 9, 10. The Heisenberg principle was originally applied in quantum mechanics. For an explanation of the principle, see David C. Cassidy, *Uncertainty: The Life and Science of Werner Heisenberg* (New York: W. H. Freeman, 1991), 226–46.

73. Schultze, *Christianity and the Mass Media in America*, 204.

74. Vest, "The Prophetic Pathos of *Crash*," para. 9.

75. One of the best collections of essays on Jacques Ellul's work is *Jacques Ellul: Interpretive Essays*, ed. Clifford G. Christians and Jay M. Van Hook (Chicago: University of Illinois Press, 1981). For a brief summary of Ellul's work, see Clifford G. Christians, "Propaganda and the Technological System," in *Public Opinion and the Communication of Consent*, ed. Theodore Glasser and Charles Salmon (New York: Guilford, 1995), 156–74.

76. Jacques Ellul, *The Presence of the Kingdom* (Colorado Springs: Helmer and Howard, 1989), 114.

77. Schultze, *Communicating for Life*, 182.

78. World Association for Christian Communications, *Christian Principles of Communication: Statement on Communication* (London: World Association for Christian Communications, 1990), 11.

79. Christian Media Research, www.christianmediaresearch.com/ripoffsunltd .html, para. 3 (accessed December 2008). Many groups like this are independently funded or operate as home-based "institutes" that seek to hold high-profile media personalities and ministries accountable for their actions.

80. Friesen, "Everything Must Change," 38.

81. L. Gregory Jones, "Faith Matters," *The Christian Century*, May 30, 2008, 35.

82. Schultze, *Communicating for Life*, 182.

83. Jones, "Faith Matters," 35.

84. Vest, "The Prophetic Pathos of *Crash*," para. 9.

85. Ibid., para. 10.

86. Van Dyk, "The Christian School," 13.

Chapter 2

1. See Scott Calhoun, "Bono's Prophetic Vox: *The Message* Author Says U2's Message is Refreshing, Faithful, and Honest," www.atu2.com/news/article .src?ID=4232, para. 5. He wrote this in the foreword to Raewynne J. Whiteley and Beth Maynard, *Get up off Your Knees: Preaching the U2 Catalog* (Cambridge, MA: Cowley, 2003). See also Laurie Ann Britt-Smith, "American Prophet: Christian Literacy Practices and Rhetorics of Social Justice" (PhD diss., Saint Louis University, 2008), ch. 5.

2. Thomas Cahill, *The Gift of the Jews: How a Tribe of Desert Nomads Changed the Way Everyone Thinks and Feels* (New York: Random House, 1998), 114.

3. See Exod. 19–24.

4. Walter Brueggemann, *Prophetic Imagination* (Philadelphia: Fortress, 1978), 32.

5. F. F. Bruce, *Israel and the Nations* (Grand Rapids: Eerdmans, 1987), 38.

6. Michael Walzer, *Exodus and Revolution* (New York: Basic Books, 1984), 91.

7. Their courage to continue was typically rooted in their confidence that they were obeying God and living within his presence. Most of the biblical commands to be courageous are tied to the assurances of the presence of God. See, for instance, Josh. 1:7–9.

8. See also 1 Kings 22:5–28; Ezek. 13:17, 19; Mic. 3:11; and Zech. 13:4. Some of the people referred to in these passages were probably sincere and even godly men whose doctrine might be based on the law of God, but they were self-deceived in that they had not been called to the prophetic office by God and were not infallible religious guides. Tests were therefore established for distinguishing the true from the false. The true prophet was recognized by signs (Exod. 4:8; Isa. 7:11, 14); by the fulfillment of his predictions (Deut. 18:21–22); and by his teaching (Deut. 13:1–5; Isa. 8:20). The true prophet's teaching was found to agree with the doctrine of the law concerning God and his nature, character, and worship.

9. Henry Snyder Gehman, *Westminster Dictionary of the Bible*, rev. ed. (Philadelphia: Westminster, 1970), 492.

10. See Joseph Blenkinsopp, *Sage, Priest, Prophet: Religious and Intellectual Leadership in Ancient Israel* (Louisville: Westminster John Knox, 1995), 128–29, 142–43. None of the fifteen classical prophets referred to themselves as *Nabi'* (prophet) and only three (Habakkuk, Haggai, Zechariah) were referred to as *Nabi'* in the superscriptions of those books. Jeremiah bears the title only in narrative passages (1:5). Amos appears to disavow the title (7:14).

11. Ibid., 144.

12. Ibid., 119. Abraham (Gen. 20:7), Moses (Deut. 18:15–18; 34:10), Miriam (Exod. 15:20), and Balaam (Num. 22–24).

13. See Gen. 20:6; 41:1; Judg. 7:13; Dan. 2:1; and Matt. 27:19.

14. See Num. 22–24. Though the prophets who are mentioned by name are few, there were many anonymous ones (1 Kings 18:4; 2 Kings 2:7–16).

15. See Titus 1:12. In the church of the New Testament there were prophets (1 Cor. 12:28). Elders and prophets are not mutually exclusive: a prophet could also be an elder, or not. In addition, some believers had the gift of prophecy. Prophets were men and women (Acts 21:9), and they were specially illumined expounders of God's revelation. They spoke by the Spirit, occasionally foretold the future (Acts 11:27–28; 21:10–11), and taught and exhorted to great edification (1 Cor. 14:3–5, 24).

16. See 1 Sam. 9:9. See also Isa. 38:5–6; 39:6–7; Jer. 20:6; 25:11; and 28:16.

17. Isa. 41:26; 42:9; 46:9; 1 Sam. 9:1–10:16.

18. 1 Sam. 10:10–13; 19:20.

19. William E. Vine, *Vine's Expository Dictionary of Old and New Testament Words* (Nashville: Thomas Nelson, 1997), 893.

20. See also Blenkinsopp, *Sage, Priest, Prophet*, 120.

21. Henry Snyder Gehman, *The Westminster Dictionary of the Bible* (Philadelphia: Westminster, 1944), 495.

22. Blenkinsopp, *Sage, Priest, Prophet*, 136.

23. Michael Walzer, *Interpretation and Social Criticism* (Cambridge, MA: Harvard University Press, 1987), 71.

24. Ibid.

25. See John Van Dyk, "The Christian School: A Prophetic Voice," *Christian Educators Journal* (February 2008): 12–13.

26. Michael Walzer, *The Company of Critics: Social Criticism and Political Commitment in the Twentieth Century* (New York: Basic Books, 2002), 5.

27. See Will D. Campbell, *Race and the Renewal of the Church* (Philadelphia: Westminster, 1962). Especially helpful is Campbell's chapter titled "The Church: Prophet and Conservator," which explores social justice and the African American church in the midst of the U.S. civil rights era (73–86). See also James H. Cone, *Speaking the Truth: Ecumenism, Liberation, and Black Theology* (Grand Rapids: Eerdmans, 1986); and Major J. Jones, *Christian Ethics for Black Theology: The Politics of Liberation* (Nashville: Abingdon, 1974).

28. L. Gregory Jones, "Faith Matters," *The Christian Century*, May 30, 2008, 35.

29. Walzer, *Interpretation and Social Criticism*, 84–85.

30. Walter Brueggemann, *Prophetic Imagination*, 2nd ed. (Minneapolis: Fortress, 2001), 41, 46.

31. Bono qtd. in Bill Flanagan, *U2 at the End of the World* (New York: Dell, 1996), 171.

32. Brueggemann, *Prophetic Imagination*, 2nd ed., 45.

33. Ibid., 40.

34. According to Walter Brueggemann, the "themes of prophetic hope are fairly consistent. There is nothing here that is private, spiritual, romantic, or otherwordly. It is always social, historical, this-worldly, political, economic" (Walter Brueggemann, *Hope within History* [Atlanta: John Knox, 1987], 75).

35. Walzer, *The Company of Critics*, xiii.

36. Ibid., xiii.

37. Walzer, *Interpretation and Social Criticism*, 79–80.

38. Ibid., 38–39.

39. Ibid., 82–83.

40. Scot McKnight, "Five Streams of the Emerging Church," *Christianity Today*, February 2007, 36.

41. See John Jalsevac, "Modern Day Prophet, Moral Crusader, Critic of Both West and East, Alexander Solzhenitsyn, Dies at 89," LifeSiteNews.com, August 5, 2008, www.lifesitenews.com/ldn/2008/aug/08080507.html, para. 4. See also Cal Thomas, "Death of a Prophet," CalThomas.com, August 6, 2008, www.calthomas.com/index .php?news=2339 (accessed January 2010).

42. British playwright Harold Pinter's Nobel Prize acceptance speech in 2005 was similarly prophetically provocative; see Harold Pinter, "Harold Pinter: Art, Truth & Politics," Nobelprize.org, December 7, 2005, http://nobelprize.org/nobel_prizes/ literature/laureates/2005/pinter-lecture-e.html (accessed September 2009).

43. See Ezek. 3:7–9.

44. See Amos 3:7–9; 6:4–6.

45. Hosea, for instance, remarks, "For I desire mercy, not sacrifice, and acknowledgment of God rather than burnt offerings" (6:6). Hosea uses deliberate overstatement; God does not forbid temple worship.

46. Brian McLaren qtd. in McKnight, "Five Streams of the Emerging Church," 36.

47. Cornel West, *Prophetic Thought in Postmodern Times* (Monroe, ME: Common Courage, 1993), 6.

48. Abraham Joshua Heschel, *God in Search of Man* (New York: Farrar, Straus & Giroux, 1976), 74–75.

49. Qtd. in Walzer, *The Company of Critics*, 20.

50. See Isa. 6:5; Jer. 1:6.

51. Heschel notes that our "greatest passion" should be "compassion." Abraham Joshua Heschel, *I Asked for Wonder: A Spiritual Anthology*, ed. Samuel H. Dresner (New York: Crossroad, 2001), 69.

52. Walzer, *The Company of Critics*, xv.

53. Quentin J. Schultze, *Christianity and the Mass Media in America: Toward a Democratic Accommodation* (East Lansing, MI: Michigan State University Press, 2003), 198.

54. West, *Prophetic Thought in Postmodern Times*, 5.

55. See scriptural texts with a grand scope of value categories: Mic. 6:8 (justice, kindness, humility) and Matt. 23:23 (justice, mercy, faithfulness).

56. Clifford G. Christians, "Technology and Triadic Theories of Mediation," in *Rethinking Media, Religion and Culture*, ed. Stewart M. Hoover (Thousand Oaks, CA: Sage, 1997), and "Redemptive Media as the Evangelical's Cultural Task," in *American Evangelicals and the Mass Media*, ed. Quentin J. Schultze (Grand Rapids: Zondervan, 1990).

57. The Center for Public Integrity, "About Us," www.publicintegrity.org/about/, para. 1.

58. Organizations like Indymedia.org mobilize citizen reporters, and sites like *Now Public: Crowd Powered Media*, "Front Page," www.nowpublic.com/ (accessed February 2009), allow readers to promote and contribute stories they find most valuable. This is not the same as public journalism (see chapter 4), in which professional journalists shed some of their cloak of objectivity and report as community members.

59. See Calhoun, "Bono's Prophetic Vox," para. 7.

Chapter 3

1. Abraham Joshua Heschel, *The Prophets*, vol. 1 (New York: Harper, 1962), 3–4.

2. See Amos 6:4–6.

3. Walter Brueggemann, *Prophetic Imagination*, 2nd ed. (Minneapolis: Fortress, 2001), 55.

4. See Nah. 3:16.

5. See Jer. 6:13. Likewise, Jesus confronted the scribes and Pharisees (Matt. 23) who sought preservation of their own prominence and esteem.

6. See Isa. 10:12–13.

7. Heschel, *The Prophets*, 4.

8. Brueggemann, *Prophetic Imagination*, 2nd ed., 55.

9. Ibid., 48. Though Jeremiah saw the wound of Israel as devastatingly deep, priests and false prophets dressed the wound as though it were superficial. See Jer. 6:14; 8:11.

10. See Amos 6:6.

11. See Brueggemann, *Prophetic Imagination*, 2nd ed., 57. Exceptions of course, would include King David (Ps. 51) and Hezekiah, who "cried" to God together with Isaiah during the threats of Assyria's King Sennacherib against Judah (2 Chron. 32:20). Hezekiah also "wept bitterly" to God when Isaiah told him that he, Hezekiah, was going to die (2 Kings 20:3).

12. Philip Yancey, "God, the Jilted Lover," *Christianity Today*, May 16, 1986, 72. Yancey points out that two dominant metaphors in Jeremiah are God as "spurned parent" and "jilted lover," both conditions that provoke God's lament of misery over Israel's (and humanity's) plight.

13. Heschel, *The Prophets*, 5.

14. Jonathan Edwards, "Excerpts from Religious Affections" in *Devotional Classics*, ed. Richard Foster and James Bryan Smith (San Francisco: HarperSanFrancisco, 1993), 20.

15. A phrase associated with the song "Comfortably Numb" from the rock band Pink Floyd; see Pink Floyd, "Comfortably Numb," *The Wall* (New York: Columbia Records, 1979).

16. Brueggemann, *Prophetic Imagination*, 2nd ed., 56.

17. Ibid., 46.

18. Ibid., 49.

19. For instance, when Jesus saw the crowds and had compassion on them, it was prefaced by his realization of their need. It was their lost condition, and his recognition of their plight, that gave rise to his compassion. This is also typically true of acts of repentance: they are preceded by grief over the sinful condition. Grief in this case is caused by the realization that something is missing or needed. It precedes both compassion and repentance. Note that the apostle Paul distinguishes between a "godly sorrow" that "brings repentance" and a "worldly sorrow" that "brings death" (2 Cor. 7:10). The point seems to be that when grief does not lead to repentance and subsequent good deeds, it merely becomes an end in itself, leading to death (2 Cor. 7:8–10). The apostle Paul also alludes to this realization of neediness, of incompleteness and weakness, as essential to experiencing the power of Christ (2 Cor. 12:9–10). Interestingly, Paul does not grieve over his "weaknesses," but "delights" in them.

20. Brueggemann, *Prophetic Imagination*, 2nd ed., 56.

21. Marvin A. McMickle, *Where Have All the Prophets Gone? Reclaiming Prophetic Preaching in America* (Cleveland: Pilgrim, 2005), 16.

22. Jay Howard, "Let the Weak Say I Am Strong: Contemporary Worship Music and God's Concern for Righteousness and Social Justice," in *The Message in the Music: Studying Contemporary Worship Music*, ed. Robert H. Woods Jr. and Brian D. Walrath (Nashville: Abingdon, 2007), 73.

23. "An oft-cited example of a target profile was developed by Rick Warren at the Saddleback Church. There, the targeted unchurched person is called 'Saddleback Sam,' a well educated young urban professional. He is self-satisfied, and comfortable with his life. He likes his job and where he lives. He is affluent, recreation conscious, and prefers the casual and informal over the formal. He is interested in health and fitness, and he thinks he is enjoying life more than 5 years ago, but he is overextended in time and money, and is stressed out. He has some religious background from his childhood, but he hasn't been to church for 15 or 20 years, and he is skeptical of 'organized religion.' He doesn't want to be recognized when he comes to church." George G. Hunter, III, *How to Reach Secular People* (Nashville: Abingdon, 1992), 155.

24. For a discussion of the "health and wealth" gospel, see Quentin J. Schultze, *Televangelism and American Culture* (Grand Rapids: Baker Books, 1991), 134. The reference to "cheap grace" comes from Dietrich Bonhoeffer, *The Cost of Discipleship* (New York: Macmillan, 1963), 45.

25. This phrase, "the power of positive thinking," appears as the title of the popular book by minister and author Norman Vincent Peale (*The Power of Positive Thinking* [New York: Prentice-Hall, 1952]). For information on the increasing popularity of Christian self-help books, see Lynn Garrett, "What's Inside," *Publishers Weekly*, August 2007, S2; Raya Kuzyk, "Brave New Genre: The Religious Partners with the Secular in a Singular 21st Century Friendship," *Library Journal*, May 2006, 8–12.

26. Søren Kierkegaard, in *Either/Or*, trans. Alastair Hannay (New York: Penguin Classics, 1992), observed that the poet is "(a)n unhappy man who in his heart harbours a deep anguish, but whose lips are so fashioned that the moans and cries which pass over them are transformed into ravishing music" (43).

27. Brueggemann, *Prophetic Imagination*, 2nd ed., 11.

28. For Christians, spiritual disciplines are found in the Bible and throughout church history. See Dallas Willard, *The Spirit of the Disciplines: Understanding How*

God Changes Lives (New York: HarperOne, 1990); Richard J. Foster, _Celebration of Discipline: The Path to Spiritual Growth_, 3rd ed. (San Francisco: HarperSanFrancisco, 1988).

29. "Fearless heart" is a common phrase and appears powerfully in the prayer of John Hus (John Bruce L. Shelley, _Church History in Plain Language_, 2nd ed. [Nashville: Thomas Nelson, 2007], 232).

30. Jonathan Edwards asserted that these metaphors described the process of the work of religion over a lifetime; that is, becoming incrementally better as a runner and "wrestler" with God.

31. We offer our students over a dozen different media-related fasts, hoping to help them evaluate their media encounters. These fasts range from daily fifteen minute walks to fifteen days without television. Students often report that the fasts assist them in realizing the extent to which they look to media as relief from boredom, as inadvertent distractions from their sense of godly calling. If you want more details on the additional media fasts not discussed in this book, you may contact Paul Patton at ppatton@arbor.edu.

32. John Teter and Alex Gee, _Jesus and the Hip-Hop Prophets: Spiritual Insights from Lauryn Hill and 2PAC_ (Downers Grove, IL: InterVarsity, 2003).

33. Arthur and Barbara Gelb, _O'Neill_ (New York: Dell, 1960).

34. Sam Shepard, _Seven Plays_ (New York: Dial, 1984).

35. David Mamet, _The Cabin: Reminiscence and Diversions_ (New York: Turtle Bay, 1992), 6.

36. David Skeele, "The Devil and David Mamet: Sexual Perversity in Chicago as Homiletic Tragedy," _Modern Drama_ 35, no. 4 (1993): 512–18.

37. Mel Gussow, "Real Estate World a Model for Mamet: His New Play Draws on Life," _New York Times_, March 28, 1984, C19.

38. Dennis Carroll, _David Mamet_ (New York: St. Martin's Press, 1987), 32.

39. Jack V. Barbera, "Ethical Perversity in America: Some Observations on David Mamet's _American Buffalo_," _Modern Drama_ 24 (September 1981): 270.

40. David Mamet, _Speed-the-Plow_ (New York: Grove, 1994).

41. See Jer. 1:7.

42. Rob Rock, Official MySpace, "The Voice of Melodic Metal," www.myspace.com/robrock1 (accessed October 2008). For full lyrics of "Something's Wrong with the World" see metrolyrics.com, "Something's Wrong with the World," www.metrolyrics.com/somethings-wrong-with-the-world-today-lyrics-rob-rock.html (accessed October 2008).

43. Neal Conan, _Talk of the Nation: Reality TV_, NPR, January 29, 2003. The German word _Schadenfreude_ explains the human propensity for taking delight in the misfortunes of others. For research that discusses this propensity as it relates to reality television, see Robert H. Woods Jr. and Samuel Ebersole, "Motivations for Viewing Reality Television: A Uses and Gratifications Analysis," _Southwestern Journal of Mass Communication_ 23, no. 1 (2007): 23–42.

44. Deborah Emin, "Another Prophet Dies: Kurt Vonnegut (1922–2007)," _The Huffington Post_, April 12, 2007, www.huffingtonpost.com/deborah-emin/another-prophet-dies-kur_b_45719.html (accessed October 2008).

45. Vonnegut, "Address to the American Physical Society," in _Wampeters, Foma & Granfalloons (Opinions)_ (New York: Delacorte, 1974).

46. Francis A. Schaeffer, _Art and the Bible_ (Downers Grove, IL: InterVarsity, 1973), 56.

47. See, for example, David Dark, *Everyday Apocalypse: The Sacred Revealed in Radiohead, The Simpsons, and Other Pop Culture Icons* (Grand Rapids: Brazos, 2002).

48. See Jer. 17:9.

Chapter 4

1. To put this into perspective: "Suppose a violent movie could be shown to cause .001% of the viewers to act more violently. Although the percentage may be minuscule, .001% of an audience of 20 million is still 200 people!" (Richard J. Harris, *A Cognitive Psychology of Mass Communication*, 4th ed. [Mahwah, NJ: Lawrence Erlbaum, 2004], 257). For an extensive review of research related to media uses and effects, see Jennings Bryant and Dolf Zillmann, eds., *Media Effects: Advances in Theory and Research*, 2nd ed. (Mahwah, NJ: Lawrence Erlbaum, 2002).

2. Since the 1940s, researchers have argued that we selectively expose ourselves to media messages that are most familiar to us and retain messages that confirm values and attitudes we already hold. For these reasons, as explained in chapter 1, we suggest that popular media play a priestly rather than prophetic role; that is, they reinforce existing behaviors and attitudes rather than challenge them. In addition, many media researchers under the heading of Cultural Studies adopt critical-cultural approaches toward popular media. In so doing, they move further away from all-powerful media models that describe viewers as passive victims of potent messages toward approaches that view audiences as active interpreters of messages within unique communities of discourse. They focus on how people make meaning, apprehend reality, and order experiences through their use of cultural symbols in popular media. See James W. Carey, *Communication as Culture: Essays on Media and Society* (Boston: Unwin Hyman, 1988); Shearon Lowery and Melvin L. DeFleur, *Milestones in Mass Communication Research: Media Effects* (New York: Longman, 1983), 34–35; James W. Carey and Albert L. Kreiling, "Popular Culture and Uses and Gratifications: Notes toward an Accommodation," in *The Uses of Mass Communications: Current Perspectives on Gratifications Research*, ed. Jay G. Blumler and Elihu Katz (Beverly Hills, CA: Sage, 1974), 234–35.

3. G. K. Chesterton, *Orthodoxy: The Romance of Faith* (New York: Image, 1991), 15.

4. Karl Menninger, *Whatever Became of Sin?* (New York: Bantam, 1973).

5. Jean M. Twenge, *Generation Me: Why Today's Young Americans Are More Confident, Assertive, Entitled—and More Miserable Than Ever Before* (New York: Free Press, 2006).

6. Quentin J. Schultze, "The 'God-Problem' in Communication Studies," *Journal of Communication and Religion* 28 (2005): 1–22.

7. Michael Jindra, "The Passions of Electronic and Alternate Media Universes," in *Passions in Economy, Politics, and the Media: In Discussion with Christian Theology*, ed. Wolfgang Palaver and Petra Steinmair-Pösel (Vienna: Lit Verlag, 2006), 423–46.

8. See Steven B. Johnson, "The Long Zoom," *The New York Times Magazine*, October 8, 2006, www.nytimes.com/2006/10/08/magazine/08games.html?_r=2 (accessed October 2006); Nick Farrell, "Spore Could Be the Greatest God Game So Far," *The Inquirer: News, Reviews, Facts and Friction*, March 2006, www.theinquirer.net/inquirer/news/1012339/spore-could-be-the-greatest-god-game-so-far.

9. See Keturah Gray, "Celebrity Worship Syndrome Abounds: Is America's Obsession with Stardom Becoming Unhealthy?" *ABC News*, Entertainment, September 23, 2003, http://abcnews.go.com/Entertainment/story?id=101029&page=1 (accessed November 2008).

10. DSM IV-TR, "Diagnostic Criteria for 301.81, Narcissistic Personality Disorder," www.behavenet.com/capsules/disorders/narcissisticpd.htm (accessed October 2008).

11. See Charles Taylor's significant work on the historical and sociological evolution of self-perception in *Sources of the Self: The Making of Modern Identity* (Cambridge, MA: Harvard University Press, 1989).

12. Su Holmes and Sean Redmond, *Framing Celebrity: New Directions in Celebrity Culture* (London: Routledge, 2006).

13. Patrick Huguenin, "On Reality TV, Losing Your Dignity Has Never Been Easier," *Daily News/Television-Radio*, November 1, 2008, www.nydailynews.com/entertainment/tv/2008/11/02/2008-11-02_on_reality_tv_losing_your_dignity_has_ne.html (accessed November 2008).

14. Daniel Boorstin, *The Image: A Guide to Pseudo-Events in America* (New York: Vintage Books, 1992), 3–6.

15. See Amos 2:6–7. Justice in the courts is out of reach for the oppressed who are unable to pay the required bribery demands. Such was the evolved state of the systems of justice in Israel, court systems birthed with heaven's promise of *shalom* only a few centuries earlier. A most vivid portrayal of Israel's vulgar state of affairs was the prophet's description of the adulterous scandal of the "father and son" using "the same girl" (v. 7). To Amos, all of these were examples of why God's wrath will not be withheld.

16. The preface to the Ten Commandments (Exod. 20) reminds the newly freed Israelites that their Maker freed them and that obedience to his commands will keep them free of all potential enslavements, whether prisons of the mind or the body. The "wages" of sinful choices is the "wrath" of God (Rom. 1:18; 2:2–3, 5, 8).

17. Quentin L. Schultze, *Communicating for Life: Christian Stewardship in Community and Media* (Grand Rapids: Baker Academic, 2000), 76.

18. Internet and television addictions are well-documented compulsive disorders. Despite the educational benefits of many video games, millions of Americans suffer from video game addiction. The American Medical Association recently debated whether video game addiction should be classified as a disorder alongside bipolar disorders or schizophrenia. See "Emotional and Behavioral Effects, Including Addictive Potential, of Video Games: Report of the Council on Science and Public Health," *American Medical Association*, December 2007, www.ama-assn.org/ama1/pub/upload/mm/467/csaph12a07.doc (accessed October 2008).

19. George Barna, "More People Use Christian Media Than Attend Church," *The Barna Update*, www.barna.org/barna-update/article/5-barna-update/183-more-people-use-christian-media-than-attend-church; see also Kathy Bruner, "Thinking Outside the Tribal TV Box," in *Understanding Evangelical Media: The Changing Face of Christian Communication*, ed. Quentin J. Schultze and Robert H. Woods Jr. (Downers Grove, IL: InterVarsity, 2008), 47.

20. Scott Stossel, "The Man Who Counts the Killings," in *Mass Media Issues*, ed. Denis Mercier, 7th ed. (Dubuque, IA: Kendall/Hunt, 2001), 321. Of course, we recognize that it is common to see short, human interest puff pieces about heroes

and kittens on the evening news. And few advertisers—except for insurance agents, maybe—want bleeding to be on people's minds when the commercials start. Yet news that bleeds (and other stories with a negative tone) still dominates local and national news coverage.

21. Aletha C. Huston, Edward Donnerstein, and Halford Fairchild, *Big World, Small Screen: The Role of Television in American Society* (Lincoln: University of Nebraska Press, 1992). Other sources place the count higher. See Stossel, "The Man Who Counts the Killings," 318.

22. See George Gerbner and Larry Gross, "The Scary World of TV's Heavy Viewer," *Psychology Today* 10, no. 4 (1976): 41–45, 89; George Gerbner, Larry Gross, Michael Morgan, and Nancy Signorielli, "The 'Mainstreaming' of America: Violence Profile No. 11," *Journal of Communication* 30, no. 3 (1980): 10–29; Nancy Signorielli, "Television's Mean and Dangerous World: A Continuation of the Cultural Indicators Perspective," in *Cultivation Analysis: New Directions in Media Effects Research*, ed. Nancy Signorielli and Michael Morgan (Newbury Park, CA: Sage, 1990), 85–106. Regarding specific cultural stereotypes, Hispanics are consistently portrayed as un-educated and unambitious. African Americans continue to be portrayed most often as criminals, victims, or less-than-respectable people. See, for example, Eoin Devereux, ed., *Media Studies: Key Issues and Debates* (Thousand Oaks, CA: Sage, 2007); Travis L. Dixon, "Psychological Reactions to Crime News Portrayals of Black Criminals: Understanding the Moderating Roles of Prior News View and Stereotype Endorse-ment," *Communication Monographs* 73 (2006): 162–87; Travis L. Dixon, Cristina L. Azocar, and Michael Casas, "Race and Crime on Network News," *Journal of Broadcasting and Electronic Media* 47 (2003): 495–520.

23. L. Rowell Huesmann, Jessica Moise-Titus, Cheryl-Lynn Podolski, and Leonard D. Eron, "Longitudinal Relations Between Children's Exposure to TV Violence and Their Aggressive and Violent Behavior in Young Adulthood: 1977–1992," *Develop-mental Psychology* 39, no. 2 (2003): 201–21.

24. Schultze, *Communicating for Life*, 81.

25. Ibid. Also, S. I. Hayakawa's *Language in Thought and Action*, 4th ed. (New York: Harcourt Brace Jovanovich, 1978), 244, notes that advertising, in general, is a "symbol manipulating" enterprise. Symbols of "fashion and elegance," for instance, are employed to sell clothing lines and cosmetics. This is one form of attempting symbolic dominance: if not "forcing," then strongly suggesting a newly forged as-sociation between symbol and commercial product.

26. For instance, African American and Latino newspapers, magazines, and broadcast networks made considerable gains, although overall minority ownership of broadcast stations still remains low. Recent industry consolidation has resulted in many minority owners selling their stations to larger groups. See Larry Irving, "Minor-ity Commercial Broadcast Ownership Report," *National Telecommunications and Information Administration* (Washington, D.C., 1998). Historically, African Ameri-cans and Native Americans were two groups at the forefront of the alternative press movement, also called the *dissident press*. See Lauren Kessler, *The Dissident Press: Alternative Journalism in American History* (Beverly Hills, CA: Sage, 1984).

27. See, for example, Paul M. Lester and Susan D. Ross, eds., *Images that Injure: Pictorial Stereotypes in the Media*, 2nd ed. (Westport, CT: Praeger, 2003); Robert M. Entman and Andrew Rojecki, *The Black Image in the White Mind: Media and Race in America* (Chicago: University of Chicago Press, 2000); Larry Gross, John S. Katz,

and Jay Ruby, eds., *Image Ethics: The Moral Rights of Subjects in Photographs, Film, and Television* (New York: Oxford University Press, 1991).

28. Jack Nachbar and Kevin Lause, *Popular Culture: An Introductory Text* (Madison: University of Wisconsin Press, 1992), 239–40.

29. Schultze, *Communicating for Life*, 82.

30. Nachbar and Lause, *Popular Culture*, 238–39. Countertypes are stereotypes in that they are "still oversimplified views" of the group being stereotyped and are typically surface correctives, demonstrating the dominance of the stereotype in place.

31. Dr. William D. Romanowski made this point during a campus-wide presentation at Spring Arbor University in 2007 ("Christian Approaches to Popular Art" [paper presented at the FOCUS lecture series, Spring Arbor University, Spring Arbor, Michigan, March 2007]). We are grateful for Dr. Romanowski's many insights that helped to shape this section of chapter 4.

32. Mark Mulder and James K. A. Smith, "Are Men Really Wild at Heart?" *Perspectives: A Journal of Reformed Thought*, October 2004, www.rca.org/Page .aspx?pid=3382, para. 23 (accessed December 2008). Dr. Romanowski brought this quote from Mulder and Smith, along with several other quotes and sources in this section, to our attention during his presentation mentioned in note 30 above.

33. To draw attention to such concerns does not diminish the positive contributions of Eldredge's work. He encourages men to embrace masculinity, not apologize for it. He also calls attention to a tendency among some churches to embrace a feminized Jesus and push an agenda that feminizes men. But the representation of "gender ideals rooted in extreme notions of masculinity and femininity are misconceptions of God's image-bearers" (Romanowski, "Christian Approaches to Popular Art"). In the biblical record, explains Calvin College professor William D. Romanowski, "God charges the man and woman to work together in the cultivation of the creation and the advance of the kingdom." Scripture says that all "people gifted by God have a wide range and diversity of talents to be used in service of our neighbor (1 Cor. 12:14–26)." Moreover, "the woman described in Proverbs 31 is capable, caring, and morally upright, with business acumen. She is deserving of love, honor, and respect; her beauty and value lie in her integrity, character, strength, and faithfulness." And, "in contrast to the popular male code of self-reliance, the psalmist wrote, 'The Lord is my strength and my shield; my heart trusts in him, and I am helped' (Ps. 28:7)." As Romanowski concludes, "And Christians—male and female alike—are expected to exhibit the fruit of the Spirit: 'love, joy, peace, patience, kindness, goodness, faithfulness, gentleness and self-control' (Gal. 5:22–23)—characteristics that are mostly considered feminine in contemporary American culture."

34. Francis A. Schaeffer, *Pollution and the Death of Man: The Christian View of Ecology* (Wheaton: Tyndale, 1970), 82.

35. A collision with a small piece of space junk is one of several possible explanations NASA offered for the puncture that led to the crash of the space shuttle Columbia (Andrew C. Revkin, "Wanted: Traffic Cops for Space," *The New York Times* [online], February 18, 2003, http://query.nytimes.com/gst/fullpage.html?res =940DE7D81E3AF93BA25751C0A9659C8B63 &sec=&spon=&pagewanted=all [accessed November 2008]).

36. In the next several years, an estimated thirty to forty million personal computers will find such graveyards in a distant continent (Chris Carroll, "High Tech Trash: Will Your Discarded TV End up in a Ditch in Ghana?" *National Geographic.com*,

January 2008, http://ngm.nationalgeographic.com/2008/01/high-tech-trash/carroll -text.html [accessed November 2008]).

37. Neil Reimer, *The Future of the Democratic Revolution: Toward a More Prophetic Politics* (New York: Praeger, 1983), 184.

38. Bill Strom, *More Than Talk: Communication Studies and the Christian Faith*, 2nd ed. (Dubuque, IA: Kendall/Hunt, 2003), 8.

39. Christopher B. Kulp, "Demonizing Our Opponents," *Issues in Ethics* (Summer/Fall 1996): 8.

40. Schultze, *Communicating for Life*, 130.

41. The Task Force of the American Psychological Association reported recently that research demonstrates a relationship between the sexualization of girls (and young women) in the media and several mental health problems—including but not limited to eating disorders, depression, and low self-esteem (American Psychological Association, Task Force on the Sexualization of Girls, *Report of the APA Task Force on the Sexualization of Girls*, 2007, www.apa.org/pi/wpo/sexualization.html [accessed October 2008]). In addition, scholars have argued that the "trend in American culture to intensify an equation of masculinity with the capacity for violence fosters an unrealistic image of masculinity that emphasizes toughness, physical strength, and violence" (Romanowski, "Christian Approaches to Popular Art"). For instance, as one scholar explains, "When a boy tries to see his own genuine attributes, his true self, in the mirror, he cannot; he only sees how he falls short of this impossible and obsolete ideal. Is it any wonder, then, that he may later become frustrated, depressed or angry, suffer low self-esteem, fail to succeed in intimate relationships, or even turn violent?" (William Pollack, *Real Boys: Rescuing Our Sons from the Myths of Boyhood* [New York: Henry Holt, 1999], xxv).

42. Rosemarie Garland Thomson, *Extraordinary Bodies: Figuring Physical Disability in American Culture and Literature* (New York: Columbia University Press, 1997), 55–80.

43. Clifford G. Christians, Kim B. Rotzol, Mark Fackler, Kathy Brittain McKee, and Robert H. Woods Jr., *Media Ethics: Cases and Moral Reasoning*, 7th ed. (New York: Pearson, 2005), 265–71.

44. For instance, many African Americans praise the highly successful and acclaimed *The Cosby Show* for its positive and atypical representations of black culture in America. Some African Americans, however, have criticized the show because it is too atypical and therefore inaccurate. See Linus Abraham, "Media Stereotypes of African Americans," in *Images that Injure*, 2nd ed., 88–92. For additional examples of both harmful and positive images of certain ethnic groups, see chapters 11–16 of *Images that Injure*.

45. Davis Merritt, *Public Journalism and Public Life: Why Telling the News Is Not Enough* (Mahwah, NJ: Lawrence Erlbaum, 1995), 113–15. See also James W. Carey, "Afterword: The Culture in Question," in *James Carey: A Critical Reader*, ed. Eve Stryker Munson and Catherine A. Warren (Minneapolis: University of Minnesota Press, 1997), 308–45.

46. Richard Campbell, Christopher R. Martin, and Bettina Fabos, *Media and Culture*, 5th ed. (Boston: St. Martin's Press, 2007), 502. See also Paulo Freire, *Pedagogy of the Oppressed*, trans. Myra Bergman Ramos (New York: Continuum, 2000). Freire recognized that some groups in his native Brazil were denied access to the media and other social institutions. He wrote on the importance of literacy and education as

a way to empower, or give a voice to, those who were marginalized. Freire radically suggested that a community's quality of life can be measured according to the variety of voices it allows to join in public discourse.

47. Merritt, *Public Journalism and Public Life*, 113–15.

48. Pew Center for Civic Journalism, www.pewcenter.org (accessed December 2008). Some critics remain skeptical about public journalism. See Jonathan Cohn, "Should Journalists Do Community Service?" *American Prospect* (Summer 1995): 15.

49. The theoretical foundation for public journalism is communitarianism. Communitarianism focuses on the outcome of individual ethical decisions, understood not as disconnected or independent choices but analyzed as the impact of the sum of the choices on society (Clifford G. Christians, John P. Ferré, and Mark Fackler, *Good News: Social Ethics and the Press* [New York: Oxford University Press, 1993]).

50. This example originally appeared in Clifford G. Christians, Mark Fackler, Kathy Brittain McKee, Peggy Kreschel, and Robert H. Woods Jr., *Media Ethics: Cases and Moral Reasoning*, 8th ed. (New York: Pearson, 2008), 99.

51. Ibid., 102–3.

52. Seow Ting Lee, "Peace Journalism," in *The Handbook of Mass Media Ethics*, ed. Lee Wilkins and Clifford G. Christians (New York: Routledge, 2009), 258.

53. See Jake Lynch and Annabel McGoldrick, *Peace Journalism* (Gloucestershire, UK: Hawthorn, 2005), xvii, xviii, 5.

54. Michael McCarthy, "Degree's Macho Men Ads Hit Target," *USA Today* [online], April 24, 2005, www.usatoday.com/money/advertising/adtrack/2005-04-24 -degree_x.htm (accessed November 2008).

55. "Men's Deodorant Ads: What the Hell?" *The Daily Ping*, April 16, 2005, www .dailyping.com/archive/2005/04/16, para. 5 (accessed January 2009).

56. Romanowski, "Christian Approaches to Popular Art." See also Paisley Dodds, "Report: Beefy Toys Give Boys Bad Image," *The Augusta Chronicle@Augusta*, May 23, 1999, http://chronicle.augusta.com/stories/052399/bus_toys.shtml (accessed December 2008).

57. Romanowski, "Christian Approaches to Popular Art." See also Kelly D. Brownell and Melissa A. Napolitano, "Distorting Reality for Children: Body Size Proportions of Barbie and Ken Dolls," *The International Journal of Eating Disorders* 18, no. 3 (1995): 295–98. The mentioning of these body measurement absurdities is nothing new. Perhaps the problem is that we are all too aware of these measurements, and our familiarity with them has diluted what should be a godly disgust.

58. Association of Alternative Newsweeklies (AAN), "About AAN," http://aan .org/alternative/Aan/ViewPage?oid=2086, para. 2 (accessed December 2008).

59. One of the oldest African American newspapers in the country serving the African American community is the *Los Angeles Sentinel*,www.lasentinel.net (accessed December 2008).

60. Tyler Perry's work presently appears on minority and mainstream cable outlets. Perry's work is highly acclaimed for its authentic portrayal of African American communities. Perry's work first premiered on the "Chitlin Circuit," the network of black urban theaters. His early success came when urban audiences responded to the way his plays addressed their neighborhoods' everyday concerns. Perry has since produced several popular movies, including *Diary of a Mad Black Woman*, *Madea's Family Reunion*, and *Why Did I Get Married?*

Chapter 5

1. "Gordon Gekko: Address to Teldar Paper Stockholders," *Wall Street*, DVD, chapter 12, directed by Oliver Stone (Century City, CA: Twentieth Century Film Corporation, 1987).

2. Abraham Joshua Heschel, *The Prophets*, vol. 1 (New York: Harper, 1962), 5. To avoid a "spirit of acceptance," Heschel advises that we need "to recover sensitivity to the divine, we must develop an uncommon sense, rebel against (the) seemingly relevant, against conventional validity, to unthink many thoughts, to abandon many habits, to sacrifice many pretensions" (Abraham Joshua Heschel, *Moral Grandeur and Spiritual Audacity*, ed. Susannah Heschel [New York: Farrar, Straus & Giroux, 1996], 31).

3. See Jer. 1:17–19.

4. Heschel, *The Prophets*, 10.

5. As Walter Fisher, one of the leading scholars of narrative communication, explains, the most compelling stories have narrative rationality. Put another way, the story must be well told and it must resonate with us; it must match up with our own beliefs and experiences and, hence, portray the world we live in. Justification systems help stories to match up with our own beliefs and experiences (Walter Fisher, *Human Communication as Narration: Toward a Philosophy of Reason, Value, and Action* [Columbia: University of South Carolina Press, 1989]).

6. For a provocative explanation of the "Story of Stuff," see the twenty-minute short film titled "The Story of Stuff" by activist Annie Leonard, available online at www.storyofstuff.com (accessed January 2009).

7. Victor Lebow, "Price Competition in 1955," *Journal of Retailing* 31, no. 1 (1955): 7.

8. Walter Brueggemann, *Prophetic Imagination* (Philadelphia: Fortress, 1978), 42–43.

9. Undoubtedly, technological advancement fosters improvements in our quality of life, including greater comfort, luxury, convenience, and choice—all of which function as proof of progress and efficiency. Instead of seeing conspicuous consumption of lavish goods and luxuries as "superficial indulgence" that contributes to personal debt and bankruptcy, supporters of commercial culture promote it as a "strangely democratic and unifying force." Luxury, once exclusive to the upper class, is now available to everyone: "limited-edition coffee at Starbucks or Michael Graves tea kettles at Target." Thus, the purchase of luxury items is not simply "one-dimensional or shallow. If what you want is peace on earth, a unifying system that transcends religious, cultural and caste differences, . . . here it is. Our system is closer to equitable distribution of rank than what other systems have provided" (Patricia Cohen, "In Defense of Our Wicked, Wicked Ways," *The New York Times* [online], www.nytimes.com/2002/07/07/style /in-defense-of-our-wicked-wicked-ways.html?sec=&spon=&pagewanted=all, paras. 5 & 6 [accessed December 2008]). See also James B. Twitchell, *Living It Up: America's Love Affair with Luxury* (New York: Columbia University Press, 2003).

10. See also Daniel Boorstin's essay "Extravagant Expectations," in *The Image: A Guide to Pseudo-Events in America* (New York: Vintage Books, 1992), 3–6.

11. Kenneth A. Myers, *All God's Children and Blue Suede Shoes: Christians and Popular Culture* (Wheaton: Crossway Books, 1989), xiv–xvi.

12. Donna Bee-Gates, *I Want It Now: Navigating Childhood in a Materialistic World* (New York: Palgrave Macmillan, 2006).

13. See Stephen Ellington, *The Megachurches and the Mainline: Remaking Religious Tradition in the 21st Century* (Chicago: University of Chicago Press, 2007); Gustav Niebuhr, "Where Religion Gets a Big Dose of Shopping-Mall Culture," *The New York Times* [online], April 16, 1995, http://www.nytimes.com/1995/04/16/us/where-religion-gets-a-big-dose-of-shopping-mall-culture.html (accessed December 2008); Os Guinness, *Dining With the Devil: The Megachurch Movement Flirts with Modernity* (Grand Rapids: Baker Books, 1993). For a defense of megachurches and their cultural impact, see Scott Thumma and Dave Travis, *Beyond Megachurch Myths: What We Can Learn from America's Largest Churches* (San Francisco: Jossey-Bass, 2007).

14. George Barna qtd. in RaeAnn Slaybaugh, "Church Trends, 2000: The Broad Picture of Interdenominational Attendance, Giving, Member Involvement and More," *Church Solutions*, September 1, 2000, www.churchsolutionsmag.com/articles/091Feat1 .html, para. 15 (accessed December 2008).

15. George Barna, "Is America's Faith Really Shifting?" *The Barna Update*, February 24, 2003, www.barna.org/barna-update/article/5-barna-update/116-is-americas -faith-really-shifting, para. 18 (accessed December 2008).

16. Richard Cimino and Don Lattin, "Choosing My Religion," *American Demographics* (April 1999): 62. See also Wade Clark Roof, *Spiritual Marketplace: Baby Boomers and the Remaking of American Religion* (Princeton: Princeton University Press, 1999).

17. Terry York, *America's Worship Wars* (Peabody, MA: Hendrickson, 2003).

18. Marva Dawn, "Worship Is Not a Matter of Taste," *Creator* 21 (November 1999): 5–9.

19. Marva Dawn, *Reaching Out without Dumbing Down: A Theology of Worship for the Turn-of-the-Century Culture* (Grand Rapids: Eerdmans, 1995). See also Sally Morgenthaler, *Worship Evangelism: Inviting Unbelievers into the Presence of God* (Grand Rapids: Zondervan, 1995); and York, *America's Worship Wars*.

20. Brueggemann, *Prophetic Imagination*, 43.

21. Ibid., 16–17. We explain Moses's alternative consciousness in chapter 2. See also Thomas Cahill, *The Gift of the Jews: How a Tribe of Desert Nomads Changed the Way Everyone Thinks and Feels* (New York: Random House, 1998), 114.

22. Brueggemann, *Prophetic Imagination*, 35.

23. F. F. Bruce, *Israel and the Nations* (Grand Rapids: Eerdmans, 1987), 38.

24. Brueggemann, *Prophetic Imagination*, 43.

25. Cohen, "In Defense of Our Wicked, Wicked Ways," para. 27.

26. BlackChristianNews.com: Breaking News from a Black Christian Perspective, "Detroit Churches Pray for a Bailout with SUVs at the Altar," December 8, 2008, www.blackchristiannews.com/news/2008/12/detroit-churches-pray-for-a-bailout-with -suvs-at-the-altar.html, para. 16 (accessed December 2008).

27. Nick Bunkley, "Detroit Churches Pray for 'God's Bailout,'" *The New York Times* [online], December 7, 2008, http://www.nytimes.com/2008/12/08/us/08pray .html, para. 12 (accessed December 2008).

28. See Marvin A. McMickle, *Where Have All the Prophets Gone? Reclaiming Prophetic Preaching in America* (Cleveland: Pilgrim, 2006), 112. As McMickle explains, prosperity preachers encourage viewers to "sow a seed," with the promise that any financial gift sowed into a particular ministry will result in a benefit for the donor. "Proof" that the formula works is delivered through on-air testimonies from

individuals who received ten-fold after giving the little they had to give. See also Brian Grow, "Church of the Mighty Dollar," *Business Week* [online], May 23, 2005, www.businessweek.com/magazine/content/05_21/b3934016_mz001.htm (accessed December 2008).

29. Robert M. Franklin, "The Gospel of Bling," *Sojourners* [online], January 2007, www.sojo.net/index.cfm?action=magazine.article&issue=soj0701&article=070120 (accessed December 2008).

30. In *Habits of the Heart*, Robert Bellah et al. identify "Sheilaism" as a form of the American obsession with individualism and self-worship. "Sheilaism" is the private, personal faith of an American nurse with the pseudonym Sheila Larson. Sheila's perception of God is not much more than the "self magnified" (Robert N. Bellah, Richard Madsen, William M. Sullivan, Ann Swidler, and Steven M. Tipton, *Habits of the Heart: Individualism and Commitment in American Life* [Berkeley: University of California Press, 1985], 221).

31. David Mamet, "The Question," *Tikkun*, November 1999, 31.

32. It is important to note that such a widespread habit of self-deification is only possible within an affluent society. See Jacques Ellul, *Money and Power*, trans. LaVonne Neff (Downers Grove, IL: InterVarsity, 1984), 47–48.

33. Paul Heelas uses the phrase "triumph of the therapeutic" in "The Limits of Consumption and the Post-modern Religion of the New Age," in *The Authority of the Consumer*, ed. Russell Keat, Nigel Whiteley, and Nicholas Abercrombie (London: Routledge, 1994), 112.

34. Christopher Lasch, *The Culture of Narcissism: American Life in an Age of Diminishing Expectations* (New York: W. W. Norton, 1978), 7. Lasch contrasts the therapeutic self with traditional religion. America's religion of optimism makes it difficult to squarely confront the negations of life—such as death, murder, divorce, children on drugs, war, poverty, hunger—since such negations are exceptions rather than part of our optimistic social reality.

35. Fosdick qtd. in T. J. Jackson Lears, "From Salvation to Self-Realization: Advertising the Roots of the Consumer Culture, 1880–1930," in *The Culture of Consumption: Critical Essays in American History, 1880–1980*, ed. Richard Fox and T. J. Jackson Lears (New York: Pantheon, 1983), 6.

36. Heschel, *The Prophets*, 7.

37. The prophets' impatience with excuses touches upon all human self-justification formats. The prophet Jeremiah barks his displeasure at the false prophets of Israel who "prophesy lies" and the priests who "rule by their own authority" (Jer. 5:31). At the same time, he will not allow the masses of individuals to ultimately shift responsibility for their self-destructive behavior by pointing to the infidelity of their leaders: "From the least to the greatest, all are greedy for gain; prophets and priests alike, all practice deceit" (6:13).

38. Lebow, "Price Competition in 1955," 7. www.citizenrenaissance.com/the-book/part-two-where-have-we-come-from/chapter-four-the-century-of-the-all-consuming-self/churning-consumption.

39. "The most urgent task is to destroy the myth that accumulation of wealth and the achievement of comfort are the chief vocations of man" (Heschel, *Moral Grandeur*, 31).

40. Vincent J. Miller, *Consuming Religion: Christian Faith and Practice in a Consumer Culture* (New York: Continuum, 2003), 193.

41. Ibid., 128. See also the classic work on consumer motivation by Ernest Dichter, *The Strategy of Desire* (New York: Doubleday, 1960).

42. Augustine, *On Christian Teaching*, trans. R. P. H. Green (New York: Oxford University Press, 1997), 9.

43. Thomas Aquinas qtd. in James Weisheipl and Fabian R. Larcher, trans., *Commentary on the Gospel of John*, Aquinas Scripture Series, 4 (Albany, NY: Magi Books, 1980), 242.

44. Augustine, *On Christian Teaching*, 9. See also Col. 3:1–5.

45. Miller, *Consuming Religion*, 18.

46. David Dark, *The Gospel According to America: A Meditation on a God-blessed, Christ-haunted Idea* (Louisville: Westminster John Knox, 2005), 10.

47. Heschel, *The Prophets*, 10.

48. Abraham Joshua Heschel describes one function of religion as the "critique of all satisfaction. Its end is joy, but its beginning is discontent, detesting boasts, smashing idols" (*Moral Grandeur*, 265).

49. Dark, *The Gospel According to America*, 10.

50. Brian Ross and Rehal El-buri, "Obama's Pastor: God Damn America: U.S. to Blame for 9/11," *ABC News* [online], March 13, 2008, http://abcnews.go.com/blotter/story?id=4443788, paras. 1, 6 (accessed December 2008).

51. Ibid., para. 6.

52. Martin Luther King Jr., "Beyond Vietnam: A Time to Break Silence," Riverside Church, New York City, April 4, 1967, *Hartford Web Publishing*, http://www.hartford-hwp.com/archives/45a/058.html, paras. 9, 11 (accessed December 2008). http://faithinactiononline.com/2008/03/19/why-america-needs-the-uncensored-prophetic-voice-of-the-black-church-by-adam-taylor/.

53. Martin Luther King Jr. qtd. in Marian Wright Edelman, "America's Sixth Child," *Bayview: National Black Newspaper* [online], December 17, 2008, http://www.sfbayview.com/2008/america%E2%80%99s-sixth-child/ (accessed December 2008).

54. Stephen L. Carter, "First Things First," *Christianity Today*, July 2005, 54. "Patriot pastors," who are recruited heavily throughout the South and Midwest to increase the evangelical vote, view the policies of a particular political party as representing authentic Christian faith. Such partisan allegiance certainly makes it difficult to critique the actions of certain public officials. For a description of "patriot pastors," see Daniel Eisenberg, "The Posse in the Pulpit," *Time* [online], May 16, 2005, www.time.com/time/magazine/article/0,9171,1061529,00.html?promoid=googlep (accessed December 2008). Patriot pastors sound like Hananiah who assured King Zedekiah that nothing Jeremiah said was true and that God was on the king's side (Jer. 28:1–4, 11). They also sound like the prophet Amaziah, whose ultimate loyalty was not to God but to the king of Israel (Amos 7:10–13).

55. Bob Dylan, for instance, labeled a "reluctant prophet" by *Relevant* magazine, has spent a career confronting the spirits of the age and the powers that bind (Scott M. Marshall, "The Real Bob Dylan: An Honest Look at the Life and Faith of Folk's Greatest Legend," *Relevant*, December 2007, 56–61). His song "With God on Our Side" gives an American history lesson in a few minutes, listing each American war's great justification, proclaiming the Almighty had already signed up with us against them, every time. Bob Dylan, "With God on Our Side," *These Times They Are a-Changin'* (New York: Columbia, 1964). See also Ron Everman and Andrew Jamison,

Music and Social Movements: Mobilizing Traditions in the Twentieth Century (New York: Cambridge University Press, 1998).

56. James W. Carey, ed., *Communication as Culture: Essays on Media and Society* (Boston: Unwin Hyman, 1989), 113, 141.

57. Quentin J. Schultze, *Communicating for Life: Christian Stewardship in Community and Media* (Grand Rapids: Baker Academic, 2000), 118.

58. Similar grandiose claims were made about alphabetic writing, print, and the printing press. See, for example, Elizabeth Eisenstein, *The Printing Press as an Agent of Change* (Cambridge: Cambridge University Press, 1980); Walter J. Ong, *Orality and Literacy: The Technologizing of the Word* (New York: Routledge, 1982); Eric Havelock, *The Literature Revolution in Greece and Its Cultural Consequences* (Princeton: Princeton University Press, 1987); and Barry Sanders and Ivan Illich, *ABC: Alphabetization of the Popular Mind* (New York: Vintage Books, 1989).

59. See Quentin J. Schultze and Robert H. Woods Jr., eds., *Understanding Evangelical Media: The Changing Face of Christian Communication* (Downers Grove, IL: InterVarsity, 2008). A common rhetoric of reverence toward technology among evangelicals is identified throughout media history. For instance, Proclaimers responded quickly to the "intoxicating effects" of Samuel Morse's telegraph. The telegraph brought a promise of "unity of interest, people linked by a single mind, and the worldwide victory of Christianity" (Daniel J. Czitrom, *Media and the American Mind: From Morse to McLuhan* [Chapel Hill: University of North Carolina Press, 1982], 10). Proclaimers premiered the first "radio church" in 1923, when Reverend R. R. Brown asked his listeners to join the "World Radio Congregation" (Mark Ward, *Air of Salvation: The Story of Christian Broadcasting* [Grand Rapids: Baker Books, 1995], 228–29). Similar rhetoric is identified in books discussing evangelical activity in cyberspace. See Douglas Groothuis, *The Soul in Cyberspace* (Grand Rapids: Baker Books, 1997); Edward Veith and Christopher L. Stamper, *Christians in a .com World: Getting Connected without Being Consumed* (Wheaton: Crossway, 2000); and Andrew Careaga, *eMinistry: Connecting with the Net Generation*, 2nd ed. (Grand Rapids: Kregel, 2001).

60. Billy Graham, "The Future of TV Evangelism," *TV Guide* 31, no. 10 (1983): 8.

61. Jimmy Swaggart, "Divine Imperatives for Broadcast Ministry," *Religious Broadcasting*, November 1984, 14.

62. Ben Armstrong, *The Electric Church* (Nashville: Thomas Nelson, 1979), 8–9; 172–73.

63. Quentin J. Schultze, *Redeeming TV: How TV Changes Christians—How Christians Can Change TV* (Downers Grove, IL: InterVarsity, 1992), 19.

64. See Robert S. Fortner, *Communication, Media, and Identity: A Christian Theory of Communication* (New York: Rowman & Littlefield, 2007), 137–60.

65. Myers, *All God's Children and Blue Suede Shoes*, 22. Even in formalized worship settings, a growing number of leaders rely on slick entertainment strategies and spectacle to entice a potential group they call "the unchurched." For such reasons, some critics suggest that Christians have defined themselves primarily as evangelists and only secondarily as worshipers. See Tex Sample, *The Spectacle of Worship in a Wired World* (Nashville: Abingdon, 1998); and Sally Morgenthaler, *Worship Evangelism: Inviting Unbelievers into the Presence of God* (Grand Rapids: Zondervan, 1999).

66. Today much Christian film and theater is like Communist theater in the United States during the Great Depression and World War II, when playwrights were weighed down by Marxist dogma and feared offending the party bosses. With rare exceptions, Marxist plays became elaborate, acted-out tracts lambasting the bourgeoisie—uninteresting propaganda disguised as stories heavy on persuasion and instruction and weak on narrative delight (Malcomb Goldstein, *The Political Stage: American Drama and Theater of the Great Depression* [New York: Oxford University Press, 1974], 82–85).

67. Schultze, *Redeeming Television*, 20. See also Fortner, *Communication, Media, and Identity*, 161–84.

68. As Walter Brueggemann explained, the dominant consciousness requires the "annulment of the neighbor as a life-giver in our history" (*Prophetic Imagination*, 43).

69. Ibid.

70. Quentin J. Schultze, *Habits of the High-Tech Heart: Living Virtuously in the Information Age* (Grand Rapids: Baker Academic, 2002), 75. See also G. K. Chesterton, *Orthodoxy: The Romance of Faith* (New York: Image Books, 1990), 48.

71. Emergent Village, "Leadership," www.emergentvillage.com/about-information /leadership, para. 1 (accessed January 2009).

72. Another tradition countervoice is the Roman Catholic Theology on Tap (TOT) ministry: "a speaker and conversation series for people in their 20s and 30s to learn more about the Catholic faith, make connections between faith and everyday life, and enter into conversation with your peers" (Archdiocese of Chicago, "Young Adult Ministry," http://www.yamchicago.com/ [accessed January 2009]). The program seeks to reconnect Catholics with the rich tradition of their faith. TOT recognizes that the "baton" of tradition "has not been successfully passed to the next generation" of Catholics. TOT often meets in bars or local pubs, realizing that young adults may "crave spirituality but don't necessarily look for it in the institutional church" (Eric Gorski, "Theology on Tap/ Catholic Church Targets 20- to 30-somethings," *The Colorado Springs Gazette* [online], Jan 19, 2002, http://findarticles.com/p/articles/mi_qn4191/ is_/ai_n10001293?tag=artBody;col1, paras. 14, 16 [accessed January 2009]).

73. Quentin J. Schultze, *Christianity and the Mass Media in America: Toward a Democratic Accommodation* (East Lansing, MI: Michigan State University Press, 2003), 92.

74. Ibid., 99.

75. See 1 Thess. 5:18.

76. See Ps. 136:1–3; 30:12.

77. See Luke 22:17–19.

78. Schultze, *Habits of the High-Tech Heart*, 80. In fact, recent research demonstrates that the cultivation of gratitude may reduce materialistic strivings and consequently diminish the negative effects of materialistic strivings on psychological well-being (Emily L. Polak and Michael E. McCullough, "Is Gratitude an Alternative to Materialism?" *Journal of Happiness Studies* 7 [2006]: 343–60).

79. See Alasdair MacIntyre, *After Virtue: A Study in Moral Theory*, 2nd ed. (Notre Dame, IN: University of Notre Dame Press, 1984).

80. "Demonstrating Gratitude," *The Washington Times* [online], http://assets .mediaspanonline.com/prod/287320/Gratitude%202.pdf (accessed December 2008).

81. Robert Emmons, *Thanks! How the New Science of Gratitude Can Make You Happier* (Boston: Houghton Mifflin, 2007).

82. Paul A. S. Harvey, "Interpreting Oshin-War, History and Women in Modern Japan," in *Women, Media, and Consumption in Japan*, ed. L. Skov and B. Moeran (Honolulu: University of Hawaii Press, 1995), 75–110. See also Jerome Johnston and James S. Ettema, *Positive Images: Breaking Stereotypes with Children's Television* (Beverly Hills, CA: Sage, 1982); William J. Brown and Arvind Singhal, "Ethical Considerations of Promoting Prosocial Messages through the Popular Media," *Journal of Popular Film and Television* 21, no. 3 (1993): 92–99.

Chapter 6

1. This actually happened in 2008 at Westwinds Church, Jackson, Michigan, as reported to the authors by the church's pastor, David McDonald.

2. See Ezek. 4.

3. Reinhold Niebuhr, *Faith and Politics: A Commentary on Religious, Social and Political Thought in a Technological Age*, ed. Ronald H. Stone (New York: George Braziller, 1968), 23.

4. The Hebrew word for prophet, *Nabi'*, originally meant "to bubble forth," or spring forth, like a spring of water. *Nabi'*, which appears three hundred times in the Old Testament, communicates the forceful intensity and passion of the prophets' focus. See John M'Clintock and James Strong, eds. *Cyclopaedia of Biblical, Theological, and Ecclesiastical Literature*, vol. 2 (New York: Harper and Brothers, 1868), 637; William E. Vine, *Vine's Expository Dictionary of Old and New Testament Words* (Nashville: Thomas Nelson, 1997), 893.

5. Abraham Joshua Heschel, *The Prophets*, vol. 1 (New York: Harper, 1962), 7.

6. Brian Swarts, "'Prophetic Art' and the Politics of Jesus," *The Spectrum Blog*, November 27, 2006, http://spectrummagazine.typepad.com/the_spectrum_blog/2006/11/prophetic_art_a.html, para. 1 (accessed December 2008).

7. Morris Massey's management training program from the 1970s famously described the changes brought about by an emotional invasion of a person's or culture's value program. See, for example, "What You Are Is Where You Were When—The Massey Triad, Revised Program No. 1," The Richardson Company, www.rctm.com/Products/change/5712.htm (accessed December 2008).

8. Walter Brueggemann, *The Prophetic Imagination*, 2nd ed. (Minneapolis: Fortress, 2001), xxiii.

9. Shock advertisements, sometimes called *shockvertisements*, understand the power of visual images to motivate viewers. They overpower audiences by violating cultural norms as a way to break through the "clutter" and, in some cases, also to bring awareness to certain public issues. For instance, Italian clothier Benetton displayed bare human buttocks and limbs tattooed with the words "HIV Positive." Although shock ads like these demonstrate defiance of the accepted social code, they also can increase attention and memory, and positively influence behavior. See Darren W. Dahl, Kristina D. Frankenberger, and Rajesh V. Manchanda, "Does It Pay to Shock? Reactions to Shocking and Nonshocking Advertising Content among University Students," *Journal of Advertising Research* 43 (2003): 268–80.

10. For Abraham Joshua Heschel, the ability to be shocked was so important to individual repentance and reconciliation that he lamented over the inability of

most individuals to be shocked: "Should we not pray for the ability to be shocked at atrocities committed by man, for the capacity to be dismayed at our inability to be dismayed?" (Abraham Joshua Heschel, *Moral Grandeur and Spiritual Audacity*, ed. Susannah Heschel [New York: Farrar, Straus & Giroux, 1996], 262).

11. See Jer. 2:35.

12. Flannery O'Connor, *Collected Works* (New York: Library of America, 1988), 949. Thanks to Christina Bieber and her work, described in endnote 13 below, which pointed us to the quote from O'Connor.

13. Christina Bieber, "The Prophet as Story-teller," in *Prophetic Ethics*, ed. Robert B. Kruschwitz (Waco: Baylor University Press, 2003), 75–82. See also Matthew Schobert, "Study Guide for The Prophet as Story-teller," Center for Christian Ethics, Baylor University, www.baylor.edu/christianethics/PropheticEthicsstudyguide6 .pdf, para. 3 (accessed December 2008).

14. The translation of Jer. 7:8–11 in *The Message* captures the essence of a direct pronouncement's indictment-threat-oracle structure like few others: "Get smart! Your leaders are handing you a pack of lies, and you're swallowing them! Use your heads! Do you think you can rob and murder, have sex with the neighborhood wives, and tell lies nonstop, worship the local gods and buy every novel religious commodity on the market—and then march into this Temple, set apart for my worship, and say, 'We're safe!' thinking that the place itself gives you a license to go on with all this outrageous sacrilege? A cave full of criminals!"

15. See Jon. 3:3–4. In addition, a variation of direct pronouncement is found in Ezra's reading of the Book of the Law of Moses (Neh. 8:1–10). The huge crowd in Jerusalem stood before Ezra who, standing on a platform built for the occasion, read directly God's laws from "daybreak to noon." The mere reading and explaining of the Scriptures provoked in the listeners the shocking realization of the depth of the nation's self-induced tragedy. Their consciences were crushed, and they displayed deep emotions of grief. This cacophony of grief-filled wailing among many thousands was provoked by the direct hearing of the laws of Moses and provides an Old Testament setting for the New Testament understanding of the prophetic role in the church of the public reading and explaining of the Word of God.

16. See 2 Sam. 12:1–7.

17. William Shakespeare, *Hamlet Prince of Denmark*, in *The Works of William Shakespeare* (Roslyn, NY: Walter J. Black, 1937), 2.2.762.

18. Thomas Jemielity, *Satire and the Hebrew Prophets* (Louisville: Westminster John Knox, 1992), 23.

19. Kelvin Friebel, "A Hermeneutical Paradigm for Interpreting Prophetic Sign-Actions," *Didaskalia* 12, no. 2 (2001): 25–45. In postmodern society we lean toward *symbolic language* that is concerned with feelings, imagination, and experience. This approach was common in the ancient world. It accounts for the indirect communication style of the prophets and also recognizes the emphasis on stories that much of the Old Testament uses to deliver its message (Pierre Babin, *The New Era in Religious Communication* [Minneapolis: Fortress, 1991], 149–51).

20. Daniel Block, *The Book of Ezekiel, Chapters 1–24* (Grand Rapids: Eerdmans, 1997), 166.

21. J. J. M. Roberts, *The Bible and the Ancient Near East* (Winona Lake, IN: Eisenbrauns, 2002), 228–31; Robert P. Gordon, *Hebrew Bible and Ancient Versions: Selected Essays of Robert P. Gordon* (Farnham, UK: Ashgate, 2006), 140.

22. Many people in our culture think of profaneness most typically as it relates to *profanity*, or vulgarity and coarse language. But there are many other forms of profanity. To "profane" the name of God would be to make his name equal to the pantheon of Greek gods or to treat it with irreverence. To "profane" the image of God, his human creation, would be to speak or act in a dehumanizing way. The concept is most easily grasped from a biblical perspective as meaning the opposite of *holiness*. To be holy means to be "set apart" for God's service (Charles F. Pfeiffer, *The New Combined Bible Dictionary and Concordance* [Grand Rapids: Baker Books, 1961], 228). When we refer to the "sacred use of the profane," we assert that in God's wisdom and economy sometimes the profane—that which is not typically associated with being "set apart" for God's service—is, in fact, used for wonderfully sacred purposes.

23. According to Barry Sanders's *Sudden Glory: Laughter as Subversive History* (Boston: Beacon, 1995), 43, the only truly joyous laughter, a "belly laugh," in the Old Testament is after Abraham was told by God that his elderly wife, Sarai, would bare him a son (Gen. 17:17).

24. Jemielity, *Satire and the Hebrew Prophets*, 22.

25. See 1 Kings 18:27.

26. Jemielity, *Satire and the Hebrew Prophets*, 22.

27. Even the well-known admonition of Amos, "Let justice roll on like a river, and righteousness like an ever-flowing stream" (5:24 NEB) "assumes added force if it is read as a satire on the [pagan] rite of pouring water as a rain-charm" (Theodor Gaster, *Myth, Legend, and Custom in the Old Testament*, vol. 2 [New York: Harper & Row, 1975], 648–49).

28. Jeremiah satirically ridicules the false gods with whom Israel is smitten. His mockery pushes the audience to respond to his series of snapshots about their religious devotion: cutting a tree from the forest, carving a tree trunk into a large phallic symbol, adorning it with precious jewels, and fastening it to a platform so the phallic idol will not wobble (Jer. 10:3–5). The prophet hopes for a reaction from his audience—something, almost anything but passive disregard.

29. The prophet Habakkuk satirically describes the craftsman carving his idol as worshiping his own creation; he mockingly points out the absurdity of asking wood or stone to wake up or speak (Hab. 2:18–20).

30. See Derek Krueger, *Symeon the Holy Fool: Leontius's Life and the Late Antique City* (Berkeley: University of California Press, 1996).

31. In the New Testament, Jesus Christ—whom Christians acknowledge as the most righteous embodiment of prophet, priest, and king—carries forward the Old Testament prophet's use of satire and irony as he confronts the Pharisees in some of the gospel's most dramatic discourses (for example, the seven woes in Matt. 23). The Pharisees' shock and outrage at Jesus's accusations, we suggest, were the result of Christ's redemptive shock therapy in that moment of woe-filled confrontation. Even the apostle Paul mocks his opponents in Corinth, satirically describing them as "strong," while he is weak, mocking their "wisdom," while glorying in his own weakness (1 Cor. 4:10).

32. Frederick Buechner, *Telling the Truth: The Gospel as Tragedy, Comedy, and Fairy Tale* (New York: Harper & Row, 1977), 5.

33. Charles Taylor, *Sources of the Self: The Making of Modern Identity* (Cambridge, MA: Harvard University Press, 1989), 98.

34. Sarah Lodwick, "Art's Prophetic Burn, Part 2," *Theology Forum*, http://theology forum.wordpress.com/2008/04/10/arts-prophetic-burn-%C2%BB-part-2/ (accessed January 2009).

35. Robert Hughes, *Goya* (New York: Alfred A. Knopf, 2003), 181.

36. Goya qtd. in ibid.

37. See Frederick Hartt, *Art: A History of Painting, Sculpture, Architecture*, vol. 2 (Englewood Cliffs, NJ: Prentice-Hall, 1976), 317; Wolfgang Kayser, *The Grotesque in Art and Literature*, trans. Ulrich Weisstein (Bloomington, IN: Indiana University Press, 1963); Wolfgang Stechow, "Hieronymus Bosch: The Grotesque and We," in *The Grotesque in Art and Literature: Theological Reflections*, ed. James Luther Adams and Wilson Yates (Grand Rapids: Eerdmans, 1997), 113–24.

38. Reverend Billy, The Church of Stop Shopping, "About Us," www.revbilly .com/about-us, para. 1 (accessed January 2009).

39. Reverend Billy, The Church of Stop Shopping, "The Stop Shopping Gospel Choir," www.revbilly.com/about-us/the-stop-shopping-gospel-choir, para. 2 (accessed January 2009).

40. Peter Gabriel, "Big Time," *So* (Santa Monica, CA: Geffen Records, 1986).

41. Steve Taylor, "Cash Cow (A Rock Opera in Three Small Acts)," *Squint* (Nashville: Warner Brothers / Wea, 1993).

42. Alex Shakar, *The Savage Girl* (New York: Harper Perennial, 2002), 60, 179, 141.

43. Ibid., 43, 145.

44. John Alberti, ed., *Leaving Springfield: The Simpsons and the Possibility of Oppositional Culture* (Detroit: Wayne State University Press, 2003), xxiv.

45. Duncan Stuart Beard, "Local Satire with a Global Reach: Ethnic Stereotyping and Cross-Cultural Conflicts in 'The Simpsons,'" in *Leaving Springfield*, 273–91.

46. For an online version of *The Wittenburg Door*, see www.wittenburgdoor.com (accessed January 2009).

47. Robert Darden, "Loser," *The Wittenburg Door*, special 20th anniversary issue, http://archives.wittenburgdoor.com/archives/loser200.html, para. 41 (accessed January 2009).

48. Ken Waters, "What Would Mohammed Drive?" in *Understanding Evangelical Media: The Changing Face of Christian Communication*, ed. Quentin J. Schultze and Robert H. Woods Jr. (Downers Grove, IL: InterVarsity, 2008), 75.

49. Mark Allan Powell, "Jesus Climbs the Charts: The Business of Contemporary Christian Music," *Christian Century*, December 2002, 21.

50. Ibid.

51. Dead Artist Syndrome qtd. in Powell, ibid. See also Jay Howard and John Streck, *The Apostles of Rock* (Lexington: University Press of Kentucky, 1999); and Mark Allen Powell, *The Encyclopedia of Contemporary Christian Music* (Peabody, MA: Hendrickson, 2002).

52. See, for example, Jan Lance Bacon, "A Fondness for Supermarkets: Wise Blood and Consumer Culture," in *New Essays on Wise Blood*, ed. Michael Kreyling (New York: Cambridge University Press, 1995), 25–50.

53. Flannery O'Connor, *Wise Blood* (New York: Farrar, Straus & Giroux, 1990), 153.

54. Motes's name is derived from the word "mote" in the New Testament. The term is taken from the King James translation of the Bible, Matt. 7:3. It is translated

"speck of sawdust" in the New International Version (translation) and is part of Jesus's penetrating description of the human habit of focusing on the sins of others—that is, the mote or specks of sawdust in someone else's eye—while ignoring the plank of wood in one's own.

55. O'Connor, *Wise Blood*, 55.

56. Brueggemann, *Prophetic Imagination*, 2nd ed., 41.

57. Augustine, *The Confessions of St. Augustine,* trans. Edward B. Pusey (New York: Pocket Books, 1951), 45.

58. The book of Ecclesiastes addresses this issue in detail. After describing life's unpredictable complexity (Eccles. 9:11), the writer asserts that "no man knows when his hour will come" (v. 12). Then he goes on to list the possibility of certain unexpected horrifying tragedies that could occur without warning or without an immediately identifiable reason: "As fish are caught in a cruel net, or birds are taken in a snare, so men are trapped by evil times that fall unexpectedly upon them" (v. 12).

59. See W. David O. Taylor, "The Horrors!" Christianity Today Movies.com, April 5, 2005, www.christianitytoday.com/ct/movies/commentaries/2005/horrors.html, paras. 39–40 (accessed January 2009); see also Terry Lindvall, *Sanctuary Cinema: Origins of the Christian Film Industry* (New York: New York University Press, 2007).

60. Namaan Wood, "Important Trivialities and Sweeping Allegations: Redemptive Criticism and Michael Moore's Rhetoric of Civic Paradox" (paper, annual convention of the National Communication Association, San Diego, November 22, 2008), 2.

61. Tony Campolo, personal correspondence to authors, January 2009. Special thanks to our Spring Arbor University faculty colleague Mary Darling for her help in securing the details of this illustration.

62. Edward Knippers, "Artist Statement," www.edknippers.com, para. 3 (accessed January 2009).

63. *Sister Camille's Kaleidoscopic Cabaret* received the 1996 prize for "Best Full Length Play" from the Christians in Theater Arts (CITA). For additional information on Paul Nicholas Mason see Dramatic Publishing, "Paul Nicholas Mason," www .dramaticpublishing.com/AuthorBio.php?titlelink=9622 (accessed January 2010).

64. Mason's material is for theaters that "wish to promote a religious worldview without appearing to preach," a point made in the play's preface; see Paul Nicholas Mason, *The Discipline Committee* (Woodstock, IL: Dramatic Publishing, 1995). When premiered at Trinity House Theater in Livonia, Michigan, the publicity made sure to include that the play was inappropriate for children. (Then again, some of Ezekiel's art was inappropriate for children as well.)

65. See 1 Kings 19:1–18.

Chapter 7

1. Jacob Bronowski, *Science and Human Values*, rev. ed. (New York: Harper & Row, 1965).

2. Recent notable exceptions include Shane Hipps, *The Hidden Power of Electronic Culture: How Media Shapes Faith, the Gospel, and Church* (Grand Rapids: Zondervan, 2006), and *Flickering Pixels: How Technology Shapes Your Faith* (Grand Rapids: Zondervan, 2009); Quentin J. Schultze, *Habits of the High-Tech Heart: Living Virtuously in the Information Age* (Grand Rapids: Baker Academic, 2002), and *High Tech Worship? Using Presentation Technologies Wisely* (Grand Rapids: Baker

Books, 2004); Tex Sample, *The Spectacle of Worship in a Wired World: Electronic Culture and the Gathered People of God* (Nashville: Abingdon, 1998); Eileen D. Crowley, *Liturgical Art for a Media Culture* (Collegeville, MN: Liturgical, 2007); Robert S. Fortner, *Communication, Media, and Identity: A Christian Theory of Communication* (New York: Rowman & Littlefield, 2007); James McConnell and Frances Trampiets, eds., *Communicating Faith in a Technological Age* (New York: Hyperion, 1990); and Stephen V. Monsma, ed., *Responsible Technology: A Christian Perspective* (Grand Rapids: Eerdmans, 1986). French scholar Jacques Ellul provides some of the earliest and most influential work on the philosophy of technology and technological culture from a Christian perspective. See Jacques Ellul, *Presence of the Kingdom*, 2nd ed. (Colorado Springs: Helmers and Howard, 1989); *The Technological Society* (New York: Vintage Books, 1964); *Perspectives on Our Age*, trans. Joachim Neugroschel (New York: Seabury, 1981); and "Symbolic Function, Technology and Society," *Journal of Social and Biological Structures* (October 1978): 216. American Jesuit Walter J. Ong is another early and influential Christian thinker in this area. See Walter J. Ong, *Orality and Literacy: The Technologizing of the Word* (New York: Routledge, 1982); "Worship at the End of the Age of Literacy" in *Faith and Contexts*, vol. 1., *Selected Essays and Studies, 1952–1991*, ed. Thomas J. Farrell and Paul A. Soukup (Atlanta: Scholars Press, 1992), 175–88; and "Communications Media and the State of Theology" in *Faith and Contexts*, 154–74.

3. See Nicholas Wolterstorff, *Until Justice and Peace Embrace* (Grand Rapids: Eerdmans, 1983), 69–72.

4. Of course, as the medium of television has evolved since its inception in the late 1940s, screen sizes have both expanded and shrunk, from fifty-inch flat screens to palm-sized models. Regardless of size, the television medium still has difficulty matching film's wide-screen expansiveness. Television scenes are still shot for viewing in the privacy and intimacy of a home. Also, the television medium has evolved not only in screen size but in its interfacing with other communication media: for instance, in viewer voting by phone for reality television contestants, or online shopping, or downloading television programming to view on computer. Such interfacing, we suggest, intensifies television's inherent properties of intimacy and immediacy. For an introduction to the wildly changing media convergence landscape, see Henry Jenkins' *Convergence Culture: Where Old and New Media Collide* (New York: New York University Press, 2006).

5. Several sources have critiqued how religious television shapes culture and how culture shapes religious television, for better or worse. For example, see Malcolm Muggeridge, *Christ and the Media* (Grand Rapids: Eerdmans, 1977); Stewart M. Hoover, *Mass Media Religion: The Social Sources of the Electronic Church* (Newbury Park, NY: Sage, 1988); Gregor T. Goethals, *The Electronic Golden Calf: Images, Religion and the Making of Meaning* (Cambridge, MA: Cowley, 1990); Stewart M. Hoover, ed., *Religious Television: Controversies and Conclusions* (Westport, CT: Greenwood/Ablex, 1990); Quentin J. Schultze, *Televangelism and American Culture* (Grand Rapids: Baker Books, 1991), and *Redeeming Television: How TV Changes Christians—How Christians Can Change TV* (Downers Grove, IL: InterVarsity, 1992); Hal Erickson, *Religious Radio and Television in the United States, 1921–1991: The Programs and Personalities* (Jefferson, NC: McFarland, 1992); Heather Hendershot, *Shaking the World for Jesus: Media and Conservative Evangelical Culture* (Chicago: University of Chicago Press, 2004).

6. Words, in contrast to images, present propositions and allow for abstract thought—making television's concrete, sensate world an inferior medium for philosophical thought or argument. Some critics argue that this "image over word" bias presents a challenge to anyone who wants to present the gospel on television. For instance, Malcolm Muggeridge, in *Christ and the Media*, argued that the television camera always lies because, quite simply, it cannot capture everything but only what is shot on screen. See also Jacques Ellul, *The Humiliation of the Word* (Grand Rapids: Eerdmans, 1985); Ong, "Communications Media and the State of Theology."

7. Dorothy G. Singer and Jerome L. Singer, *Imagination and Play in the Electronic Age* (Cambridge, MA: Harvard University Press, 2005).

8. Schultze, *Redeeming Television*, 86.

9. See Neil Postman, *Amusing Ourselves to Death: Public Discourse in an Age of Show Business* (New York: Viking, 1985), 99.

10. See, for example, Lynn Spigel, *Make Room for TV: Television and the Family Ideal in Postwar America* (Chicago: University of Chicago Press, 1992); Leslie Savan, *The Sponsored Life: Ads, TV, and American Culture* (Philadelphia: Temple University Press, 1994); Jennings Bryant, ed., *Television and the American Family*, 2nd ed. (Mahwah, NJ: Lawrence Erlbaum, 2000); Raymond Williams, *Television: Technology and Cultural Form* (New York: Routledge, 2003).

11. Television's language also includes properties common to all visual media, such as realism and reduction. For a description of television's unique visual language, including properties it shares with other visual media, see Herbert Zettl, *Sight, Sound, and Motion*, 5th ed. (Florence, KY: Wadsworth, 2007); John Fiske, *Television Culture* (New York: Routledge, 1987); John Fiske and John Hartley, *Reading Television*, 2nd ed. (New York: Routledge, 2003); Ken Smith, Sandra Moriarty, Gretchen Barbatsis, Keith Kenney, and Kenneth L. Smith, eds., *Handbook of Visual Communication: Theory, Methods, and Media* (Philadelphia: Lawrence Erlbaum, 2004); Robert Edmonds, *The Sights and Sounds of Cinema and Television: How the Aesthetic Experience Influences our Feelings* (New York: Teachers' College Press, 1982). See also Clifford G. Christians, "The Sensate in Sorokin and in Primetime Television," *Et cetera: A Review of General Semantics* (Summer 1981): 189–201; Horace Newcomb, *TV: The Most Popular Art* (New York: Anchor Books, 1974).

12. Schultze, *Redeeming Television*, 88–95. See also Horace Newcomb, *TV: The Most Popular Art*, 243–65.

13. We recognize that with high definition (HD), news stations must now find more graphic content to fill the sides of the screen and background. And, in dramatic programming with HD production, set designers must now pay closer attention to props and scenery. Yet it is unlikely that increased attention to such superfluous elements as a result of HD will detract from television's bias toward a character's face. News and dramatic television are still driven by personalities and characters. It is more likely that HD will bring increased attention to the lines and subtle expressions visible on a character's face. When we saw an HD version of our favorite show for the first time, we were not drawn to the props in the room but to the wrinkles and color spots on our favorite actor's face that we had never noticed before. (It was clear that he could not pass for the younger age of the character he was playing!) Throughout the show, we paid even more attention to his face than in previous non-HD episodes, gaining new appreciation for how he controlled the meaning of the dialogue with

subtle facial cues. In any case, it is too early to determine the full effects of HD on television's inherent biases toward intimacy and immediacy.

14. Para-social Interaction (PSI) is a perceived relationship of friendship or intimacy by a media consumer with a remote media "persona" (Donald Horton and R. Richard Wohl, "Mass Communication and Para-Social Interaction: Observation on Intimacy at a Distance," *Psychiatry* 19 [1956]). PSI may take many forms, for example, "seeking guidance from a media personality, imagining being part of a favorite program's social world, and desiring to meet media performers" (Alan M. Rubin, Elizabeth M. Perse, and Robert A. Powell, "Loneliness, Parasocial Interaction, and Local Television News Viewing," *Human Communication Research* 12 [1985]: 156–57). PSI goes beyond simple identification with the characters to include a desire to form actual relationships or be more intimate with the target of one's identification in real-life settings.

15. *Newsweek*, December 9, 1963, 88.

16. Visual immediacy through television allows people from all over the country to share their common experiences. There are few similar conversations, for instance, among generations past about their common moment of shock at only hearing by radio or finding out in the newspaper that Pearl Harbor was attacked in December 1941. Having not *seen* the attacks, "it didn't feel as if it had happened to them, personally, at all. Such is the power of television's visual immediacy" (Thomas de Zengotita, *Mediated: How the Media Shapes Your World and the Way You Live in It* [New York: Bloomsbury, 2005], 6).

17. Ibid., 7.

18. Schultze, *Redeeming Television*, 98.

19. Todd Hertz, "Get 'Lost': Acclaimed Show Asks Big Questions," *Christianity Today Magazine* [online], January 21, 2009, www.christianitytoday.com/ct/2009/february/8.60.html, para. 4 (accessed January 2009).

20. Chris Seay, *The Gospel According to Tony Soprano: An Unauthorized Look into the Soul of TV's Top Mob Boss and His Family* (Lake Mary, FL: Relevant Books, 2002).

21. Liane Bonin, "'Arc' Angels," *Entertainment Weekly* (EW.com), February 18, 2004, http://www.ew.com/ew/article/0,,592041,00.html, para. 5 (accessed January 2009).

22. Jean Paul Sartre, *The Family Idiot: Gustave Flaubert, 1921–1957*, vol. 1 (Chicago: University of Chicago Press, 1981), ix.

23. John Calvin, *Institutes of the Christian Religion*, ed. John T. McNeill (Philadelphia: Westminster, 1960).

24. Another example includes the miniseries about President John Adams on HBO. The seven-part miniseries, broadcast in 2008, is based on the book by David McCullough. The miniseries covers the first fifty years of the United States.

25. Schultze, *Redeeming TV*, 115–17, 123–24.

26. See, for example, Neil Vidmar and Milton Rokeach, "Archie Bunker's Bigotry: A Study in Selective Perception and Exposure," in *All in the Family: A Critical Appraisal*, ed. Richard P. Adler (New York: Praeger, 1979), 123–38.

27. See, for example, Horace Newcomb, ed., *Television: The Critical View*, 7th ed. (New York: Oxford University Press, 2007); Victoria O'Donnell, *Television Criticism* (Thousand Oaks, CA: Sage, 2007); Susan Murray and Laurie Ouellette, *Reality TV: Remaking Television Culture*, 2nd ed. (New York: New York University Press,

2008); John Fiske, *Reading Television* (New York: Routledge, 1990); Robert Allen, ed., *The Television Studies Reader* (New York: Routledge, 2003); and Jason Mittell, *Genre and Television: From Cop Shows to Cartoons in American Culture* (New York: Routledge, 2004).

28. See, for example, Chris Seay, *The Gospel According to Tony Soprano*; William D. Romanowski, *Pop Culture Wars: Religion and the Role of Entertainment in American Life* (Downers Grove, IL: InterVarsity, 1996); Craig Detweiler and Barry Taylor, *A Matrix of Meanings: Finding God in Pop Culture* (Grand Rapids: Baker Academic, 2003); William D. Romanowski, *Eyes Wide Open: Looking for God in Popular Culture*, rev. and exp. ed. (Grand Rapids: Brazos, 2007); David Dark, *Everyday Apocalypse: The Sacred Revealed in Radiohead, The Simpsons, and Other Pop Culture Icons* (Grand Rapids: Brazos, 2002); and Brian Godawa, *Hollywood Worldviews: Watching Films with Wisdom and Discernment* (Downers Grove, IL: InterVarsity, 2002).

Conclusion

1. The apostle Peter's first epistle was addressed to "God's elect" (1:1) whom he later describes as "being built into a spiritual house to be a holy priesthood" (2:5) and a "chosen people, a royal priesthood" (2:9).

2. See Tracey Mark Stout, "Would That All Were Prophets," in *Prophetic Ethics*, ed. Robert B. Kruschwitz (Waco: Baylor University Press, 2003).

3. Quentin J. Schultze, *Communication for Life: Christian Stewardship in Community and Media* (Grand Rapids: Baker Academic, 2000), 171.

4. John A. Thompson, *The Book of Jeremiah: The New International Commentary on the Old Testament*, ed. R. K. Harrison (Grand Rapids: Eerdmans, 1980), 88.

5. The great preacher Charles Spurgeon, for instance, was given to periods of depression, which sometimes left him bedridden and able to rise only to preach on Sundays. Spurgeon said, "Fits of depression come over most of us. Usually cheerful as we may be, we *must* at intervals be cast down. The strong are not always vigorous, the wise not always ready, the brave not always courageous, and the joyous not always happy" (Susan Verstraete, "Mingling Groans of Pain and Songs of Hope: Charles Haddon Spurgeon on Depression," BulletinInserts.org, Christian Communicators Worldwide, www.bulletininserts.org/spurdepr.html, para. 2 [accessed January 2009]).

6. Jacques Ellul, *The Presence of the Kingdom*, 2nd ed. (Colorado Springs: Helmers and Howard, 1989), 9–10.

7. See 1 Kings 19:1–4.

8. The prophetic sensibility, which includes the willingness to be self-critical, should be ever vigilant in resisting the temptation of arrogance. Simply put, arrogance distorts our perception of reality in two ways. First, arrogance minimizes our absolute dependence upon God. The ability to make wise and compelling critical decisions that produce prophetically faithful analysis or memorable artwork is a gift of God. Every component that makes the work possible is a gift from God. Second, arrogance distorts by minimizing our absolute interdependence with the rest of God's earthly creation. It is our dependence upon God and our interdependence with the rest of God's earthly creation that defines who we are and what we do as part of the prophethood of all believers.

9. For instance, related to pornography, there is no way around the necessity of applying Jesus's metaphoric admonition in Matt. 5:27–30. Immediately after warning

against committing mental adultery, Jesus says, "If your right eye causes you to sin, gouge it out and throw it away" (v. 29). A prophetic sensibility should be increasingly aware of what needs to be "gouged out" in order to live a holy life.

10. 1 Cor. 6:12; 10:23. Kenneth A. Myers, *All God's Children and Blue Suede Shoes* (Wheaton: Crossway, 1989), 87, suggests that these texts from 1 Corinthians offer a constructive orientation for our interactions with popular culture.

11. See 1 Cor. 10:13.

12. Cornel West, *Prophetic Thought in Postmodern Times* (Monroe, ME: Common Courage Press, 1993), 6.

13. As one critic observes, "Perhaps there is one common mark of the critical enterprise. It is founded in hope; it cannot be carried on without some sense of historical possibility" (Michael Walzer, *The Company of Critics: Social Criticism and Political Commitment in the Twentieth Century* [New York: Basic Books, 2002], 17).

14. M. Scott Peck suggests that some depression is healthy. His emphasis is that depression is a sign that an idea, a wish, or assumption about ourselves has to be given up. The "giving up" is often part of the continual process of "growing up" (*The Road Less Traveled* [New York: Simon & Schuster, 1978], 69). For those committed to developing a prophetic sensibility, sometimes the depression is associated with having to surrender the notion that their words and actions have an immediate and immediately identifiable redemptive effect.

15. Abraham Joshua Heschel, *I Asked for Wonder: A Spiritual Anthology*, ed. Samuel H. Dresner (New York: Crossroad, 2001), ix.

16. The comprehensiveness of God's purposes includes giving meaning even to the smallest act; see Mark 9:41.

17. Jesus's repeated emphasis about prayer is simply that we should keep praying, and that our prayer lives should be characterized by persistence, especially when we are discouraged; see Matt. 18:1–8.

18. Brother Lawrence, *The Practice of the Presence of God and the Spiritual Maxims* (Mineola, NY: Dover, 2005), 5.

19. Throughout the Bible, the call to courage is typically followed by the reminder that the "Lord your God will be with you wherever you go" (Josh. 1:9). In the Gospel of Matthew, Jesus's final admonition was to remind his disciples, "Surely I am with you always" (Matt. 28:20). The psalmist noted that even though he was walking in the "valley of the shadow of death," he would "fear no evil" (Ps. 23:4). Why? David simply believed that God was present with him (Ps. 23:4).

20. As cultural critic Kenneth A. Myers, *All God's Children and Blue Suede Shoes*, notes, "The most significant question raised by pop culture concerns the most edifying way to spend one's time" (53).

21. Of course, as with any memorization challenges (thinking of the regular demands of actors on the stage and screen), if you do not commit yourself to reviewing the verses you have memorized, many will be forgotten. We encourage reviewing them sometime each day during your stream-of-consciousness time: that time when you are not thinking about anything in particular. Memorization and review of the Scriptures helps, in part, to practice the presence of God.

22. In some Christian communities there is a specific, designated role of *prophet* within the functioning church structure. It appears that this role is not self-designated either, but that it comes from the discernment of the elders within the congregation.

23. Dr. Martin Luther King Jr. described Heschel as "one of the truly great men of our day and age, a truly great prophet." The quote appears on the back cover of Abraham Joshua Heschel, *Moral Grandeur and Spiritual Audacity* (New York: Farrar, Straus & Giroux, 1996).

24. Heschel, *Moral Grandeur*, 301–2. In his eulogy at Niebuhr's funeral, Heschel uses the same language in describing Niebuhr as he used in describing the Hebrew prophets: "He appeared among us like a sublime figure out of the Hebrew Bible. Intent on intensifying responsibility, he was impatient of excuse, contemptuous of pretense and self-pity" (302).

25. West, *Prophetic Thought in Postmodern Times*, 5.

26. See Acts 10:34; Deut. 10:17; 2 Chron. 19:7; Job 34:19; Rom. 2:11; Gal. 2:6; Eph. 6:9; Col. 3:25; 1 Pet. 1:17. Jesus commands his followers to "love your enemies" (Matt. 5:44) as participation by grace in the impartiality of God. God provides for those who acknowledge the wisdom and power of his presence through obedient service, as well as for those who defiantly disregard him. The sun and rain, necessary for the existence of humanity, are to be seen as signs of God's indiscriminate loving care for all of his creation. Jesus tells his followers that their lives are to be similarly characterized. For godliness is indiscriminate in the giving of grace: to enemies as well as friends, to strangers as well as soul mates, to the weak as well as the wise, to the anonymous as well as the famous; see Matt. 5:43–47.

27. Yahweh "defends the cause of the fatherless and the widow, and loves the alien, giving him food and clothing" (Deut. 10:18). Then comes the divine invitation to partner with God's concern for the alien by loving the alien as his Creator loves (v. 19). The human creation is God-designed to capably care about justice and mercy for all of the citizens of the earth, regardless of the categorical differences that too often justify our disregard for justice, mercy, and peace.

28. For instance, for a prophetic approach to storytelling in film, see Christine Gunn-Danforth, *Transforming Culture: A Model for Faith and Film in Hollywood* (Eugene, OR: Wipf & Stock, 2008). Several additional case studies are cited throughout our book's extensive endnotes; for example, Laurie Ann Britt-Smith, "American Prophet: Christian Literacy Practices and Rhetorics of Social Justice" (PhD diss., Saint Louis University, 2008), examines the rhetoric of Dorothy Day, Martin Luther King Jr., and Bono. James Darsey, *The Prophetic Tradition and Radical Rhetoric in America* (New York: New York University Press, 1997), includes in-depth analyses of several historical and literary figures. See also Harold R. Landon, ed., *Reinhold Niebuhr: A Prophetic Voice in Our Time* (Greenwich, CT: Seabury, 1962).

29. Quentin J. Schultze, *Here I Am: Now What on Earth Should I Be Doing?* (Grand Rapids: Baker Books, 2005).

30. C. S. Lewis, *The Screwtape Letters* (New York: Macmillan, 1943), 112.

Index